# NORTH AMERICAN EXPLORATIONS

## TEN MEMOIRS OF GEOGRAPHERS FROM DOWN UNDER

Edited by Leslie J. King

2007

Trafford
PUBLISHING

Order this book online at www.trafford.com/07-0945
or email orders@trafford.com

Most Trafford titles are also available at major online book retailers.

Note for Librarians: A cataloguing record for this book is available from Library
and Archives Canada at www.collectionscanada.ca/amicus/index-e.html

Printed in Victoria, BC, Canada.

ISBN: 978-1-4251-2751-0

*We at Trafford believe that it is the responsibility of us all, as both individuals
and corporations, to make choices that are environmentally and socially sound.
You, in turn, are supporting this responsible conduct each time you purchase a
Trafford book, or make use of our publishing services. To find out how you are
helping, please visit www.trafford.com/responsiblepublishing.html*

*Our mission is to efficiently provide the world's finest, most comprehensive
book publishing service, enabling every author to experience success.
To find out how to publish your book, your way, and have it available
worldwide, visit us online at www.trafford.com/10510*

www.trafford.com

**North America & international**
toll-free: 1 888 232 4444 (USA & Canada)
phone: 250 383 6864 ♦ fax: 250 383 6804
email: info@trafford.com

**The United Kingdom & Europe**
phone: +44 (0)1865 722 113 ♦ local rate: 0845 230 9601
facsimile: +44 (0)1865 722 868 ♦ email: info.uk@trafford.com

10 9 8 7 6 5 4 3

# Contents

# THE CONTRIBUTORS

## William A. V. Clark

Bill Clark graduated in geography from Canterbury College of the University of New Zealand (B.A. 1960, M.A. 1961). He completed his Ph.D. in geography at the University of Illinois in 1964 and then, after appointments at the University of Canterbury and the University of Wisconsin, in 1970 he joined the Geography Department at U.C.L.A. where he teaches today. His research on residential segregation, housing choice and migration has won him many academic honors, and also appointments as an expert witness in school desegregation law cases. He received an Honors Award from the Association of American Geographers (1987), an honorary doctorate from the University of Utrecht (1992), a Guggenheim Fellowship (1994/5), and a D.Sc. from the University of Auckland (1994). In 1997 he was elected an Honorary Fellow of the Royal Society of New Zealand, and in 2003 a Fellow of the American Academy of Arts and Sciences. In 2005 he was a recipient of the prestigious Decade of Behavior Research Award in the United States.

## Reginald G. Golledge

Reg Golledge graduated in geography from the University of New England, Australia (B.A. 1959, M.A. 1961). After teaching at Canterbury University for two years he went to the University of Iowa where he completed his Ph.D.(1966). Appointments at the University of British Columbia and Ohio State University then preceded his move in 1977 to the University of California, Santa Barbara where he teaches today. His pioneering research in behavioral geography was acknowledged by his receipt of an Honors Award of the Association of American Geographers (1981), a Guggenheim Fellowship (1987/88), the Australia-International Medal of the Institute of Australian Geographers (2000), honorary doctorates from the universities of Goteborg, Sweden, and Simon Fraser, Canada (2001), and the Grosvenor Medal for Geographic Education (2002). He is an Honorary Life Member of the Institute of Australian Geographers, a Fellow of the American Academy of Arts and Sciences, and a past President of the Association of American Geographers (1999). In 2007 the latter association honored him with a Lifetime Achievements Award.

## Peter G Holland

Peter Holland is Professor Emeritus at the University of Otago, New Zealand. He is a geography graduate of the University of New Zealand (B.Sc. 1961), the University of Canterbury (M. Sc. 1963), and the Australian National University (Ph.D. 1967). He was a member of the Department of Geography at McGill University in Montreal, Canada from 1967 to 1979, and during that time spent two years on secondment in Kenya and another two years on research and study leave in South Africa. He returned to join the Department of Geography at the University of Canterbury, and then in 1982 he took up the Chair of Geography at the University of Otago. He was Associate Editor of the *Journal of Biogeography* from 1982 to 2004. Since his retirement in 2002 he has retained close research and teaching links with the Department of Geography, and continued to serve as an academic auditor for tertiary institutions and educational organizations throughout New Zealand. Awarded the Paul Harris Fellowship of Rotary International in 1988 and elected an Honorary Member of the New Zealand Institute of Surveyors in 1996, he was President of the New Zealand Geographical Society in 2002.

## Leslie J. King

Les King is Professor Emeritus at McMaster University, Canada. He completed his B.A. (1955) and M.A.(1957) in geography at the Canterbury College of the University of New Zealand. After receiving his Ph.D. from the University of Iowa in 1960 he taught at Canterbury University, McGill University and Ohio State before becoming the Chair of Geography at McMaster University in 1970. Subsequently, he served there as Dean of Graduate Studies (1973-79) and Vice-President, Academic (1979-89). An advocate for the use of quantitative methods in human geography, he was the founding editor of *Geographical Analysis: an International Journal of Theoretical Geography.* He was the recipient of a Fulbright Award (1957), the Distinguished Service Award of the American Association of Geographers (1976), the Queen's Silver Jubilee Medal (1977), the Award for Scholarly Distinction of the Canadian Association of Geographers (1984), and a Commonwealth Prestige Fellowship in New Zealand (1986). A past President of the Canadian Association of Geographers (1986-87), he was elected a Fellow of the Royal Society of Canada in 1988, and in 2002 was awarded an honorary LL.D. by McMaster University.

## Malcolm I. Logan

Mal Logan is Professor Emeritus, Monash University, Australia. He graduated in geography from the University of Sydney with a B.A. and Ph.D.(1965). He taught at that University and then at the University of Wisconsin, Madison, with visiting appointments at the University of Nigeria, Ibadan, and the London School of Economics. In 1969 he was appointed to the Chair of Geography at Monash University where he later served as Vice-Chancellor from 1987 to 1996. He has been a consultant and advisor to many national and international bodies concerned with urban policy and regional development, notably as a member of the OECD's Expert Group on Japanese urban policy (1984-86), as Chairman of the Task Force on Human Resources Development in the Asia-Pacific Region (1989-96), as a director of the Melbourne Docklands Authority (1991), and as Chairman of the Australian Housing and Urban Research Institute (1991). He has twice served as President of the Institute of Australian Geographers of which he is an Honorary Life Member. He is a Fellow and past member of the executive of the Australian Academy of the Social Sciences. In 1996 he was appointed a Companion of the Order of Australia, and was named as 'Australian of the Year' by the *The Australian* newspaper.

## Terry McGee

Terry McGee is Professor Emeritus, University of British Columbia, Canada. He graduated in geography from Victoria University, Wellington (B.A., M.A., Ph.D.), and taught there and at the Universities of Malaya and Hong Kong, and the Australian National University, before moving to the University of British Columbia in 1978 as Professor of Geography and Director of the Institute of Asian Research (1978-98). His research on Asian urbanization and related development and planning issues led to his inclusion in the volume *Fifty Key Thinkers on Development* (Routledge, 2006), and to appointments as consultant and advisor to many different policy groups and development agencies, including the UNDP, the Asian Development Bank, IDRC and CIDA. He is a member of the *Expert Panel on Urbanization in Developing Countries* established by the American Academy of Sciences in Washington, and a member of the International Geographical Union's Task Force on *Megacities.* He is a Fellow of the Academy of Social Sciences of Australia, and in 2003 was awarded the President of Vietnam's medal for distinguished contributions to Vietnamese social science. He is a Past President of the Canadian Association of Geographers (1990-92).

## Janice Monk

Jan Monk is currently Research Social Scientist Emerita and Professor of Geography and Regional Development at the University of Arizona, Senior Fellow with the Association of American Geographers, and Adjunct Professor at Macquarie University, Australia. Jan graduated in geography from the University of Sydney (B.A. 1958) and the University of Illinois ( M.A. 1963, Ph.D. 1972). She stayed on at Illinois as a faculty member until 1980 when she moved to the University of Arizona where she teaches today. Her research on feminist/gender issues, social relations, and faculty and curriculum development in higher education has won her an Honors Award (1992) and a Lifetime Achievements Honor (2000) from the Association of American Geographers, the Australia-International Medal of the Institute of Australian Geographers (1999), and the Taylor and Francis Award of the Royal Geographical Society (2003). She is a past President of the Association of American Geographers (2001).

## Warren Moran

Warren Moran is Professor Emeritus at the University of Auckland. After completing his B.A.(1957) and M.A.(1959) in geography at Auckland he took up a high-school teaching position in Toronto, Canada, where he stayed for five years. He returned to a lectureship at the University of Auckland where he later completed his Ph.D. (1976). He was appointed Professor of Geography, and from 1992 to 1997 served as Dean of Arts at the University. He has had visiting appointments at a number of North American and French universities. His research on the New Zealand and international wine industries has won him a James Cook Fellowship, election as a Fellow of the Royal Society of New Zealand, one of the inaugural Distinguished New Zealand Geographer Medals of the New Zealand Geographical Society (2001), and an honorary membership of France's Societe de Geographie. He served two terms as a Vice-President of the International Geographical Union (1992 -2000), the second as First Vice- President.

## Brian Murton

Brian ('Charley') Murton is Professor Emeritus at the University of Hawaii. He received his B.A (1960) and M.A. (1961) from the University of Canterbury, and his Ph.D. (1970) from the University of Minnesota. After teaching at York University in Toronto, in 1969 he joined the geography department at the University of Hawaii and later served as its chair from January 1986 to July 1992. Among his several visiting appointments, he taught at Madras as an Indian University Grants Commission Visiting Professor. He has held the Ames Fellowship in the Historical Geography of South Asia at the University of Minnesota, and Junior and Senior Fellowships (twice) from the American Institute of Indian Studies. His research focused on various aspects of the historical geography of southern India, including agrarian change from the eighth to the nineteenth century and famine issues. He was Vice-Chair of the International Geographical Union Working Group, *Transformation of Rural Habitat in Developing Countries*, and was a member of the Union's Study Group on *Famine Research and Food Production Systems*, as well as serving on the Editorial Board of the *Cambridge World History of Food*. From the mid 1990s he has been heavily involved in Waitangi Tribunal claims in New Zealand.

## Robert H. T. Smith

Bob Smith is Professor Emeritus, The University of New England, Australia. He completed his B.A. at Armidale, his M.A. at Northwestern University in the U.S. and his Ph.D. at the Australian National University (1962). He then held appointments at the University of Melbourne, the University of Wisconsin, Queens' University (Ontario), Monash University and the University of British Columbia. At each of the last three universities he served as Head of the geography department. His involvement in university administration widened with his appointment as Vice President (Academic) and President *pro tem* at the University of British Columbia, with his subsequent appointments as Vice Chancellor of first, the University of Western Australia (1985-89) and then the University of New England (1990-93), and with his current role as Chancellor of the University of Ballarat. He has served on many national bodies concerned with higher education in Australia, and has chaired the National Board of Employment, Education and Training (1989-90). He also served as Executive Director and President of the Australian Education Office in Washington, D.C.(1994-97). His honors include two Fulbright awards, a Guggenheim Fellowship (1964/5), Fellowships in the Australian Academy of Social Sciences (1974) and the Australian Institute of Management (1987), Honorary Life Membership in the Institute of Australian Geographers, and an honorary doctorate from Southern Cross University (1995). In 1998 he was appointed a Member of the Order of Australia.

# INTRODUCTION

THIS IS A collection of memoirs written by persons who graduated in geography from Australian or New Zealand universities in the 1950s and 1960s and who then went on to pursue successful university careers that were shaped, to varying degrees, by their experiences in North America.

The subject of geography which the authors studied as undergraduates had been part of their universities' curricula for only a few decades. It had first achieved recognition as a university discipline in Australia with the appointment of Griffith Taylor as a lecturer in the subject at the University of Sydney in 1920 and then in New Zealand with the appointment of George Jobberns to teach the subject at Canterbury College in 1937. In the decades that followed, programs and departments were established in all of the major universities in the two countries (see, Spate and Jennings 1972, Johnston 1984, Johnston and Holland 1987, 1-12).

Those institutions down under were modeled on the British university and many of the senior staff positions in them, in most disciplines, were held first by British-born or British-educated scholars. In geography, Jobberns, born and educated in New Zealand, was a clear exception to this pattern; Taylor, of British birth but educated in Australia, was only slightly less so; but those who joined them later, the senior figures in geography at the universities throughout Australia and New Zealand, were all graduates of British universities.[1] Cumberland (2007) provides interesting testimony on the important consultative role played by R.O. Buchanan, a New Zealander who held appointments at University College, London, and the London School of Economics, in the early development of academic geography in his native land.

Given the strength of these British traditions and links, it was not surprising that most of the graduates of the young geography departments in New Zealand and Australia who sought either to do post-graduate studies or to take research leaves overseas, did so in British universities.[2] There they could work in well-established geography departments that offered the specializations in regional analysis or the different sub-fields of human or physical geography that they were interested in studying.

---

1   Notably, K. Cumberland and J. Fox at Auckland; B. Garnier and R. Lister at Otago; K. Buchanan and H. Franklin at Victoria; G. Lawton at Adelaide; G. Butland at Armidale; R. Greenwood at Brisbane; O. Spate and J. Jennings at Canberra; J. Andrews at Melbourne; J. Mabutt at New South Wales; J. Holmes and G. Dury at Sydney, and P. Scott at Tasmania

2   From Canterbury, for example, W. Packard, S. Duncan, J. Rose, W. Johnston, and M. McCaskill, at one time or another, studied and/or lectured in England ; so too did G. Ward from Auckland.

This orientation of Australian and New Zealand geography towards Britain changed only slowly in the years preceding the Second World War. Griffith Taylor made one of the earliest and more significant moves in changing it when he left Sydney in 1928, and after a short stay at the University of Chicago, took up the appointment as foundation Professor of Geography at the University of Toronto in 1935. He was joined there a year later by Ann Marshall from Melbourne who later completed an M.A. at Berkeley before returning to Australia. George Jobberns visited Columbia University in 1939 on a Carnegie grant though his contacts there were mainly with geology.

With visiting geography lecturers from the United States appearing in New Zealand departments as early as 1940 (Johnston 2004), and with the launching in 1946 of the Fulbright scholarship scheme that widened the opportunities for post-graduate study in the United States, it was inevitable that more young geographers from down under would begin to favor North American universities over British ones as the entry points for their future academic careers. Indeed, by the time the New Zealand contributors to this volume were graduating, three of their countrymen had already obtained doctorates in geography from U.S universities and returned to university positions down under.[3]

For most of the authors here however, a career in university research and teaching was far from their minds when they first enrolled as undergraduates. Many of them were supported by bursaries or scholarships provided by the national Departments of Education and these entailed commitments to future careers in school teaching. An emphasis on good teaching subjects such as geography and history was a common feature of many of their undergraduate programs. The factors behind their subsequent decisions to pursue further university studies overseas rather than embark on high-school teaching careers were many and varied— the stirrings of ambition prompted by undergraduate success, the advice and suggestions of colleagues and teachers, the opportunities provided by Fulbright awards, the excitement of going overseas.

They entered post-graduate studies in geography at a time when the discipline in North America was undergoing some marked intellectual changes. The so called 'quantitative revolution' and the associated development of behavioral geography were the major factors driving these changes and these prompted a great deal of debate, some of it quite acrimonious, between older established geography departments, steeped in the traditions of regional description and qualitative analysis, and those other centers that had taken up the quantitative and social-science oriented approaches (Livingstone 1992, 304-46). The majority of the authors here were caught up in these developments, some embraced them and played significant roles in fashioning and promoting the changes.

Notwithstanding these changing intellectual currents, all of the authors made

---

3    K. Thompson, M.A. and Ph.D.(University of Washington, 1949 – 1953); C. Duncan, Ph.D. (Ohio State University, 1955), and G. Lewthwaite, Ph.D. (Wisconson, 1956).

good of their opportunities once they were overseas.. The education that they had received as undergraduates and their specialization in geography stood them in very good stead. Whether as graduate students or professors they adapted to the North American university environment very easily and enjoyed considerable success. In time, many of them were honored by professional societies and academies, some received honorary degrees and a number served as Presidents of national geography societies. Further, although they were members of an academic discipline, geography, that frequently was, and often still is, the subject of diatribes and critiques about whether it belongs in the academy, some of the authors succeeded in being appointed to senior administrative positions within the university, two even to vice-chancellorships or presidencies.

A feature apparent in many of the accounts is that in the North American context the young geographers found a freedom and flexibility of approach in their academic work that provided entry into career opportunities wider than what they might have experienced back home. For some this meant the chance to work on funded research projects in developing countries, southeast Asia, India and Nigeria, and to become acknowledged experts on aspects of those societies. For others, it meant taking up the challenges of working in the domain of public policy, fashioning urban development policies, becoming involved in legal cases having to do with residential segregation, and championing the cause of women's and minority rights. That those involved were able to enjoy success in these endeavors speaks well of their training as geographers.

The experiences captured in this volume are special only in the sense that they relate to a particular phase in the development of academic geography down under when its ties with North America were widened and strengthened, and to a period in North American geography when the discipline there was seeking to achieve recognition as a legitimate social science (King 1993). In those changing circumstances, the individuals identified here adapted well and made their marks on the discipline. There were others of their contemporaries who joined them in their trans-Pacific journeys, a few of them unfortunately have passed on, some others chose not to contribute to this volume.

Later generations of young geographers from down under have followed the path to North America, and many of them now enjoy success there or elsewhere. The discipline of geography that these younger scholars now engage with in North America is markedly different from that which their predecessors encountered in the 1960s; it is much more pluralistic in character, far less introspective in regard to its nature and identity, and generally more tolerant of deviation and dissent. Whether these later arrivals in North America will match the achievements of those whose lives are recalled here, only time will tell. In the future, their stories should be told.

**REFERENCES**

Cumberland, K. B. 2007 'Kenneth B. Cumberland: A memoir' *New Zealand Geographer* 63, 62-68

Johnston, W. B. 1984 'An overview of geography in New Zealand to 1984' *New Zealand Geographer* 40, 20-33

Johnston, W. B. 2004 'New Zealand and American geography: Geographical cycles' *GeoJournal* 59, 33-38

Johnston, W. B. and Holland, P. G. eds. 1987 *Southern approaches. Geography in New Zealand* (Christchurch: New Zealand Geographical Society)

King, L. J. 1993 'Spatial analysis and the institutionalization of geography as a social science' *Urban Geography* 14(6), 538-551

Livingstone, D. N. 1992 *The geographical tradition* (Oxford: Blackwell)

Spate, O. H. K. and Jennings, J. N. 1972 'Australian geography 1951-1971' *Australian Geographical Studies* 9, 197-224

# REFLECTIONS ON A CHANGING WORLD AND A CHANGING DISCIPLINE

## William A. V. Clark

'ALL VISITORS ASHORE'[4] booming over the ship's loudspeaker was the signal for the accompanying visitors to leave their friends who were bound for London and other European cities. Paper streamers and rolls of toilet paper stretched from the ships rails to the waiting groups below. As the tug nosed the ship away from the pier, the gathered fare-welling friends sang 'Now is the Hour' a popular 1940s and 50s song of farewell, and the ship slipped gently away from the Auckland harbor pier. The ship was filled with young New Zealanders anxious to begin their 'OE' (overseas experience), in my case to travel via the Panama Canal to Ft Lauderdale and Urbana-Champaign to take up further graduate work at the University of Illinois. It was planned to be a three-year voyage of discovery and learning with a return to university teaching and research in New Zealand after getting a Ph.D. in geography. Of course it did not turn out quite that way. As the saying has it, 'life happens while you are making plans.'

It is perhaps not surprising if you grow up on the 'other side of the world' that you will be drawn eventually to discover what is out there across the ocean. Distant echoes of New Zealand at war brought the first inklings of a wider world 'out there' to be followed by glimpses from travel documentaries at the movies and stories from older cousins who had seen service in the Korean War. Later, New Zealanders who had been in the Second World War in Italy, North Africa and Egypt, who were older returning students to the university, added their stories of these far away places. Despite the required geographical study in elementary school and even in high school, it all seemed remote, especially exotic cities and towns in Europe. But while Egypt and Italy were remote, Britain was ever present in the Christmas cards we sent, with snowy scenes while it was in the 70s (Fahrenheit), visits of the new Queen and other royal family members, and the links of the New Zealand legal and university systems to their origins in England.

My grandparents, like the majority of New Zealanders of my generation, were of English, Irish, Scottish stock — McDonalds, McGees, and Clarks were mixes of these groups with a dash of French, the latter the impact of the ill-fated activities

---

4    It is also the title of an evocative book on growing up and leaving New Zealand in the 1950s by Carl Stead, one of New Zealand's fine novelists.

of Bonnie Prince Charlie. My grandparents got to New Zealand in a variety of ways, but fairly early on, before the big flows of settlement in the 1860s and 1870s. The family folklore, probably not to be trusted, is that we were related to the Pigeons (people, not birds) of Pigeon Bay in Banks Peninsula. The ships took four to six months to reach New Zealand; I often look down on the Pacific from some Boeing 777 and think about those vessels traveling around the Cape of Good Hope, crossing the Indian Ocean, and finally reaching New Zealand. Even when I left New Zealand in 1961, it took only three weeks to reach Florida.

Growing up in the 1940s and 1950s provided, looking back, an almost idyllic childhood — an intact family until my father's death at the incredibly young age of 50, concerned parents, concerned in particular about doing well in school but all tempered by family vacations to the sea in the summer. We were left to invent our own days with cousins and friends. The long summer days always seemed golden, though we had lawn mowing jobs and worked in various places in the summers to provide the extras for our bicycles, our main means of transportation to and from school and further afield.

## Getting Started

The early education in elementary school in New Zealand in the late 1940s and early 1950s was both circumscribed and expansive, a strange mixed bag that nevertheless seemed to work. It was strongly focused on reading and writing, what we might now call literacy and numeracy, but it was all leavened with field trips to museums, the ocean, and parks to collect grasses, butterflies, shells and a myriad other 'natural objects'. It was, either with forethought or by accident, a design and approach which now could be viewed as a calculated process of imbuing a scientific bent to our education. Classification was clearly a big part of all those collecting enterprises, and I wish I could find those countless boards with mounted shells and sundry other collectibles, but they have long since vanished. Of course, the New Zealand education curriculum was very much influenced by New Zealand's British origins. Still there was a heavy flavor of the immigrant experience — clearing the land and establishing the agricultural practices that are still the backbone of the New Zealand economy. The *New Zealand School Journal* gave us the same sanitized version of the country's settlement as American school children used to get of the settlement of America. There was a lot of 'jingoism' and rally around the flag in that version of the settlement of New Zealand. The Maori, like the Native Americans in North America, were viewed as an inconvenience in the way of white settlement. How much has changed today in New Zealand with the attention to Maori rights and the attempts to redress past wrongs! Still, back then along with the sanitized version of conquest, we were proud to learn that New Zealand was notable for being the first country to extend the vote to women, to create special parliamentary seats for Maori, to establish childbirth care for women, and to introduce universal education and health care.

Although education was indeed open to all, and although all children were required to stay in school until 15 years of age, it was clear by the middle of the elementary school years that there was a two tier education system and strongly ingrained 'streaming' by ability within the grades. Once at the high school level, students were directed either to schools that were preparatory for the university and the professions or to high schools that provided more practical training, including a heavier dose of what in North America would be called 'shop'. But in New Zealand they were wood-working and practical courses that would be useful to students who were going to become carpenters, electricians, mechanics and plumbers . This is not to say that students from the more professional high schools did not also travel the apprentice route and that students from the technical schools did not go on to university. The beauty of the New Zealand education system then, was its flexibility and adaptability. In hindsight, it seems a very different system than the US emphasis on a liberal education, and though I may be seeing the whole system through rose-colored glasses, the professional and the vocational paths still managed to provide a good sense of the classic 'English' literature.

The streaming continued in the high school where a standardized exam was used to sort us into one of eight beginning classes for the five years of high school. There was little privacy, names were read out in assembly and students moved to their assigned groups. I have wondered since whether it was better to be at the bottom of the first group or the top of the second group. Even within classes, we were ranked in order; you were 1st or 2nd and so on out of 35, perhaps even 35th on each of the subjects. Science was a serious business in high school. The classes were designed to prepare us for the first of the national tests , the third year school certificate. English, history and mathematics were required for the exam, other subjects were optional. School certificate was followed a year later by the university entrance exam which was often awarded on the basis of performance rather than a specific exam. However, without school certificate, it was not possible to advance to the university, though there were special provisions for 'mature' students beyond the age of 21 to gain entry without it.

I was unsure of my long term goals during the high school years, though high school teaching seemed like a good idea and in those days certainly offered status, a good salary and the possibility of administrative advancement. I took history, English, mathematics, French and science. Again, field trips and science were important parts of that long five-year high school apprenticeship. At its end, we had a reading knowledge of French though we never spoke the language — a failing of language teaching in the New Zealand system then I believe— good mathematics skills including two years of calculus, and a nodding acquaintance with some physical and biological processes. The two years of calculus were very useful later when I wanted to push the 'quantitative envelope' in graduate school, an experience that I think has been common to most British students who came to North America to do graduate work. Sadly, I note thatthe emphasis on good mathematics skills seems not to be so important in my field at the present time.

The freedom of university worked well for me, but for some of my high school friends the lack of structure was a problem. No one required you to be at lectures at a particular time, there was no enforced ritual of class attendance, and unlike high school, lectures were only two or three times a week across three ' subjects', hardly an onerous schedule. I actually found the political science classes and the English ones more interesting than the geography offerings which were extremely traditional, at the level of Russell and Kniffen's *Culture Worlds*, if I recall correctly. It offered little that was exciting compared to the ideas of the political philosophers we discussed in political science. Cotton's books that presented a 'Davisian' view of New Zealand's geomorphology were much more interesting, and I can see why some of my cohort were attracted to physical rather than human geography. Those who also took geology classes quickly became interested in the science of geomorphology and embarked on what seemed like exciting trips to the mountains and the sea studying rocks and rivers. But, I wanted to marry history and geography, and during the three years of undergraduate work at Canterbury I was able to do just that. I opted for courses where I could bring space into history. I became enamored of Plumb's *English Social History* and mapped 'travel accessibility' in England in the 18th century from descriptions given there and in other sources. I took a course on the Risorgamento taught by a vivacious New Zealander who had lived in Italy and was then the most exotic woman I had ever met. I mapped the struggle for territory as Italy moved towards unification.

Even in the last year of my undergraduate program, I was still pointed to high school teaching but the 'pull of far away places with strange sounding names' was growing stronger. 'How to do it' became the question of the moment. Despite the strength of the geography program at the Canterbury College of the University of New Zealand, now the University of Canterbury, there was not a huge amount of information about studying abroad. The faculty who had been abroad mostly had been to England. Murray McCaskill, then lecturer in the Department and later founding professor at Flinders University in Adelaide, Australia, had studied for a year in London but completed his Ph.D. in New Zealand while teaching full time. Similarly, Barry Johnston and Bill Packard had both spent time in England. However, my MA advisor to be, Leslie Leigh Pownall had studied in the US for a year at Madison, Wisconsin, and traveled widely in Europe but he too completed his Ph.D., on the New Zealand town, back in New Zealand. Still, there was enough general information and some encouragement to apply for further graduate work. As I have written elsewhere, it was a laborious process with multiple carbon copies and manual typewriters.[5] When you went through that process, you truly understood the meaning of cut and paste.

Leigh Pownall, who was later to be Vice-Chancellor of the University of Canterbury and then an officer of the University of London, taught the first urban geography course in New Zealand. He had already been applying the ideas and techniques of Howard Nelson (who will return later in the narrative) and William Steingenga to the classification of towns in New Zealand. His first course in urban geography taught to a half dozen of us plowed through the newly published book by Mayer and Kohn, *Readings in Urban Geography*. What a change from Russell and Kniffen and some of the other texts we had suffered through. I am certain I missed more than I understood, but here was the first whiff of change in geography, and the articles were not just by geographers but by economists, planners, sociologists and demographers. Of course, some of the papers were already 'old'; the Harris and Ullman work having been published in the late 40s and in sociology. It was an exciting year.

## *A visitor's experiences*

I wanted to study at the University of Minnesota where John Borchert was involved in a mix of analytic and policy-work that was later to become the hallmark of my own career and contributions in geography. I do not think that I could have articulated it as well then as I can now, but in hindsight it was all about translating theory to practice and evaluating (testing) hypotheses drawn from theoretical interpretations. That approach is still central to my practice of geography.

Then I was an unknown quantity, with a degree but without an associated grade point system that could be evaluated. Minnesota turned me down while holding out the possibility of a position if someone else declined. Later I shared a laugh with faculty at Minnesota over the way the world turns. It was a good thing that Les King had returned from Iowa in 1960 to take up a lectureship at Canterbury because he was quick to point out that applying only to Minnesota was at the very least short-sighted, and he encouraged me to apply elsewhere. He did not think the Iowa program (already strongly quantitative) would suit me with my broad interests in historical and urban geography, though it may have, and suggested Washington, Syracuse, where Evelyn Dinsdale (later Dame Evelyn Stokes) was studying, Illinois and UCLA. I received offers of admission from Illinois and UCLA, a peremptory rejection from G. Donald Hudson at Washington who added some gratuitous comments about my unsuitability for their highly quantitative and cutting-edge program, and a decline from Syracuse. Illinois was in the center of the country, a good base for traveling around, and I had read Jerry Fellman's recent paper in the *Annals*. It seemed

---

5    A forthcoming essay , 'Geography and the life course: Reflections on choices and places', covers some of the same ground as this essay but here I am more concerned to explore my own paths in the light of the changing disciplinary foci of the 1960s and 1970s.

like a good opportunity and I accepted their offer. Fulbright provided a travel grant and I would have a fellowship for the first year—no multi-year guarantees in those early days.

So it was that I sailed on the 'Fairsky' bound for Fort Lauderdale (essentially the docking for passenger ships calling at Miami) via the Panama Canal. We stopped at Pitcairn Island, of 'Mutiny on the Bounty' fame, and then Panama City on the west coast of Panama before the Canal passage. The shore excursion in Panama City started what was to become a life long travel bug. I missed the ship-organized shuttle to Panama City, but to my great delight I was picked up by a local military attache stationed there, who not only helped me buy a duty free camera, but took me home for lunch and drove me about showing me the sights of Panama City. Ah, the days of trust on both sides of the equation. The passage through the Canal, the Gatun Locks and the raising and lowering of the ship to reach the Atlantic are still vivid memories. We stopped in Jamaica, another exotic experience, before docking in Ft. Lauderdale and waiting the day to catch the overnight train to Jacksonville.

In some sense, the experiences of Jacksonville were to emerge later in my own reaction to race and society in the United States. My wife and I were young, and I realized very quickly that we had had very little experience of any other culture, nor had we met any black (African Americans as we say now) people. There was a small Maori population in New Zealand, but in Christchurch there was little contact with them and for me the only other 'different people' were the Chinese shop keeper at the end of the street and later my fellow high school student who was Indian- Pakistani. It was a pretty circumscribed world. So it was strange to be suddenly in contact with so many black people and as I recall we rode on the train in the same carriages as the local traveling black people, which suggests that at least interstate transportation had been integrated by September of 1961. Of course, most of the waiters and the railway staff were black, but when we invited a black woman we met on the train to have breakfast with us, she politely pointed to the 'whites only' sign on the train station restaurant . The waiting rooms, colored and white, emphasized the separation in US society, though change was on the way and later I would be thrust into the debates over segregation and separation in urban areas and into court discussions of segregation.

My reaction to graduate school was mixed, partly because my expectations did not fit with the program at Illinois, which was traditional though changing, and mainly because I quickly realized that the University of Illinois was not on the cutting edge of the new quantitative work which was sweeping the field. I contemplated leaving for the University of Chicago where Brian Berry was working with a group of bright graduate students whom I had met at my first West Lakes regional meeting of the AAG in October, just after arriving. But leaving Illinois would have delayed my progress by a year or two and I was bent on finishing, traveling in Europe and starting a career in New Zealand. So I stayed on.

Of course, things are always more nuanced than you realize and to return to an earlier comment, life happens while you are making plans. And so it was at Illinois. By chance, the entering group of graduate students were lively, creative and full of fresh ideas. Kevin Cox had come from Cambridge, and he might have stayed in England if his undergraduate degree had got a better mark and impressed the British hierarchy. If he had not come it would have been my loss and a loss to US geography. Along with Janice Jones (Monk) from Sydney, the only woman in the entering group as I recall, and Lorne Russwurm and Alex Blair from Canada we joined a group of US students, including Bob Altschul and Rainer Erhardt .Warwick Armstrong from Auckland had already paved the way and was probably the reason that the Illinois Department was willing to take the risk on foreign students. Some other older students were finishing up though our cohort tended to spend time together arguing about space and place and the changing nature of our discipline. Although we were all in the geography program we had very different perspectives and substantive interests as our later careers have shown. Kevin's political interests, my urban interests and Janice's anthropology focus were all accommodated in the program.

I talked my way out of the required field trip, a six-week requirement for all graduate students. It was not that I wanted to avoid field work— I did a study of the developing ex-urbanization and large lot development that was going on around Champaign as part of my first year program — it was just that I had to do German in the summer to keep up. Illinois like most US PhD programs required two languages and that was in addition to the statistics courses I wanted to do outside the department. They were all extras, so to speak.

By then, science, broadly speaking, had captured my attention. Outside of geography, in economics and psychology, statistical analysis and more importantly, theory were much more central than in geography. Could we have theory in geography? What was our central question? We debated these issues without much resolution but trips to the West Lakes meetings made us aware that other graduate students such as Larry Bourne, Jim Simmons and Peter Goheen at Chicago, and Barry Garner at Northwestern were arguing about the same issues. Reg Golledge came to Iowa to work with Harold McCarty and through my earlier friendship with him, I met graduate students at Iowa. Ron Boyce came to Illinois to the Community Analysis Bureau and later was appointed to the faculty. He had been trained at the University of Washington with Art Getis, John Nystuen and Dick Morrill, and he brought some of the excitement of analytic geography. Later, when he moved to the University of Iowa in the summer of 1964, he hired Reg Golledge, Gerry Rushton and myself to work on the spatial structure of geographical activities in Iowa. Later, Gerry wrote his Ph.D. dissertation on the spatial behavior of consumers in Iowa. That summer was an intense experience of work, discussion and play, and we formed a lasting bond, though we eventually moved into quite different substantive areas. The summer ended with my attendance at a two-week summer internship/workshop at

Northwestern University where Brian Berry, Michael Dacey, Ed Thomas and Ned Taaffe tried to enhance our quantitative skills.

The graduate years passed quickly enough and I accepted a position, according to my long-term plan, as lecturer in geography back at Canterbury. I had contemplated going to MIT to pursue a planning degree, but funding fell through and the pull of home and family was strong. I began a research program which extended my interests in population patterns and processes but more pattern than process. I was interested in land use patterns and how populations were distributed. Did New Zealand's land tax system have an impact? Were New Zealand cities sprawling in the same manner as US cities? I was very much influenced by the classification work on cities and commercial centers that Brian Berry had published from his work in Washington and later in Iowa. The distribution of retail centers in Iowa was a seminal volume in directing my thinking about theory in geography.

## A search for context and theory

On my return to Canterbury, I taught the usual run of courses from introductory geography to an urban seminar. Les King was still on the faculty but about to leave for McGill University and my fellow undergraduate student, Roger McLean, had returned from McGill where he had completed a Ph.D. in physical geography. It was a collegial time, and I was given free rein to introduce a quantitative series for second and third year geography students. The undergraduates at Canterbury were getting more analytic geography than many undergraduates in American geography departments. But it is not surprising that I returned to the United States. There was a growing demand there for quantitatively trained geographers, departments were expanding and remodeling their curricula, and so I was only one of many US trained Ph.Ds who returned to the US after a period teaching 'back home' in Britain, Australia or New Zealand. Some were not persuaded to return and stayed to make careers in Britain and Australia. Some came back and left again. British departments too were beginning to change, often with American trained geographers, and Canadian departments also were able to draw on a rich and able group of US trained students.

Geography was changing rapidly and the publication of *Locational Analysis in Geography* in 1965, Peter Haggett's masterful summary of work inside and outside of geography, set a standard for all of us interested in science — as he puts it 'with the need to look for pattern and order in geography'. He also looked ahead to the arguments about how we impose our own biases on research to note that order and chaos are not part of nature but part of the human mind and that we bring order to analyses with the systems and models we use. I was lucky to visit Peter Haggett and Dick Chorley at Cambridge in 1964, as they were doing the layouts for the book that would be published a year later in Britain, though most of us did not get a copy until 1966. I realized at lunch with them that while I had good technical skills, I did not have any notion of a substantive theory to provide a platform for what I wanted to do. Peter Haggett's work on the diffusion of diseases was already central in the structure of his ideas and influenced the questions he asked and how he answered them. Bill Bunge's monograph, *Theoretical Geography*, had been published in 1962 and was widely read. Indeed, it played a major role in my interest in the classification of shapes in research that I did in graduate school, but it was geometrically inspired and did not have the broad appeal of *Locational Analysis*.

It was not that I was dissatisfied with the research and articles I had completed as a graduate student, or soon after, but I continued to feel that there was no unifying theme; no bigger research picture into which to fit the disparate pieces of research that I was completing. And if citation is the criterion, not much of that early work is cited now. Nor did my unease change much with my move back to the University of Wisconsin in 1966. I arrived with a cohort of new assistant professors including Norb Psuty and David Ward to join Bob (RHT) Smith, Bill Denevan, and of course the senior distinguished faculty of Arthur Robinson, Andy Clark and Richard Hartshorne. Glen Trewartha had just retired. They were already legends for their wide-ranging contributions to geography and to the profession. Andrew Clark had spent time in New Zealand and while there had written *Patterns on the Land*. Arthur Robinson had both physical and cartography text-books and Hartshorne's '*The Nature*' if no longer the bible, was certainly still a force in the field though increasingly as a target rather than as a reference. We were welcomed with our new ideas, but it was clearly a highly structured department. The subsequent hiring within a short space of time of Mal Logan, George Dury, Tom Eighmy and eventually John Hudson, further changed the structure of the department and brought some tensions between old and new ideas. The combination of contentious personalities was probably unsustainable and within a couple of years many left to find other opportunities but David Ward stayed and was instrumental in rebuilding the department in the 1970s and he was to hire one of my first Ph.D. students, Martin Cadwallader in 1974.

The late 1960s were heady times, with colloquia, special sessions at the regional and national meetings and a mimeo-graphed literature of new and exciting analytic ideas. Les King and Ned Taaffe founded *Geographical Analysis* as an outlet for new quantitative work in 1969, the same year that Alan Wilson launched *Environment and Planning* which later grew into several sub journals. Departments who wished to re-vamp their programs invited our cohort to visit and present our research and talk about appointments. At the AAG, department heads hunted for new talent (and that has not changed much except that it is harder to separate the wheat from the chaff now in what seem to be a thousand or so concurrent sessions). In the late 1960s Chicago was the premier department in the country but Northwestern, Ohio State and Penn State were developing strong departments and there was a good deal of rivalry. Now sadly there is no geography to speak of at Chicago nor at Northwestern.

The years at Wisconsin and the conversations with David Ward, Bob Smith, and John Hudson provided the basis for some of my first moves to a focus on population processes and the beginnings of a more articulated theory of residential and neighborhood choice. But as for so many of us who thought of ourselves as quantitative geographers, geometry ruled and powerfully influenced our work.

## Changing locations and directions

In January 1970 I left for UCLA where Howard Nelson had arranged a two-quarter visiting position for me with a promise of a tenured associate professorship beginning in July. I had earlier in 1968 interviewed at UCLA but at that time had decided to stay at Wisconsin. Now I was going through personal life changes and thought I might stay three or four years in Los Angeles and then move on. Again life happens and interrupts the best-laid plans.

UCLA was going through change. There was a push to reconnect with the city and city planning and administration, and to increase the urban contribution that the university made to the city, essentially to bring the insights of the academy to the planning process. At least some of this push came from the enthusiasm of Harvey Perloff and John Friedman (before his post-modern flirtations) who were re-vitalizing the urban planning program at UCLA. The weekly brown bag lunches brought together academics and practicing planners and a veritable who's who of the academic community's urban specialists — Manual Castells, Kevin Lynch, Peter Hall, Martin Dykman and others too numerous to list here. Werner Hirsch, an urban economist in the economics department at UCLA was running the Institute of Government and Public Affairs (later to become the Social Science Research Institute) and that research unit offered related opportunities for young faculty and graduate students. Perloff's contacts with 'Resources for the Future' and other Washington groups brought in projects and funding and provided a grounded experience for those of us struggling with the relevance of our research agendas. I nearly joined the planning program, but my involvement was thwarted by internal politics in the geography department.

Despite the proliferation of research projects, I still did not have a good organizing theme for what I was doing: my research was episodic and data driven, and I had yet to write a convincing paper on migration or mobility. But three things changed my direction and provided the missing structure, and set me off on the path that I still follow. First, within a couple of years of arriving in Los Angeles, I was supervising a group of four talented Ph.D students (Karen Avery, Martin Cadwallader, John Everitt and Gary Gaile). They did not all do migration research, indeed Gary Gaile refused to study a wonderful Milwaukee data set that I had and went off to East Africa to look at regional development. But all of them challenged my thinking about how I was doing research. Then, secondly, there was the change in the UCLA department. We hired Jim Huff and Phil

Lankford, graduates of Northwestern and Chicago respectively, who were both extremely well trained. Phil and I did not always see eye to eye but I learned a lot from him. Eventually, he pursued a successful non-academic career with urban government in the Bay Area. Jim Huff became a collaborator with me, a critic and friend. I am still proud of the work we did together, especially that which we and Jim Burt ( a physical geographer) did on migration and behavior. The third factor was that the first large- scale data sets on migration and mobility from the federal 'Housing and Urban Development' department, and from some local urban planning agencies, were coming on line, and these made it possible to examine analytically some of the ideas about neighborhood change and residential mobility.

Eric Moore had published an excellent monograph on residential mobility in the Northwestern Geography Department monograph series and had provided a rich set of new ideas about residential behavior.

It was an exciting time, and my rapidly developing professional career was matched by a change in my personal life. Remarriage, step-children and a new child changed any thoughts I may have had of leaving and re-focused my energies. Buying a house and moving highlighted the quirkiness of how residential moves intersect with the larger urban context. I was heavily into 'search patterns' and their impacts for residential change at the time, but the house we bought and still live in was outside my 'search area.' At the time, however, it was large enough for the four children and household help, and close enough to campus to allow me to go back in the evening to keep up with research projects, so we bought it anyway. It has served us well though now it is an 'empty nest'.

My interest in population change and population movements began to co-alesce around ideas of neighborhoods and how they changed as families moved in and out of them. Why did households choose particular places? Why did they move when they did? These and a related set of questions became more important during the 1970s as I, alone, or in collaborative enterprises tried to work out a consistent set of answers to these seemingly simple questions. I had not yet formulated a coherent theoretical approach to residential change and mobility, but bit by bit as I sought to explain residential mobility and its outcomes that differed across neighborhoods and communities, I fashioned an approach which had both a theoretical structure and the ability to deal with policy issues from poverty to segregation.[6]

Two events in the 1970s helped cement these developing ideas and set up what was to be my research agenda for the next two decades. First, Waldo Tobler helped me obtain a small grant from the Mathematical Social Sciences

6    I have written more extensively elsewhere about the role of science and the development of a structured approach to residential mobility and residential patterns. Also, in 'Geography, space and science: perspectives from studies of migration and geographical sorting', to be published as part of an International Geographical Union sponsored special issue on the development of quantitative methods in geography, I show the continuing relevance of an informed scientific approach to geographical questions.

Board to hold a conference at UCLA in 1976 on mobility and population. Eric Moore, Waldo, John Quigley, Bill Frey, Duncan MacLennan (from Glasgow), Stephen Gale and Ralph Ginsberg spent three days in Los Angeles reading papers and discussing mobility processes. The workshop led, with John Hudson's help, to an edited Northwestern University monograph.

The second, and perhaps more defining event was a much larger conference again at UCLA funded by 'Housing and Urban Development' (HUD) with additional funding from Howard Freeman, then the director of the Institute for Social Science Research. While the papers from the first conference were almost entirely abstract, though data based, the second conference had an avowed focus on policy issues. Could research on residential mobility contribute to policy outcomes? Eric Moore who was visiting UCLA at the time, had been deeply involved with the HUD sponsored EHAP (Housing Allowance Program) projects and brought his experience in those projects to bear on the discussion. We co-edited the volume from the conference and though we argued in the first chapter that there was a need to show how our analysis could be used in policy frameworks, we concluded that the evidence and results were a very mixed bag. Recent studies with the MTO (Moving to Opportunity) project of HUD tend to have similar findings. For many participants in that conference such as Eric Moore the challenge of translating social science discoveries into practical use remains an important issue; for some of the other participants such as Michael Dear a move into 'post-modernism' has proven more attractive.

In their different ways, both conferences struggled with the important questions of what social science can contribute. Little did I know that within a few months of the conference I would be thrust into the middle of a real-world application of social science models and analysis. It was to be a series of events which would lead me to a better grasp of the relevant theory, the models to examine those theories, and the day-to-day context of the intersection of law, policy and academic expertise.

## Two Themes

My research was shifting from a primarily urban geographic focus to a broader population one, though they were never clearly separated because I was always interested in populations in urban areas. Still, I was increasingly concerned with individual behavior and less with flows and structures. One such new theme was to seek to understand individual decision making about where to move and what house and location to choose. With a graduate student in planning, Jun Onaka, we developed nested logit models of choice, and with some European colleagues, especially Frans Dieleman, a series of models of tenure choice and housing selection. In this work, it was wonderful to have the involvement of a mathematician, Rinus Deurloo, who always brought us back to the questions of what was new in what we were doing, and what were we contributing. He was a sceptic and a critic whose insights continually stimulated our thinking.

I now had a theoretical structure into which I could fit the varying and some-time contradictory behavior of individuals and discern some order in their decisions and choices. I was dealing with what is now called the 'life course' and how intersecting behaviors arise. It was increasingly clear from events in my own life and of those around me, that the decision to move was much more than a search for housing and space; it intersected with decisions about marriage and divorce, having children and changing jobs. That is a pretty obvious statement, but working it out in a modeling framework was a lot more complicated. Further, any such an advances in the understanding of individual decision making behaviors did not do much to explain the aggregated changes in the urban fabric. Why are there concentrations of African Americans and Hispanics, of Asians and the myriad new nationalities that have been thronging into North American cities?

A second new theme in my research then was to seek to understand these changing aggregate patterns and it was in this work that the intersection of the academic and the policy realms become more apparent. In 1978, I was asked to participate in a Federal Court case on desegregation. It was the first 'metro-case' (a decision about the city and the surrounding suburbs) since the Millikin v Bradley decision against cross-district busing in Detroit in 1973. What followed for me was a twenty-five year 'roller coaster' of court room testimony and legal participation. That history is too long to recount here but a part of it is relevant to my story of science and the study of residential change.

For the case, I was to map the patterns of the black population in Atlanta over the past three decades and offer opinions on why the black population was almost entirely in the southern sections of Fulton County. At an interpretive level, I was to discuss the importance of affordability, personal choice, urban structure and discrimination as explanations for the spatial patterns I observed. The patterns of black concentration were little different from those in most US cities, and I viewed the task very much in the context of an introductory urban geography exercise. However, it turned out not to be so simple. It became more complex when I was asked a seemingly simple question by the presiding judge - why do people live where they do?

The plaintiffs in the case, a combination of lawyers and experts from the American Civil Liberties Union (ACLU) and the Legal Defense Fund, argued that the explanation for the concentrated black population was white racism and discrimination by private, white individuals and local and federal government agencies. Prejudice and discrimination, intolerance and red-lining, they insisted were the only explanations for the patterns of separation in the Atlanta metropolitan region. Clearly, racism and *de jure* (by law) segregation were powerful forces in the segregation of the races in the past — who could deny it? Certainly not I, who had witnessed it first-hand in Jacksonville, Florida, on my arrival in the US seventeen years earlier. But, the more I poked and pushed at the issue of residential segregation the more it seemed contextual and more a function of a complex set of forces including discriminatory acts. But residential patterns seemed also to be intertwined with other forces, including housing costs and incomes and residential preferences and the ties to neighborhood friends and facilities.

In that 1978 Armor v Nix trial in an Atlanta Federal Court room, we struggled with the issues of residential segregation; it was geography and sociology transferred from the classroom to the courtroom. In the end, the case, as so often in Federal trials about desegregation, turned not so much on whether we could determine why African Americans were concentrated in south Fulton County as on the issue of whether or not the suburban school districts around the County had created these patterns of residential separation. Even then, the plaintiffs wanted the court to find that the suburban districts by their actions had prevented African Americans from moving out of Fulton County. But there was no evidence that they had and the Court ruled for the school districts and against the ACLA and the Legal Defense Fund. It was only the first salvo in what developed into a 25-year battle over whether school districts were responsible for creating residential segregation and whether they had done enough to redress past cases of *de-jure* segregated school systems.

The outcome of the struggle over what school districts should do pitted some very well trained people (on both sides of the question) against one another. It was always contentious and sometime verged on being a 'Perry Mason' circus. The response in the academy more generally to my involvement in these cases (often testifying for defendant school boards who were seen as the 'enemy' by plaintiffs experts) was often unpleasant. How could you say anything that would hinder 'poor blacks' and other minorities, friendly colleagues asked. The unfriendly ones accused me, *sotto voce* of course, of bias and racism. One newspaper article, which I learned later was instigated by a well-known Harvard academic and supporter of busing, reported that I was unremittingly opposed to desegregation. That was certainly not true. For most of the academy, the politically correct position favored racial balancing across schools and busing and the elimination of segregated schools. Never mind that most black parents did not want their children bussed all over the district. And, what was the evidence that busing improved school outcomes— scant as it turned out.

I am not going to argue that I was without my viewpoints in this work, we all bring our agendas and intellectual baggage to the table. But the turn to relativism and post modernism I believe has done society and social science a disservice. We do need to make decisions based on the best evidence available to us but some experts tailored their reports and rendered opinions that could not be supported by the data. It seemed to me then, and even more so now, that the debates over residential segregation were not black and white issues. Living in Los Angeles, I was acutely aware of the increasing Hispanic presence in the city, the growing Asian numbers and new flows from Iran, after the fall of the Shah. The west side of Los Angeles has a huge mixed foreign-born population — my hairdresser is from Iran, my internist from Armenia and the nurses who greet you at the clinic are Russian and Philipino. Often these groups live in enclaves, clusters and, in the case of many Iranians, in gated communities. Are they all the victims of white racism? I don't think so.

Throughout the 1980s in several successive cases and studies in Cincinnati, Omaha, Kansas City, Milwaukee and Los Angeles I collected data on residential preferences. But I was still struggling with the Atlanta judge's question and with the inadequate sociological explanations of residential segregation. I began re-reading Thomas Schelling's 1969 article in the *Journal of Mathematical Sociology* and his 1971 book on *Micromotives and Macro Behavior* and that provided me with important new insights.[7]

Schelling posits that a household prefers to be a square on a checkerboard arrangement of two colors in which half or more of the eight nearest neighbors are of a similar color, in essence that people want to be near people like themselves. Hardly rocket science in one sense—' birds of a feather flock together' as one cocktail wag suggested when I described my research. Still, as far as I could tell, no one had attempted to apply Schelling's insights empirically. I had the data to do it. A paper in *Demography* in 1991 outlined an empirically based analysis of Schelling's preference tolerance schedules and a second paper a year later showed that the preference tolerance curves for blacks and whites could be replicated in broad terms for Hispanics and Asians. There are many versions of this work which are not relevant to my discussion here, but these papers fulfilled my search for theoretically informed empirical analysis and they have been widely cited. My study of concentration and separation has continued with new collaborative work that has introduced agent based modeling as a formal extension of both Schelling's theory and preference analysis as a fundamental explanation for the outcomes we see in the residential fabric.

## *Parallel careers*

Research and teaching are enough to consume an academic life but inevitably with age you drift up the hierarchy, to chair, Dean, administrator. I was a little more senior than some chairs when I became head of department at UCLA in 1987. I discovered then that the department was not viewed as favorably by the UCLA administration as we believed was our due. Indeed, the dean was thinking of our amalgamation with anthropology who would not have liked it any more than we would have. In the end, we remained separate and intact and now are well respected for our activities and contributions.

Chairing a department is a strange ritual in the North American context and it is often joked that it is about 'herding cats.' Certainly it was difficult to direct twenty or so people with very different views of geography, to create a common

---

7   Elsewhere I have written at length on the issue of residential preferences, most recently in a forthcoming paper in the Proceedings of the National Academy of Sciences.

vision and to deal with their everyday irritations and concerns. The sum is clearly greater than the individual parts, but it is hard to create the sum. It was made more complicated by the dual structure of the geography degree at UCLA which offers geography and an environmental science degree. We are lucky to have the environmental program and to have warded off efforts in the past by the then Dean of physical sciences, a geologist, to capture it to bolster a failing geology program. Now that sustainability science is the flavor of the month, it is good to have it in geography.

I was chair for four years in the mid to late 1980s and then again for two years in the mid 1990s. When I first became chair, I wrote proposals for a future larger department (it did not happen but we got back to a reasonable size), argued for resources, and did all the things one might expect of a new chair. We were allowed to advertise for four new positions in the first year, had a dozen interviews and appointed faculty who are now the backbone of our department. We later hired four women to assistant professorships, the first women hired in the department in the last thirty years, and three of them are now senior faculty members. They changed the image of the department and our standing in the profession

Looking back, I ask myself, 'did I have a vision of the department I wanted?' I think I did, but like the search for theory I think it evolved differently and took paths that were not always expected. I did have the view that we should hire young faculty who were committed to a scientific enterprise broadly defined and I believe we did that. Interestingly, the physical geography program once less strong than the human program, is now a very talented one. The appointment to it of Larry Smith from Cornell during my second term as chair still has me marveling at how much difference one individual can make to a program.

I was succeeded after my first term as chair by my colleague, Nick Entrikin, whom I had helped hire in 1975 and who was a former student at Wisconsin. During our eight years as chairs, the Department evolved into the strong one that it is now. I think we can both take credit for that transformation, but of course it will be forgotten as new people put their stamp on the program. I worry about whether the future replacements of those of us who are no longer young will maintain the focus and interest on science in human geography.

Whether by luck or timing, I did not 'drift' further into administration. I am not sure had I been offered a Dean's job that I would have declined, but I am on reflection glad that it did not happen. I like my research projects too much to give them up and I have truly enjoyed teaching a diverse, smart and creative group of graduate students. My recent Ph.D. students, mostly women given the changing demographics of our graduate programs, have joined programs across the country and internationally and are busy making names for themselves. While my first graduate students have in turn chaired departments and moved into senior administration in some cases, these new graduates are just beginning their research careers. I am pleased that they have been trained to keep the analytic tradition alive and to do research which is not so different than that which has been at the heart of my own contributions.

But it is not only graduate students to whom we leave the legacy of continuing the scientific tradition. I have enjoyed teaching my undergraduate classes on population growth and dynamics to hundreds of undergraduates over a thirty or so year career at UCLA. From time to time, I get those letters reminding us that teaching is a critical part of our role in the university: a letter thanking me for opening a door to new ideas, a note to tell me that someone has been made partner in a law firm, a thank you for suggesting graduate school studies in public health as a way of returning 'home' and being of service in a developing country. These letters remind me that the influence of our teaching extends beyond our discipline and also that a commitment to the scientific context is a thread that binds us all together.

It is a changing world and geography a changing discipline but one with a lot to offer the wider research community and our undergraduate students, whether they be those whose contact is through only one or two undergraduate geography classes or those who train to be future professionals in our changing world. The New Zealand I left decades ago has changed too. The multiple daily flights have drawn it closer to the once far away places, and although I visit there often and sometimes think of returning, the ties that bind are on both sides of the Pacific now.

# BUILDING ON THE DOWN UNDER EXPERIENCE

## Reginald G. Golledge

I WAS BORN at the end of the great depression in avery small town, Dungog, in the Hunter valley of New South Wales. The few memories I have of my earliest years were of feeding kookaburras on the back steps of our home and gorging myself on mandarins at my grandparents' home. My father worked on the government railways, an 'essential industry' when war came, and unlike several of his brothers he did not go to war. But we all grew up with tales of how the uncles were doing in France, in Egypt, and later in New Guinea.

My father's job resulted in the family moving frequently throughout the state, first to Katoomba and Lithgow in the Blue Mountains west of Sydney, to Tocumwal on the Murray River, to Cootamundra a thriving town in the 'Riverina' area and then to Yarra where we lived on a small sheep farm. I learned to love open country, the hundreds of bird varieties (mostly parrots), and growing our own vegetables. But I disliked the poisonous brown snakes that infested the house and yard, the primitive outdoor toilet, the carrying of containers of water from a nearby creek when our water tanks were low, and the fording of swollen streams and riding bicycles through pouring rain to the nearby city of Goulburn where I went to high school.

At high school, I did not have good study habits until my English teacher, Mr. Jack Plews, took me aside one day and gave me a strong lecture about work ethics and the importance of achieving a good education. He went on to become Principal of Goulburn High School and later received a Queen's Honors award for his outstanding work with young people in the local community. I respected him greatly and am still indebted to him for his mentoring and advice that have stood me in good stead.

In the school holidays I worked, running trap lines for rabbits and foxes and working as a farm laborer. I loved the outdoor life and roamed around the near and distant countryside, developing a keen sense of orientation and way finding. With only candles and a kerosene lamp at night in our home, school homework was hard to do, and often I fell so far behind that I received rebukes from my teachers. But those years instilled in me a sense of independence, a confidence in my ability to survive, and a keenness to learn about life and the world.

The only high school subjects I thought I was good at were geography and geometry but in my final year my statewide Leaving Certificate exam results were a surprise: I got first class honors in history and only second class in geography. I found out about my results when my history teacher, a Mr. Edwards, rode his bicycle out to our farm with a copy of the newspaper stuffed in his shirt; he was ecstatic that one of his students had got a 'first'. The results were enough to get me a Commonwealth Scholarship and a Teacher's College Scholarship to attend the college of my choice. I did upset my geography teacher, though not intentionally, by asking Jack Plews what I should get with the small monetary prize I won for geography. I had thought about an atlas, but he convinced me that a dictionary would be more appropriate. I bought a Concise Oxford English dictionary which I still have.

Having grown up in very small towns in different parts of the rural environment in Australia, the 'outback', I elected to go to the University of New England, located a few miles outside of Armidale. Going away to university did not start well. I traveled by train from Goulburn via Sydney and Newcastle to Armidale. We got to Newcastle in time to encounter one of the worst floods in the region with rail lines, roads, and bridges either inundated or washed away. We had to leave the train and were packed into army trucks which slowly made their way along dirt roads through the coastal hills and into the upper Hunter River valley where the flooding was less serious. After a five-hour ride we were put on a train again, in the middle of the night, and packed into such a small number of carriages for our trip north that several people in each car had to share the space in the toilets, an arrangement that made for continual disruption.

## *The University of New England experience*

The total number of freshmen entering the University of New England (then a college of the University of Sydney) was eighty-one and the total student population was only slightly more than two hundred. This resulted in intense and often very personal contact with the lecturers and professors teaching the various courses, even from the first day of class.

I did not immediately follow Jack Plew's advice and become a hard working undergraduate. Instead, I did enough work to get reasonable grades and spent a great deal of my time playing rugby, chess and cards. However, the people that I associated with in the student union included not only my peers in each year, but also those who were senior and junior to me, as well as the very small number of graduate students in the university at that time. There were more of the latter in the hard sciences, particularly physics and chemistry, than in the humanities and social sciences, and this exposure helped make me aware of the gaps in the knowledge I had accumulated during high school.

My first year courses reflected my interests in high school and consisted of geography, history, English, and an interesting new experience, psychology. In my second year, I took geography, history, and English and in my third year, geography and history. My results were such that I was one of two persons invited to stay on for a fourth year and complete the geography honors program. By doing so, and then enrolling the following year in the geography M.A. program (I was the first to enter and complete this degree at UNE), I abandoned my original plans to attend the local teacher's college and earn a Diploma in Education and thereby forfeited the bond associated with the Teacher's College Scholarship that I had received. I was required to repay to the Department of Education the sum of £500 (about the same amount as my father earned in a single year when working for the New South Wales government railways) and as I note later I received some generous help in meeting this commitment.

The instructional system at the University of New England combined lectures and intense small group tutorials with all professors participating, even the more senior and distinguished ones. The faculty of the various departments in which I enrolled obviously had a tremendous impact on my life. In geography, Ellis Thorpe the chairman of the department, sponsored me for the honors degree and was a strong supporter of my later work at the Masters level, even though it was well outside his areas of interest, which were surveying and cartography. He became a longtime friend and associate and many late afternoons were spent socializing with him in enjoyable surroundings. He also took me on gem hunting trips where I found some beautiful blue sapphires.

Edward (Ted) Chapman introduced me to transportation geography—a specialty that has stayed with me my entire academic career—and carefully supervised me through my Masters program. He had just returned from a sabbatical at Ohio State University, and that opened a very small window for me on what US programs offered. He also was the first to make me aware of the tremendous environmental differences between Australia and the US midwest. At one point in the writing of my Masters thesis, I made a statement about the 'depths of the Australian winter.' He put huge red marks around this with many exclamation marks, noting, 'wait until you've experienced the midwest in winter—then you'll know what the depths of winter really are!' Eventually, I found out this to be only too true.

Eric Woolmington, also on the geography faculty, was a friend and remained so until his untimely death. He was interested in population, particularly demography, and taught me (along with Norm Feather in psychology) the rudiments of statistical analysis. I used some correlation and regression analysis in both my honors and Masters theses, and I was able to get one of the first papers in human geography that used statistical methods published in the *Australian Geographer*.

Herb King, an urban geographer, introduced me in 1956 to the writings of Christaller and Lösch although I did not pay much attention then to their ideas, and only became interested in learning about them later when I was at the University of Canterbury. John Holmes, another lifelong friend, taught me about regional development and change and helped me to develop a style of writing that stood me in good stead for many years. Harold Brookfield introduced me to cultural and social geography, and although this was before he became heavily involved in cultural influences on environmental perception, helped lay the foundations for a way of looking at the world that eventually led me to become a behavioral geographer. Eugene Fitzpatrick, a climatologist, helped me with statistics and was a great trout fishing partner. Iain Davis, a geomorphologist, took me on many field trips and showed me how to interpret the environment in geomorphological terms. In particular, he developed in me an interest in rivers that went beyond the only use for them I had up to that time—as places to fish.

Outside of geography, the two faculty whose influences on me were long lasting were Brian Doulton, chair of history, and Norman Feather, lecturer in psychology. I used to play occasional games of tennis with Feather, and decades later I renewed my acquaintance with him through our common interest in certain mathematical models in psychology, specifically graph theory and multidimensional scaling.

Perhaps the strongest direction in my selection of a MA thesis topic and in ways of processing data was given by Bob Smith, who had been a teaching assistant in the department in my first year while finishing his honors B.A there. As Bob discusses in his own chapter in this book, he went to Northwestern University in the U.S. for a Masters degree and then brought back to Australia a theoretical and quantitative view of transportation and human geography generally that were reflected in his PhD work at the Australian National University. When he returned there, I visited him frequently to ask his advice about my research on rail freight movements. He introduced me to market area analysis and location theory and urged me to buy the innovative book by Walter Isard on *Location and Space-Economy*, which I did, and this changed my entire outlook on the potential of theory and methods in geography. Bob also brought back another innovation that piqued my interest. He showed me how he collected data on Hollerith cards and used them in sorting and classifying information. These, of course, were the precursors of punched cards for computers which were to become an important component of my academic life. No matter how inconvenient it was, whenever I showed up at Canberra, Bob made time to talk to me, to discuss and critique my work, and explain to me what he was doing in the field of transportation.

Two other undergraduate colleagues were to become lifelong friends. One was Toni Logan whose husband, Mal, was then a lecturer in geography at the Armidale Teacher's College. He too is one of the contributors to this volume. Through Mal I later met Maurie Daly and Mike Webber, the latter then a PhD student at the Australian National University and someone who later was to play a significant role in helping me after I lost my sight, but more on that later. The second was Bob Stimson who I became acquainted with in his freshman year when I was his teaching assistant and 'moral tutor'. Bob never recovered from the latter experience but later we became close friends and collaborators (see Golledge and Stimson 1987).

## The University of Canterbury Influences

The offer of a position at the University of Canterbury came to me while I was on a field trip with Herb King in central Queensland. Unfortunately during the trip Herb suffered a heart attack and I had to drive him to the local hospital. For the next three days I lived in the department's station wagon that we had, existing on water from a nearby farmhouse and pineapples. A police car eventually showed up and I was taken to the local station, cleaned up and given refreshments. When they learned my identity, they told me that the entire Queensland police force was on the lookout for me and they produced a telegram, simply addressed to 'Reginald Golledge traveling somewhere in Queensland,' that had been sent to all police stations in the state. The telegram's message was that I had been offered a job at the University of Canterbury and asked if I was prepared to accept it. I phoned the chair of my department at UNE and indicated that I would certainly accept and asked that he telegraph Canterbury to that effect, which he did. It was not until I got back to Armidale and talked to him that I realized that the position was in New Zealand and not the United Kingdom.

I was married the day before I left for New Zealand, and spent the first ten days there touring the North Island. The diversity of landscapes impressed us. Then after a very rough ocean voyage from Wellington to Lyttelton, we traveled by train into Christchurch where we were met at the railway station by the head of the Department of Geography at Canterbury, Leigh Pownall. We learned that he had found a place for us to live and he helped us get settled in immediately. He showed us around Christchurch and described a walking route for me to get to the university. This was but a small example of how efficient and polished Pownall was, both in general as an administrator and as a mentor to his faculty. He became Vice Chancellor of the University a year or so later, and when in that role he learned that I was still paying off my Australian teacher's college scholarship, he arranged to have it paid off immediately. He certainly had my respect.

At Canterbury, I was assigned the teaching of cartography and mapping to a mix of geography and civil engineering students and I was expected to run field trips associated with the surveying and mapping components of my courses. I also ran a graduate seminar on Australia, and taught economic geography at the undergraduate and graduate levels. I was soon introduced to three other young persons in the department who became my firmest friends and remain so to this day. They were Les King who had just returned from the University of Iowa after completing a PhD there, John Rayner, a climatologist/upper atmosphere and meteorology specialist, who had gone from England to McGill University in Montreal for a M.Sc. before coming to Canterbury; and Bill Clark who had finished his M.A. and was planning to go to the University of Illinois for doctoral study.

The most influential contribution to my enlightenment and development as a geographer was provided by Les King. He had read my *Australian Geographer* article and knew of my interest in quantitative methods. He offered courses on introductory and advanced statistics to graduate students at Canterbury and invited me to sit in on them. He also had a strong interest in location theory and rekindled my interest in the subject. When Harold McCarty came as a visitor the following year, Les suggested that I teach a joint course with McCarty on location theory which we did. Les also introduced me to martinis and manhattans that complemented my experience with Australian beer and (at that time) not so good wines.

John Rayner and I jointly taught some field classes, including surveying and mapping. It was in connection with computing that John had his strongest influence on me. The university had recently bought an IBM 1620 with 32K of memory and Les and John convinced me to go with them to the programming courses taught by the IBM representative. Les kept insisting on how important computers were going to be in the future, and I slowly kept plugging away at learning about the computer environment. After Les left to go to Canada, John took me under his wing and helped me learn computer usage. At that time, I had made an arrangement with the New Zealand Government to obtain all their rail freight bills, punched onto IBM cards, for a period of 12 months and I was receiving about a million cards a month. John helped produce a program to summarize and generalize the information and we spent many a night watching the computer run through hundreds of thousands of cards while illegally drinking beer and eating pies in the computer room. I had about eight million cards processed by the time I left Canterbury in August of 1963, and though I later obtained a small grant to process the remaining cards from that year, I was never able to access the complete set of documents. I understand that the 10 or 12 million punch cards were eventually stored in a damp cellar and in time disposed of.

Two visitors to the Canterbury department also helped to shape my future career. The external examiner on my Masters thesis at the University of New England had been Professor Harold Mayer from the University of Chicago. During my first year at Canterbury, he was visiting the University of Auckland and came down to Canterbury to give a series of lectures. We talked extensively, and he urged me to come to the United States to do a PhD. An even stronger influence was that of Professor Harold H. McCarty, chair at the University of Iowa, who spent 1962 at Canterbury. Les King had been instrumental in getting 'Mac' to come out for the year. As noted earlier, we co-taught a course in economic geography which drew heavily on Isard's work. At various times during the year, McCarty urged me to come to the States and do a PhD. Initially, I was hesitant but when after his return to Iowa he offered financial support for me in the department and for my wife in the Department of educational psychology and as a teacher in the University high school, I was persuaded. I left the University of Canterbury in August of 1963 and entered the PhD program at the University of Iowa later that same year.

## The University of Iowa Period

We arrived in in San Francisco in August 1963 and from there flew on to Denver to attend the AAG conference. McCarty and King met me there, and McCarty immediately took me in tow. He introduced me to several prominent members of the discipline, some of the gods we had worshiped from afar. King in turn introduced me to some of the young 'rebels'.

From Denver, we drove in convoy across the midwest to Iowa. My Australian background surfaced when after a day or so of crossing the plains, I blurted out, 'where are all the birds?' I was so used to the constant chattering of parrots and the intermittent calls of kookaburras or other exotic species in the Australian wild that the silence of the midwest was striking. I was told in reply about the migratory habits of North American birds.

The geography faculty at Iowa consisted of Harold McCarty, Clyde Kohn, Neil Salisbury, James Lindberg, Ronald Boyce and Ken Rummage. McCarty, Lindberg, and Boyce played significant roles in my education, particularly in regard to location theory and quantitative methods. Kohn had a major part in making me realize the importance of theory and the lack of it in geography. I interacted less with Rummage and Salisbury (a physical geographer), but appreciated the latter's emphasis on process thinking.

One of the more striking impressions made on me was by Gustav Bergman in his course *Philosophy of Science* which we geography graduate students were required to take. He was a logical positivist, and introduced me to a way of rigorous thinking of which I previously had no experience. My mind felt like an opening flower. Many new lines of thought emerged. I had never properly considered the importance of assumptions in any facet of geographic work (quantitative, methodological, systematic, or theoretical). It was Bergman more than anyone else who influenced me to start looking seriously at the assumptions on which theories, laws, and generalizations were based.

Bergman had a similar influence on the other graduate students at Iowa at that time, including Gerard Rushton, Douglas Amedeo and John Hudson. The long talks I had with these three and the results of their suggestions that I take courses in marketing, computer science, psychology, and philosophy, gave me the type of multidisciplinary background that had been missing up to that point but which greatly influenced my life thereafter.

At that time Bill Clark was completing his PhD at the University of Illinois and he joined Gerry Rushton and me one summer in working for the Community and Business Research Organization at Iowa. Much of the work involved countless hours at the university computer center, punching, collating, and entering cards that contained data on the consumer behavior of an extensive sample of rural householders in Iowa with respect to the size and location of towns in which they purchased a range of goods and services. On many nights this mindless exercise was terminated when we were picked up at the computer center at about 3 a.m, taken back to Ron Boyce's home, and given food and generous libations until he could finally beat us at pool.

At Iowa, I became much more interested in psychology and took courses in learning theory and developmental psychology, as well as statistics. My interests shifted from classic transportation flow modeling to location theory and then to decision making and choice behavior. In particular, I focused on consumer behavior and found companionship particularly in the works of Rushton and Clark. In succeeding years, we published several articles resulting from our shared interests. In my own work, the transition to an interest in decision making and choice behavior led me to Herb Simon's *Models of Man*, to the work of Julian Wolpert on the irrelevance of economic or spatially rational behavior as opposed to the alternatives offered by Simon, and to Peter Gould's work on game theory showing how different results can be produced when changing attitudes toward risk or learning occurred. My PhD dissertation focused on probabilistic analyses of marketing decisions in the Iowa hog farming community and was the foundation for my interest in what later became known as behavioral geography.

I completed my PhD in 1965 and took up a position at the University of British Columbia, Canada, where I stayed for a year. But change was again in the wind. Les King had moved from McGill University to Ohio State University and was working with Edward Taaffe to build a theoretical and quantitative group. He recommended that both John Rayner and I be recruited and we were eventually appointed to positions at there.

## *The Years at Ohio State University*

Between the mid and late 60s, the Department at Ohio State University appointed Kevin Cox, Lawrence Brown, Emilio Casetti, John Rayner, and myself, among others. The department was developing a new image, that of an innovative, progressive department fully in step with the 'quantitative revolution' while also maintaining some of the best facets of traditional geography. Howard Gauthier and Taaffe taught an up-to-date series on transportation geography, Earl Brown and Henry Hunker taught economic geography and location theory; George Demko taught demography and population and had a specific regional specialty in the Soviet Union. One of the department's earlier specialties, cartography, was continued and later further developed under the guidance of Harold Moellering.

Several aspects of the Ohio State experience helped shape my career. First, my interests in theoretical and quantitative analysis were strengthened by my participation in a unique set of seminars in which faculty presented their specializations to colleagues in a colloquia type setting. At that time, I was exploring the use of different types of learning models for dynamic decision making in a spatial context and I led one of these colloquia based on the book by Bush and Mosteller, *Mathematical Models in Psychology*. Others were offered by King on multivariate analysis, Casetti on differential equations, Rayner on spectral analysis, Brown on diffusion processes and simulations, and Cox on linear programming and social network analysis.

Collaboration in research such as I had done at Iowa with Rushton and Clark flourished in the Ohio State setting. With Lawrence Brown I published a paper from my dissertation on 'Search, learning and the market decision process' and with him and a graduate student, John Odland, a paper on migration behaviors. Les King and I collaborated on an invited paper for the retirement of Harold McCarty at Iowa, on the use of Bayesian analysis in different geographic scenarios. I had the task of presenting the paper in Iowa City and I was startled to find a very large notice in the corridor outside the room in which the session was to be held, inviting all persons currently attending the 'North American Bayesian Society' meeting to come and hear the paper. But then to my relief I found out that it was one of John Hudson's 'manufactured situations'. King and I later collaborated in writing an urban geography text in which we tried to combine analytical components of urban settlement, urban structure, and urban behavior (King and Golledge 1978 ).

My friendship with John Rayner strengthened at Ohio State. As an upper atmosphere analyst, his background and training were quite different from mine, but we found a number of interesting situations where they overlapped. Consequently, we jointly obtained NSF funding for a study of the spectral analysis of settlement patterns in diverse environments, examining places as different as southwestern Pennsylvania, western Iowa, and eastern Oregon. We also ventured into the realm of mathematical psychology, presenting a paper at one of the annual meetings of the North American Classification Society and Psychometric Society. The paper included analysis of behavioral data using non-metric multidimensional scaling followed by a two-dimensional spectral analysis of scaling output. Following that conference, we obtained funding for a two-day meeting at Ohio State University at which geographers, psychologists, and people from marketing met to discuss multidimensional data analysis. The result was a jointly edited book (Golledge and Rayner 1982).

Taaffe encouraged me to pursue my interest in behavioral geography and I did so in a series of seminars and student supervisions. Kevin Cox also was developing an interest in behavioral analysis from his viewpoint as a political geographer interested in voting behavior and social networks. We organized a session at the AAG meeting in St. Louis and then published the papers as one of the first collections in behavioral geography (Cox and Golledge 1969). Although in the 1970s our interests drifted apart, we later put together a companion volume illustrating how the field had developed and changed over the decade.

Georgia Zannaras was the first of a number of students at Ohio State who pursued what at that time was labeled a 'behavioral approach' in geography. Her thesis on the perception of urban neighborhoods was one of the first analytical behavioral studies that focused on the area of cognitive mapping and the attempt to verify the externalizations of preferences and attitudes using conventional socio-demographic variables. Following her, Ronald Briggs' work on the multidimensional scaling of consumer preferences, Victoria Rivizzigno's on spatial cognition, and Aaron Spector's on analytical models used in cognitive mapping and spatial cognition were equally important.

With these students I began exploring new ways of collecting data ( for example by survey research and laboratory experiments) and new methods for analyzing them, including uni-dimensional scaling, non-metric multidimensional scaling, hierarchical clustering, multivariate analysis of variance, and so on. Attendance at conferences on these subjects brought me in touch with the work of persons such as Joseph Kruskal, Douglas Carroll, Clyde Coombs and others. Our first paper using multidimensional scaling in connection with perceptions of distance in intra-urban space was presented at the AAG meetings of 1969 and was received rather coolly by the audience though one commentator, Eric Moore, praised it.

The following year when I was on leave at the University of Sydney, I went to a talk by Coombs who also was visiting there. After his presentation, I managed to talk to him for awhile and mentioned my interest in multidimensional unfolding and scaling. I noted that I was visiting from Ohio State and in reply he said that he understood that there was a young geographer there who was interested in the same topics and that I should make sure I contacted him upon my return. When I told him that I was that young geographer, he was a little embarrassed. However, we did maintain contact for years, and I obtained many publications from him and his associate James Lingoes relating to scaling and the use of different analytical techniques on scaled data.

During the next four or five years, most of my efforts were focused on obtaining and contrasting different metric and non-metric multidimensional scaling practices. Graduate seminars proved to be an ideal place for this type of exploration and students such as Marilyn Brown, John Odland, Grant Thrall, Richard Zeller and others all made significant contributions in terms of learning and testing a variety of analytical methods that could be used on behavioral data. In the early 1970s, I received an NSF grant to look at cognitive configurations in the local area using metric and non-metric scaling, hierarchical clustering, and other analytical procedures. Unfortunately, Senator William Proxmire awarded my project one of his annual 'Golden Fleece' awards. We entered into a correspondence wherein I explained what the future significance might be of the work I was doing, and I received an unofficial apology from him.

My former associate, Gerard Rushton at Iowa had also become interested in multidimensional scaling and we were asked by Les King, on behalf of the Commission on College Geography of the Association of American Geographers, to write a resource paper on the subject. The paper which appeared in 1972 drew attention to, among other things, the work of Waldo Tobler of the University of Michigan whose innovative work in cartography had produced software that did trilateration, a parallel version of Kruskal's multidimensional scaling algorithms. His software became important in my research over the next few years and I developed a long term friendship with Tobler, to the point where we later became colleagues in the same department.

Much of the work we all did at that time was innovative and highly technical, and it was difficult to find publication outlets for it. In this respect, we were in the same boat as many others working with spatial analysis in geography. The situation led to the growth of a 'gray literature' consisting of departmental discussion papers and technical reports. The discussion papers of the University of Washington, Michigan, Northwestern, Iowa, and Ohio State University constituted the bulk of this new literature. Since these publications never achieved official status their circulation was limited. Because of this, their significance in the history of the discipline usually has been overlooked, particularly by those writing from afar who primarily rely on the conventional published literature in deciding what is important in the discipline.

One outcome was the launching of the new journal *Geographical Analysis* which Les King, its founding editor, describes in his chapter in this book. When Les left for McMaster University, I became editor and with a view towards enlarging the journal's readership I invited papers from psychologists, biologists, mathematicians and others to complement the work being produced in geography. Today the journal is still regarded in the discipline as a leading one for publishing theoretical and analytic papers and has a well-established multidisciplinary reputation and patronage.

Another activity that was important to many of us in the discipline at the time was the series of seminars in quantitative geography that Michael Dacey and his colleagues at Northwestern University obtained funding for and ran. It was at one of the seminars that I first met Peter Gould and Barry Garner, both of whom became friends for life. I was particularly interested in Gould's ideas about 'mental maps', which were, in essence, cartographic maps depicting surfaces representing people's stated preferences for living in certain environments. This idea fascinated me and led eventually to further explorations of the literature in cognitive psychology, particularly that relating to spatial cognition. It was also influential in my search for alternate ways to represent externally different knowledge structures acquired by individuals over time and led to our experiments with metric and non-metric multidimensional scaling, hierarchical clustering, and other techniques mentioned earlier.

I had retained my interest in philosophy while teaching at Ohio State, and was very concerned about finding a philosophy that was relevant to behavioral research. The strictly logical positivist point of view that I had embraced eagerly from Gustav Bergman at Iowa, and which was reflected in the book that I had written with a former Iowa colleague (Golledge and Amadeo 1975), did not fit with the idea of a cognitively organized subjective world. Thus, while exploring different methodologies for analyzing behavioral data, I also searched the literature for an appropriate philosophical base on which to ground this work. An introduction to the Michigan geographer Gunnar Olsson helped me in my quest. We discussed philosophies at length, and I began traveling to Michigan to spend weekends with him. One never knew who else would be there. His house was like a magnet and at times I found John Hudson, David Harvey, Les King, Peter Gould, as well as Michigan geographers such as Waldo Tobler and John Nystuen there and we would sit around for most of the night discussing the state of the discipline and philosophy and life in general. For some of these visits I took graduate students to Ann Arbor with me and at other times he brought groups of students down from Ann Arbor to spend a day or two at Ohio State. Out of these experiences, I slowly developed what I called my 'process philosophy of everyday life'. I use this approach to relate objective and subjective realities and to help understand the decision making processes of people in both real and imagined environments. I also began formulating my own theory of how people acquire spatial knowledge which we called 'anchor point theory' (Golledge 1978). Thereafter, it became the main framework for my work in spatial cognition and cognitive mapping and has gained some recognition in associated fields where cognitive maps are a subject of research.

In 1975 -76 an Australian student, Ashlyn Adrian, piqued my interest in disadvantaged groups and through her I met her professor, Joseph Parnicky, a social worker and social psychologist. Out of this contact came an NSF funded joint project that combined my interest in cognitive mapping with his interests in disadvantaged groups, particularly those who are borderline retarded. Our collaboration extended over a number of years and involved for a time John Rayner also.

## *The Move to the West Coast*

In 1970 while on a sabbatical leave at the University of Sydney, Australia, I became acquainted with David Simonet who was then chair of the department. He had earned the first PhD in geography from the department, and then had spent years in England and the United States in a variety of academic and business positions before returning to Sydney. He did not stay there long however and by the mid 1970s he had returned to the United States as chair of the Geography Department at the Santa Barbara campus of the University of California. He contacted me to see if I would be interested in joining their program. I went out for an interview during which Simonet took me around the university, stopping at every grove of eucalyptus trees. The sights and smells and the sunny, clear weather reminded me very much of Australia, and Simonet's enthusiastic plans for developing the department persuaded me that it would be a very interesting move. Back in Columbus, Ohio, I communicated several times with Waldo Tobler who was also being courted by Simonet and by June 1977 we had both decided to accept his offers. I have never regretted my decision though initially it involved a cut in my salary.

The department that we joined had only an undergraduate program in geography and our first challenge, working with Simonet and the other faculty, was to win approval for graduate programs at the masters and doctoral levels. It was granted in very short time. The PhD program began in 1980, the year I inherited the chair from Simonet who had been appointed Graduate Dean. I had already completely embraced his idea of a department of geography in which physical and human sciences were integrated and joined by a common knowledge and use of symbolic languages and technology.

Initially at UCSB, I continued working on projects relating to mentally challenged people that I had begun with Joseph Parnicky at Ohio State University. I was fortunate to become advisor to a group of extremely productive and bright graduate students, including G. Donald Richardson (UCSB's first PhD in 1982), Nathan Gale, Bill Halperin, C. Michael Costanzo, Peter Burley, Scott Davis, and several others. This group at first worked with me on developing a study of mentally challenged people in the Santa Barbara area that matched the work we had begun at Ohio State. This was a quite productive period, and we experimented with more of Tobler's software while producing a number of related papers and technical reports. I also continued with my work on consumer behavior, developing a joint project with Neil Wrigley of Bristol University that involved a cross-cultural study of consumer practices in Bristol and Santa Barbara.

While acting as Editor of *Geographical Analysis*, I had accepted the publication of a paper by a Wisconsin mathematical psychologist, Lawrence Hubert. I was surprised to find that he had arrived at UCSB at the same time that I moved there, and in our first year we managed to meet up over a pitcher of beer in a local bar. By the time the pitcher was finished, we had outlined two or three projects on the backs of napkins. Hubert had some brilliant ideas for analyzing spatial data sets, but lacked the primary data to test them. We had joint interests in non-metric and metric multidimensional scaling, hierarchical clustering, and mathematical and statistical analysis generally. There followed a period of about eight years of significant and productive collaboration between Hubert and my group.

Multidisciplinary collaboration was not restricted to my work with Hubert. Terry Smith, a colleague in geography, and I had found a number of overlapping interests, particularly in decision making and choice behavior. He was very interested in computer science and in an attempt to establish a cognitive science program at the university. One side effect of this was the development of a multidisciplinary interaction which included Smith and myself, Jim Pellegrino from educational psychology, and S. Marshall from psychology. Our major interest was in the development and use of computational process models in spatial domains. Two streams of work were involved, the first being the technical task of building a computational process model, in this case of spatial travel behavior, and the second was the empirical testing of such a model. As a group, we obtained NSF funding and began many years of collaborative research. In particular, Pellegrino and I collaborated for the rest of that decade on a variety of topics relating to children's acquisition of spatial knowledge by their travel in unfamiliar environments.

At this time also, a longstanding correspondence with psychologist Tommy Gärling at the University of Umeä (Sweden) blossomed. We finally managed to meet personally, and we began a long association in research which has continued to the present day. Gärling became interested in computational process models and we arranged that one of my students at that time (Sucharita Gopal), who was also working with Smith and Marshall, would spend a year with him in Sweden. The outcome of this was a series of joint papers (together with others on his faculty at Umeä) developing a computational process model format to deal with daily activity patterns of household members. Another result was the building of the model 'Scheduler' which proved to be of interest to transportation scientists in many countries who were also considering adopting an activity-based approach to transportation planning and policy making. Since that time of our first cooperation, Gärling and I have exchanged visits and worked with different groups of each other's students in the area of disaggregated behavioral modeling and spatial cognition (see Garling and Golledge 1993). We have worked also with colleagues at UC Davis and UC Irvine in adapting geographic information systems (GIS) to the 'Scheduler' model.

In 1983, while in Australia, I lost the sight of my left eye overnight. There was no warning, and I only found that I could not see out of the eye when I tried to play squash the next morning and could not hit the ball. I cut my visit short and returned immediately to the United States for treatment; there I was told not to worry, it was a freak event, and nothing else would happen for about another ten to fifteen years. Twelve months later to the day, I lost the sight of the other eye, again overnight without warning. This was a disastrous event. I could not imagine how I could possibly continue with an academic life of teaching and research that relied so much on access to printed material.

The UCSB Instructional Consultation team (Rick Johnson and Stan Nicholson) came to my rescue and for about six years they comprised a solid support team that helped me learn how to get back into the classroom. They investigated and we experimented with various technical aids that could help me with access to ongoing printed and graphic research materials in my field of interest. Rick Johnson in particular devoted much time both during and after work hours in researching and testing various forms of equipment for my possible use. This equipment included the making of video tapes of lectures that could be presented as a holistic picture instead of my (then) bumbling attempts to remember key points in appropriate sequences. It also involved experimenting with different types of cassette recorders in teaching me how to 'speed listen'. The latter turned out to be extremely important for it takes much, much longer to listen to a book than to read it by visual scanning. We used volunteers from the national organization, 'Readings For the Blind', to read class text material onto tapes. Trials were also done with different types of raised ink pens and spur wheels to try and obtain some idea of text and images through tactile scanning. Still, for several years I did not think that I would be able to continue a productive academic career in geography.

During this time, I received special support from members of the discipline. Mike Webber, then chair of geography at McMaster University in Canada, had faculty members prepare cassette tapes of their current research and send them to me. Peter Gould at Pennsylvania State University constantly sent me taped versions of material that he was writing. Several others in the profession did the same and all this helped me have some contact with what was going on in the discipline. But the most significant event occurred early in 1985 when I was visited by two psychologists, Jack Loomis and Roberta Klatzky. They walked into my office and asked if they could help in some way. At that stage, I was still rather distressed and replied that I had no idea of how they could help me. Klatzky immediately suggested that I draw on the fifteen or so years of work I had done on cognitive maps to help myself to adapt to those overwhelming problems facing those who are blind or vision-impaired, overcoming the print barrier and ensuring safe and independent travel in the general environment (Golledge 1997).

I had soon decided after losing my sight that I did not have the tactile sensitivity to read Braille. I had had carpel tunnel surgery on both hands and found that I could not readily distinguish between the patterns of dots used in Braille representation. Therefore, I decided to rely on other technical aids. This was a time when the first text scanners, text-to-speech conversion software, and other devices were being developed that would eventually lead to an enhancement of a blind person's ability to access digital material. My assistant, Karen Harp, and a friend, Jim Peters (a consulting computer scientist), worked with me to design a computer system. The result was primitive but it worked. A scanner was used to input text into the computer (though it could only scan a limited number of type fonts); a voice card allowed me to speak instructions to the computer for bringing up files and reading them; text to speech conversions were made possible by a Dektalk interpreter; and a vision enhancer enlarged the computer screen and allowed me to vary the size of symbols and text so that I could, with the limited amount of vision remaining to me, work through mathematical formulas and some images and tables. Obviously, this was an area that could benefit from further research, and I pursued it. For example, in 1986 while on sabbatical in Australia, Don Parkes of the University of Newcastle, a geographer friend for many years, came to me with the idea of producing computer-based tactile images supplemented with auditory descriptions so that I could access maps, diagrams, and images again. The result, called NOMAD, proved to be both acceptable and commercially profitable for Don and, by the early 1990s, was available in many countries throughout the world. Ten years later a visiting post doctoral fellow from Queens University,

Belfast, Dan Jacobson, suggested an upgraded and newly configured version of the NOMAD type device which could give blind or vision-impaired people access to on-screen imagery, diagrams, and tables. Research on this project called 'Haptic Soundscapes', was funded first by two grants from UCSB and then by a multi-year grant from the 'Program for Persons with Disability' of the National Science Foundation. The research focused on using force feedback or vibratory mice to explore on-screen imagery or tables with an auditory description complementing the virtual tactile experience of the shape and form of the images just accessed.

The challenge of finding a solution to the problem of ensuring safe and independent travel continues to be an important theme in my research. It has been stimulated and shaped by my interaction with the psychologists Loomis and Klatzky. For most of 1985, these two met with me weekly (Fridays for two hours), at which time they would summarize for me papers that they had read during the week that related to my interest in cognitive mapping, way finding and travel behavior, and spatial cognition generally. After almost a year of this, Loomis produced a 'white paper' for discussion that talked about a way finding guide for blind or visually-impaired people using current technology including a global positioning system (GPS), a geographic information system (GIS), and an auditory virtual reality as the interface. This led to a series of proposals which we submitted to the National Eye Institute at the NIH and we received several multi-year grants to pursue this line of research. Much of the initial work was concerned with the spatial abilities of the blind or visually impaired. We undertook extensive laboratory and field testing of the relative ability of blind persons to estimate and travel different distances, and to estimate angles and directions, including the learning of routes and spatial layouts. By 1990 Loomis had produced a working model of what we called a 'Personal Guidance System'. Our testing showed this to be extremely powerful, and for the next fifteen years we did research on various aspects of the model's capabilities while continuing with our basic research into the spatial processes involved in way finding with and without sight (Golledge 1999). Even when Klatzky became chair of psychology at Carnegie-Mellon University, we continued weekly meetings by phone and were able, with the help of some post doctoral students in psychology and geography, to produce a substantial number of papers and book chapters on our procedures and results.

One other line of research surfaced during my UCSB years. An anthropology graduate student, Carol Self, began to take my seminars and undertook a series of direct readings with me. Her interest was on sex-based differences in spatial abilities. In class, we designed and conducted a number of pilot experiments that compared sex typing of spatial activities and compared them with a study done ten years before with east coast undergraduates. Our results were very different, and we interpreted this as a reflection of the social changes resulting from the general emancipation of women in the work place, in the home, and in sporting and recreational activities. Shortly after this, we appointed a young psychologist, Dan Montello, to our faculty and he, Carol and I obtained a multi-year NSF grant to study sex-based differences in spatial abilities.

## Concluding Thoughts

I have been fortunate throughout my career in that the people who influenced me greatly have remained good friends. Bob Smith, Les King and John Rayner in the early decades, and Lawrence Hubert, Jack Loomis, Roberta Klatzky, and Dan Montello in more recent years have given me valuable encouragement and support in my efforts to pursue a multidisciplinary and integrated research career. Many others whom I should have acknowledged have also given wonderful help.

There is no doubt that my early training at the University of New England and my spell at the University of Canterbury provided me with an appropriate sense and awareness of what was going on in the academic world beyond Australia and gave me some exposure to the new theoretical and empirical research that was being undertaken in North America geography. I was fortunate in having the opportunity to become a member of the geography profession in the United States and I have not regretted my decision to do so. What would have happened had I stayed in Australia? I doubt very much that I would have developed the same research interests in spatial analysis and computers, and I certainly would not have had the levels of international activity and contacts that I have been able to enjoy by way of editorship of journals, reviewing of journal submissions and book manuscripts, and conducting joint research funded by substantial grants from agencies such as the U.S. National Science Foundation.

Like those other geographers who are part of the Australian diaspora— Bob Smith, Mal Logan,Terry Beed, John Britton, Jan Monk, and Robert Stimson— with whom I have had varying levels of contact over the years, I have been able in North America to build on the solid foundations laid in my undergraduate and graduate programs in Australia. The gradual emergence of multidisciplinary participation in my research was, I believe, a product of the encouragement I had in my early years to read widely outside of geography. My academic life has been stressful but productive and built on my down under experiences.

**REFERENCES**

Amadeo, D. and Golledge, R.G. 1975 *An introduction to scientific reasoning in geography* (New York: Wiley)

Cox, K.R. and Golledge, R.G. eds. 1969 *Behavioral problems in geography: A symposium* (Evanston, Ill.:Northwestern University Press)

Garling, T. and Golledge, R.G. eds. 1993 *Behavior and environment: Psychological and geographical approaches* (North Holland: Elsevier)

Golledge, R. G. 1978 'Learning about urban environments' in Carlstein, T., Parkes, D. and Thrift, N. eds. *Timing space and spacing time. Vol. 1 Making sense of time* (London: Edward Arnold), 76-98

Golledge, R. G. and Rayner, J.N. eds. 1982 *Proximity and preference* (Minneapolis: University of Minnesota Press)

Golledge, R. G. and Stimson, R. 1987 *Analytical behavioral geography* (London: Croom Helm)

Golledge, R. G. 1997 'On reassembling one's life:Overcoming disability in the academic environment' *Environment and Planning D: Space and Society*, 15, 391- 409

Golledge, R. G. 1999 *Wayfinding behavior: Cognitive mapping and other spatial processes* (Baltimore: Johns Hopkins University Press)

King, L.J. And Golledge, R. G. 1978 *Cities, space and behavior: The elements of urban geography* (Englewood Cliffs, N.J.: Prentice-Hall)

# STEPS ALONG THE WAY

## Peter G. Holland

IN DECEMBER 1975 I left Montreal in a mid-winter snowstorm to pay a flying visit to my home town of Waimate in South Canterbury, New Zealand. It was high summer when I arrived, and a few days later I walked along the Hunters Hills where I had done the field work for my Master of Science thesis fifteen years earlier. Memories of growing up in rural New Zealand came flooding back, spurred by the distinctive smell of damp clover, the twittering of skylarks, the big sky and distinctive topography, and the unforgettable sound of wind in tall tussock.

I recalled that experience thirty years later during a weekend research retreat in the delightfully named Pleasant Point, a rural service town in South Canterbury. At sunrise, I walked into the surrounding farmland and met another member of the research team. All we wanted to talk about was our native hearths: he was born in Fairlie, close to the northern flanks of South Canterbury, and I thirty kilometers farther south. What struck us that late spring morning were the cool dry air of dawn, the shining backdrop of snow-covered foothills and the distant Southern Alps, the closely managed farmland grazed by impossibly white sheep, and a comfortable silence punctuated by the day's first larks and the wild chortling of magpies. I had always liked South Canterbury, but that morning I understood what Yi-fu Tuan (1977) and others meant by the word 'home'.

New Zealand is characterized by its diverse environments, and South Canterbury contains examples of many of them. Childhood in Waimate County had imprinted on me a rich set of landscape references: forest remnants in damp gullies protected from runaway fire, tree ferns and *podocarps*, tussock grasses and 'vegetable sheep', some rivers that begin to rise a few hours after heavy rain sets in and others that take a day or two to respond, and the alternating hot dry and cold wet gales of spring and early summer. Three childhood experiences affected what I later chose to study. My parents had encouraged me to propagate ferns and other native forest plants, told me the names of introduced species, and allowed me to spend time on my paternal grandparents' farm on the outskirts of Waimate. Carefully trimmed gorse hedges lined the fields, and a grid of tall *macrocarpa* trees protected the house and out-buildings from gales in winter and spring. There were productive vegetable and flower gardens, a large orchard, and many different types of farm animals. All spoke of self-sufficiency and a deep respect for the land.

Mine was a bridge generation. Rather than leave high school at fifteen years of age to work in a shop or on a farm, as friends had done a few years earlier, I completed high school, went to university, graduated, and joined a profession. In the late 1950s tertiary education in New Zealand was undergoing change. Young people were faced with new social expectations, but we were offered tools that would fit us for life in a rapidly changing world.

> *..teaching and research at the university usually affect social change most profoundly in ways that are often implicit and indirect... (Pelikan 1992, 161)*

I went to the University of Canterbury in Christchurch in 1958 with the intention of graduating Bachelor of Arts then training as a high school teacher. George Jobberns, at that time Professor of Geography and Head of Department, felt that I would not do well in an Arts program and suggested that I enroll instead for the three-year Bachelor of Science degree. Despite an almost disastrous first year of undergraduate study, I discovered that he was right and reveled in botany, chemistry, geography, geology, and mathematics courses. The two-year Master of Science by coursework and thesis followed.

My last three years at Canterbury were what university should be about. Until then, the core of our instruction had respected geographic tradition: impressionistic assessments of landscapes, words rather than numbers, and photographs rather than diagrams. Abroad, however, the seas were being made choppy by academic geographers who had recently adopted and found productive the normal methods of scientific inquiry: hypotheses rooted in strong theory, well-designed experiments or programs of carefully controlled observations, appropriate methods of mathematical or statistical analysis, logically derived conclusions, and limited speculation. The geography that I knew as a school boy and as a young undergraduate stressed facts, but its successor was about principles. Without knowing it, geography students at Canterbury during the early 1960s were experiencing at first hand something of a scientific revolution, a development in the discipline that subsequently has been discussed at length.

At the University of Canterbury, the drivers of that revolution were three recent graduates: Reg Golledge from the University of New England in Armidale, Australia; Les King back in New Zealand after doctoral studies at the University of Iowa; and John Rayner from McGill University in Montreal, Canada. Together, they steered the students in my year towards a new world of ideas and provided some of the analytical and practical tools that we needed to explore it. No one who studied geography at Canterbury in the early 1960s will have forgotten the noisy 'Monroe' calculator that was housed in an airless room and required a booking to use. In my final year, the University bought an IBM 1620 computer and I learned Fortran I. But it was not all indoor work for geography students. Indeed it could not have been in a Department so committed to field inquiry and where the highest compliment to which a Canterbury geographer could aspire was for George Jobberns to say 'you have an eye for country.'

John Rayner took Jobberns' words even further when he described his and Jane Soons's plans for a network of environmental sensors in the Chiltern Valley at Cass, near the headwaters of the Waimakariri River. He showed us how to view the environment as a 'system', demonstrated the merits of a well-designed field experiment, and told us how key environmental variables could be identified and electronically measured. Reg Golledge directed us to quantitative analyses of people, their actions and economies, and Les King introduced us to a suite of powerful analytical tools that we could use in diverse situations. Their teaching, supplemented by Moroney's (1962) engagingly written introduction to the basic methods of parametric statistical analysis, opened the door to a large room full of previously unimagined ideas and potent research procedures.

A few months after I had left the University of Canterbury to study in Canberra an eminent New Zealand geographer of the old school who was visiting Australia at the time asked about my Ph D topic. It concerned the growth dynamics of mallee vegetation in the semi-arid southeast of Australia, and he visibly grew more sombre as I described how I was trying to relate shape and growth in my sample plants. He let me get to the end of a rather breathless account, stood up, said 'poor geography', then walked away.

*The plants are nothing like as fresh and green as those at home, and the landscape has a peculiar, lustreless, grey-green hue (Aurousseau 1968, 521)*

The five years I spent as a student at the University of Canterbury were stimulating, but three and a half years as a Ph D student in the Institute for Advanced Studies at the Australian National University, Canberra were a revelation. With the whole-hearted encouragement of my research supervisor, Donald Walker, I read widely and explored a research topic in depth. Four publications influenced my thinking about plants and their environments: two were early accounts of cybernetics (Ashby 1952; Weiner 1948), and the others were von Bertalanffy's (1960) survey of systems theory and Lindeman's (1942) pioneering paper on ecological energetics. Three years later the book by the theoretical physicist, Morowitz (1968), introduced me to a powerful set of mathematical and physical principles about the biosphere as an intermediate system, with its structure, persistence, and activity dependent on a steady flux of energy.

In the mid-1960s, the ANU was a young organization with a small permanent staff, many academics on fixed-term appointments and almost 200 PhD students. University House was home to all research students except those with dependent children, and it is hard to imagine a more stimulating environment. A few senior research staff and a steady stream of short-term visitors were also in residence, and many University staff had lunch there. I recall sitting next to Harry Godwin, Fred Hoyle, Margaret Meade, Linus Pauling, Stephen Runciman, and Alfred Steer, to name six in the flow of eminent scholars. All had a lasting impact on an impressionable young man only a few years out of his teens.

What made the ANU such an exciting place was the ferment of ideas and discoveries. Somewhere on campus research was underway into cosmology, DNA, the history of independence movements in the Asia-Pacific region, New Guinea languages, computer-based pattern recognition, plasma physics, plate tectonics, and quasars, and one could hear tantalizing snippets about many of them at meal times or when people gathered in the University House common room for late evening coffee and a chat. Bill Williams and Joyce Lambert had only recently published their ground-breaking paper in *Nature* about a mathematical method for identifying ensembles of species in areas with a complex vegetation cover, the Commonwealth Scientific and Industrial Research Organization was relocating many of its scientific and technical staff from Melbourne and Sydney to a greenfield site beside the University campus, and there was the pervasive sense of science going places. On several occasions while in Canberra I was interviewed about my research for the Australian Broadcasting Corporation's farmers' program. A couple of days after one interview, I was enjoying a beer in a back country pub when someone came up to me and said 'You are wrong'. He had heard me on radio, recognized my voice, and wanted to debate my research findings. The mid-1960s were a grand time to be a scientist in Australia.

I often wondered if what I was studying mattered compared with what staff and other students at the ANU were doing. My work involved an investigation into the dynamics of *mallee*, a vegetation type that many Australians during the 1960s would probably have described as boring, best converted to wheat fields, and the antithesis of dynamic. I had selected for detailed study two stands of mature *mallee* vegetation, each two hectares in extent: one at Wyperfeld Park in northwest Victoria, and the other ten kilometers south of Mount Hope in central New South Wales. My research sprung from Ovington's pioneering studies in Great Britain. The field and laboratory work entailed monitoring seasonal change in species composition and the growth of herbs and small shrubs in permanent quadrats, as well as deciding how to estimate standing crop and growth rates in the shrubby *eucalypts* that give the *mallee* its name and character. The latter part of the project quickly proved the more rewarding, and I discovered mathematical regularities in plant form and function. My starting point was a method for analyzing the stream patterns of large and small drainage basins (Horton 1945), which I had heard about while a postgraduate student at the University of Canterbury, and I treated *mallee eucalypts* as organized networks of twigs and branches in three-dimensional space.

Like others who had done research in the Australian *mallee*, I came to think of it as an integrated ensemble of two biogeographically distinct groups of species: the *mallee eucalypts*, together with the shrubs and ephemeral herbs that grew in their shade; and the *spinifex, chenopods*, and short-lived herbs that predominated under canopy gaps. I was also struck by the timing of bud-break. The *eucalypts* in my two field areas put on soft new shoots in December, just as the searingly hot summer got underway. Whenever I cut off a new shoot it would wilt in a few minutes, yet I did not see a wilted shoot on any of my tagged plants despite the serious drought then affecting the *mallee* country of southeastern Australia. That observation pointed to the dominant, tall shrubby plants having a highly efficient water economy, but it also hinted at a growth system which had evolved in a place and time with less potential for water stress during summer. Did an ancestral ensemble of woodland species spread outwards from cooler, better watered land at the close of the Pleistocene to split the habitat with *spinifex* and other arid zone species? I was unable to answer that question, but the experience of living in, observing, and thinking about the Australian *mallee* pointed to the importance of parallel inquiries at three different scales: the local scale, to uncover details of plant growth and propagation; the landform scale, to observe geographic patterns in plant distribution and check how closely they match the geomorphological elements of a landscape; and the national or continental scale, to ascertain if patterns discerned at the other two scales remain evident across the biome.

### *It is a curious city, Montreal ( MacLennan 1961, 238)*

Shortly before completing my doctoral studies in Canberra I was appointed to the staff of McGill University in Montreal, and my response upon arrival was a mixture of astonishment and unease: Montreal was bilingual, the first large city I had lived in, and situated even further from the sea than Canberra. It was also the city I quickly grew to love and still think of as one of my two 'homes'. Until then I had only seen beech, maple, and oak trees growing in parks and private gardens, but my office at McGill looked out on a tall hill covered with them and other strange plants. Even at the family level there were few similarities between the flora of the eastern deciduous forests of North America and that of either the eucalyptus forests and woodlands which I had known in southeastern Australia or the remnant *podocarp* forests in the South Canterbury hill country. In effect, I had been transplanted from one biogeographic realm to another and was faced with learning a new flora as well as coming to terms with an environment characterized by tropical heat in summer and intense cold during winter. My response was to replicate what I had done in the southeastern Australian *mallee* in the hope that it would help me come to grips with a novel flora and a different environment. While publishing the main findings of my doctoral research, I established several sets of permanent quadrats in the deciduous forest on Mont St Hilaire, which the Gault family had willed to 'McGill University and the Youth of Canada'.

In the late 1960s the Gault Estate was a forested oasis draped over an exposed mass of geologically old, intruded volcanic rocks set in the previously glaciated, intensively farmed Saint Lawrence lowlands of southern Quebec. It lay about forty kilometers southeast of Montreal, and offered recreational facilities to the public as well as secure areas to scientists for field study. Like the McGill students and staff who undertook research there, I found it a refuge from the bustle of Montreal and an area of abiding scientific interest. After a couple of summers spent on my knees periodically resurveying the flora of almost five hundred permanent quadrats, I began to appreciate what had made the eastern deciduous forests of North America so exciting to several generations of field ecologists and biogeographers. I also got to know an ephemeral forest herb, *Erythronium americanum* or 'trout lily', that was to be the focus of my research for two decades.

From what I observed in my permanent quadrats it was apparent that trout lily could form dense swards in the fertile soils of moist, shaded ground and each year could spread about ten centimeters. Although it speedily filled recently opened niches it did not strike me as a species that was especially well adapted to 'finding' and occupying dispersed sites. Most of the trout lily plants that I monitored at weekly to monthly intervals over three growing seasons were sterile, lacked flowers, and spread by runners. I also wondered if there were geographically isolated small areas on Mont St Hilaire where this species might be expected to grow but did not. Then there were the questions that had intrigued several generations of biogeographers and ecologists who had worked in the deciduous forests of eastern Canada. Did all the plant species currently found there make the same long journey from refuge areas in southern United States of America after the close of the Wisconsin glaciation 12-15,000 years ago, or did some find refuge in places closer to the ice-margin? And is post-Pleistocene recovery in species composition and vegetation structure essentially complete?

My research involved field transplant experiments, and they allowed me to decide if trout lily is occupying all possible small-area habitats on Mont St Hilaire. After more than five years of close observation on transplanted bulbs and their progeny, I was able to conclude that trout lily grew wherever its long-term, ecological requirements were satisfied. In environmentally marginal sites my transplanted bulbs failed to produce runners and were usually dead within a couple of seasons. Bulbs transplanted to damper soils, however, normally established small, apparently viable, colonies.

In the course of that research, I checked research publications about the geographical distribution of trout lily across Eastern North America and was impressed by the situation in the Atlantic Provinces, especially New Brunswick and Nova Scotia. Trout lily grows in upland parts of the belt that links the two provinces as well as in the hardwood forested hills flanking the northern and eastern headwaters of rivers draining into the head of the Bay of Fundy. It also occurs as an outlier on Cape Blomidon in Annapolis County. That distribution excited my interest. Is the geographical range of trout lily in Nova Scotia expanding or contracting? Is the outlier the consequence of bulbs having been washed down river from deciduous forested hill country inland from Truro, thence into the Bay of Fundy, and finally lodging on the flanks of the Cape? Alternatively, had someone planted bulbs in the deciduous forest on the Cape? I felt that a transplant experiment would provide useful information for answers to those questions.

At the same time I became interested in the ecology, growth behavior, and demography of trout lily across its geographic range, and measured preserved specimens held by herbariums in eastern North America. There appeared to be consistently smaller individuals from the southern states of the USA and larger from the northern states and adjacent Canada. Is that difference statistically and biologically significant and, if so, is the cause environmental or genetic? Had I remained at McGill, those questions would have driven my research for a decade or longer.

*The geographical position, and the height of the land combined to create a landscape that had not its like in all the world. There was no fat on it and no luxuriance anywhere; it was Africa distilled up through six thousand feet, like the strong and refined essence of a continent ( Blixen 1964, 3)*

The two years I spent on secondment to the University of Nairobi during the early 1970s helped me complete the mental shift from ecology to biogeography. It also reconnected me with arid zone plants and Southern Hemisphere floras. Nairobi lay close to excellent sites for field teaching and research. Riparian strips of closed canopy forest extended off the Aberdare Mountains and onto the Masai Steppe. Low hills near the regional administrative center of Machakos were fringed by sedimentary aprons with well-developed catenary sequences of topsoils: deep red earths on the gently sloping hill tops, shallow brown soils in midslope locations, and deep black clay soils on the broad flats that extend out from the toe of the slope. And widespread sheet and gully erosion showed what can happen after heavy rain falls on the unprotected bare soils of subsistence holdings. One powerful memory from that time is of a trip along the edge of farmland southeast of Machakos after heavy rain the previous day had mobilized exposed topsoil and washed it several kilometers downslope to come to rest on the highway between Nairobi and Mombassa. That morning, local people were spread out along the road with wheel barrows and shovels, picking up loads of fines and taking them back to their small holdings in the hills. An experience like that quickly shifts the need for environmental management off the pages of a textbook and into a geographer's consciousness.

The highway west from Nairobi rises gently for about thirty kilometers then suddenly drops almost a thousand meters down the eastern wall of the Great

Rift Valley. A few kilometers south, the Ngong Hills are a grandstand for an even more dramatic view: the eastern wall of the Rift Valley falling in steps down to Olorgesaille, an early occupation site for hominids in East Africa. Lava flows extend from fissures in the earth's crust, apparently extinct volcanoes rise at intervals along the floor of the Rift with large and small lakes between them, and twenty kilometers away the western wall of the Rift rises abruptly from the floor. Two high volcanoes lie to the east of the Rift Valley. Mount Kilimanjaro, with its cap of snow and ice first established during the Pleistocene and now rapidly shrinking, is the higher and younger. Mount Kenya. which looks like an ancient tooth from which the enamel has been removed, has remnant pockets of ice and snow, one of which is the Lewis Glacier named after a British geomorphologist. Mount Elgon, on the western plateau, is smaller and lower. In my day, the only place where activity normally associated with volcanic activity could be seen was at Hells Gate on the floor of the Rift Valley, where steam rose from vents in the volcanic rock.

The vegetation cover of the Rift Valley floor was dominated by grasses, thorny shrubs, and succulent plants adapted to survival in an area of almost year-round water stress. The lower walls of the Rift were covered with a dry forest vegetation, but at higher altitudes where there was more rainfall and air temperatures were cooler the forest cover had a tropical appearance and contained abundant *podocarp* trees. They were potent reminders of places I already knew in the southern hemisphere, namely the forests of southern New Zealand. Higher again, the forest gave way to dense thickets of tall bamboo. Above that, and as sharply as if the border had been cut with a scythe, an extensive moorland began. Near its lower altitudinal limits the common tall shrub was *Erica arborea*, which seemed to play an ecological role comparable to that of *manuka* in the New Zealand hill country. I was also struck by the small herbs that grew at high altitudes on Mt Kenya. Most were closely related to plants I had seen in western Ireland yet were profoundly different from the plants that grew in the wide grassy steppes between the two mountains. How and when did their ancestors make the long journey south into equatorial East Africa from the middle and high latitudes of Western Europe? And why did the ensembles of herbs and shrubby plants differ, often quite markedly, from one East African mountain top to the next?

The heathers of Eastern and Southern Africa were a biogeographic mystery. Taxonomists recognized more than 730 species of *Erica*, about fourteen of them in Scandinavia, Western Europe, and the flanks of the Mediterranean basin. *Erica arborea* is the only species in the northern half of Africa and its geographical range extends into eastern Africa, thence to southeastern Africa. South of the Limpopo River, however, what has long been treated taxonomically as *Erica* is represented by several hundred species.

A Kenyan plant that posed fewer taxonomic problems and had an interesting geography was *Euphorbia candelabrum*, a tall succulent perennial of dry woodlands on the semi-arid lower flanks and floor of the Rift Valley. It has close relations in the dry lands of eastern and southern Africa as well as in the Horn of Africa. The late Professor Alf Hove and I found that in central Kenya its local scale distribution was closely linked to soil water availability. In arid parts of the Rift Valley floor the plant was confined to shallow depressions in relatively impermeable larva that had been filled with fine sediments and where sufficient water could accumulate to meet the plant's needs through-out the year. In better watered places, however, the plant was widespread and could even be found growing in the stratified, highly permeable volca-nic ejecta that had accumulated in ancient lakes. Those observations helped me appreciate the close functional links between terrain elements and plant distributions, something that Hack and Goodlett (1960) had outlined in their classic publication. Terrain diversity is also a force for species evolution, as Ernst Mayr had shown in his stimulating accounts of species formation in the animal kingdom. A couple of years later I was later able to draw upon those ideas in a study of the geographical distribution of *Aloe ferox* in the karoo of South Africa.

*It is a country flooded by sun; lonely, sparse, wind-swept, treeless on the flats for many miles (Palmer 1966, 14)*

South Africa during the 1970s and early '80s was a challenging and stimulating country for a visiting geographer. The flora of southern Cape Province was as diverse as any I had encountered, yet biological links with far off New Zealand were evident. The notion of a Gondwana biota became comprehensible to me, and the highly diversified terrain of the southern Cape was clearly a driver for the evolution of new plant species. Taken as a whole, Africa does not have an especially large flora – climatic changes during the Pleistocene, primarily forced by shifts in global wind systems, are thought to have depleted a biota that had evolved in comparative geographic isolation during the Tertiary era – and it is theoretically possible for one expert to identify most of the trees and shrubs across large parts of the continent. What is biogeographically striking about the extreme south of the continent, however, is the very large number of species that grow in nutrient-poor soils on the metamorphosed sandstone mountains of Cape Province.

Field work in eastern and southern Africa enabled me to observe how a wide-ranging plant species tends to occupy different small area landforms at the edge of its geographical range than in the middle. The classic paper is by Boyko (1947), and it concerns the inter-fingering of three biogeographically distinctive groups of species in Palestine. Levyns (1950) extended that work in her analysis of topographic controls over the geographical distribution of Cape *schlerophyll* and karoo species in hill country near Ladismith, South Africa, and I based my research into the biogeography of *Aloe ferox* on her model.

*Aloe ferox* is inter-fertile with several other species of the genus, one of them being *Aloe arborescens*. The former is a tall, long-lived, single stemmed plant with a branched inflorescence and wide-ranging, shallow roots. The latter is multi-stemmed, has a simple inflorescence, and roots that extend well below the surface for support, water, and nutrients. One of my field areas in the southern Cape extended down a long gentle slope mantled with colluvium and ended near the top of a rocky escarpment. *Aloe ferox* grew in good numbers on the colluvium and *Aloe arborescens* was abundant amidst the rocky outcrops, but in the mosaic of colluvium and fissured rock where the two terrain units overlapped I found *aloe* plants sharing some morphological features of one species and some of the other: for example, branched plants with branched inflorescences. That cluster of morphologically intermediate individuals was almost certainly a hybrid swarm growing on intermediate terrain akin to what Anderson (1948) had observed in the southern United States of America.

A biogeographer tends to view the landscape as a dynamic stage that offers diverse ecological and evolutionary opportunities for living things. As an undergraduate I had been told about the 'misguided' views of environmental determinists, and nothing I have seen or read since then has led to a change of heart. Harlan Barrow's notion of human ecology as the intellectual core of geography strikes me as beyond dispute, but Aldo Leopold (1940) is the environmentalist whose book had the greatest initial impact on my thinking about people and environment.

*The lamentable laisser faire in regard to misuse of land and water is passing away (Guthrie-Smith 1922, 422)*

After two decades abroad I decided to return to New Zealand. By then I had a clearer understanding of the role and functions of a university in western society and was spurred by the desire to understand the profound environmental transformation by people of a part of the country that had been home to both sides of my family for five generations. Of the many early accounts of environmental transformation, and its consequences for native New Zealand plant and animal species, the best remains Guthrie-Smith's (1922) book about 'Tutira', a large sheep station in Hawkes Bay. A more general traversal, and a book that I had read while an undergraduate student at Canterbury, is Clark's (1949) survey of the transformation of New Zealand by people, plants, and animals. I had been told and had read about the speed of that process, and knew many of the introduced plant and animal species involved, but was beginning to feel that the declared certainties lacked support. Why did so many pest plant and animal species become established in New Zealand? What did the first generation of European settlers make of the New Zealand environment, and how well prepared were they for living in a small country about as far as it is possible to be from the British Isles whence so many came? What did they learn from personal experience and from the experiences of others? And how did they make use of that learning in their everyday lives? As I came to grips with recent ecological thinking about pioneer plant and animal species, what I had seen during my childhood began to make scientific and cultural sense.

An uncle used to tell me about rural life in early South Canterbury, and his words suggested a much greater intelligence at work than the popular image of country people merely bumbling through. The New Zealand climate is benign for much of the year, and there are few poisonous animals or plants. The country's position astride a major geophysical plate boundary predisposes it to earthquakes and vulcanicity, but neither is an every-day occurrence. None of these examples suggested significant and persistent problems for residents. What was, however, strange to many European settlers and hard for them to deal with were temporal and spatial variability in the weather and the way a large river can turn from a manageable flow to a raging torrent in a few hours. In the second half of the nineteenth century, some English newspapers referred to drowning as 'the New Zealand death', and it did not take only those foolhardy people who after one pot of ale too many had blundered into a deep running stream outside the taproom and drowned. Even talented and knowledgeable young persons accidentally lost their lives in flooded rivers, and the country was deprived of too many of its brightest and best at the time when they were most needed.

The words 'brave', 'interested', and 'risk-taking' came to mind whenever I thought about the first two or three generations of European settlers and how they dealt with an often capricious, occasionally unforgiving, physical environment. Poets like Blanche Baughan have written about the feelings of pioneer women giving birth and raising families in isolated huts, all the while worrying about their spouses working in the bush far from the house, and this theme winds through much of the early fictional writing. Twenty years ago I realized that I had to worm my way into the minds of the first two generations of European settlers if I hoped to discover what had driven them to clear the tussock, burn the bush, plant long straight lines of gorse and broom bushes, and establish oblong plantations of pine and *macrocarpa* trees. By their actions they were laying the foundations for the no-nonsense, economically efficient, and highly productive rural landscapes that are evident today throughout the lowlands of the eastern South Island of New Zealand.

Early newspapers have proved a good but not outstanding source of information about a time when news from outlying areas could take several days to reach the Editor's desk and when it took equally long for published newspapers to reach rural subscribers. Manuscript sources were often better. From the earliest days of organized settlement, rural people often kept written records: farm and personal diaries, letter books, accounts of income and expenditure, and the names of visitors and laborers. I decided to begin my investigations with fencing and shelter plantings. Fences and hedges lie at the heart of sound farm management. They ensure pasture is used efficiently and allow the farmer to control breeding in flocks and herds of farm animals. Along with shelter plantings and remnant patches of the original vegetation cover, they give shape and substance to a rural landscape.

*...research and instruction mutually fructify each other...( Pelikan 1992, 84)*

After twenty years passed studiously avoiding administration, the sea change came when I was appointed Professor and Head of the Department of Geography at the University of Otago. The time seemed right for a career shift. I was enjoying lecturing and research supervision, had found a fruitful and stimulating topic for my own research, and felt that I could maintain balance between those professional activities and a new suite of service responsibilities. I thought then, and still believe, that academic administrators need to be in regular contact with lecturing and technical staff in their respective disciplinary areas, supervise one or two graduate students, and remain active in research.

The first of my administrative activities at the national level, and one that gave great satisfaction, involved chairing a large expert group of high school teachers and government officials charged with producing an integrated geography syllabus for the final three years of high school. At that time, my departmental colleagues and I used to offer short residential courses – typically running from Friday evening to Sunday afternoon – to assist geography teachers in the high schools of southern New Zealand, and they deepened my appreciation of the importance of close links between high school and university for a teaching subject like geography. Within two years my job description included administration at the university and inter-university levels, and I was deeply involved with the development of tertiary education policy for New Zealand.

In 1962 the University of New Zealand comprised six semi-autonomous university colleges. That year each was granted legislated independence, but all were funded from a governmental grant administered by the University Grants Commission (UGC). The Education Act of 1989 brought further changes across the tertiary sector, notably a widening of responsibility for degree programs. The salient characteristics of each type of educational institution were specified in the Act, and the central importance of research-based teaching in degree programs was enshrined in law. The Act had a profound impact upon tertiary education, and the universities took some time to appreciate the benefits and challenges of the new policy environment. At the time, I found as others did Pelikan's (1992) reconsideration of the views of Cardinal Newman – founder of the National University of Ireland and a major nineteenth century thinker about universities and their role in education and research – to be of great assistance.

For the six years before the Education Act became law, I had represented the University of Otago on the UGC Curriculum Committee, a national body responsible for approving new study programs in the universities. An important operating principle was that there should not be unnecessary duplication of specialized study programs. A university could continue to offer a costly professional program in, for example, dentistry or electrical engineering in the reasonable expectation that another institution would not seek to duplicate it, thereby diluting the potential student intake. When the Act became law, all the comfortable old certainties changed and tertiary institutions were able to propose and offer study programs in almost any area of inquiry. Approval to proceed – in effect access to public funding for the program – required satisfactory completion of a sequence of steps controlled by the Universities Vice-Chancellors Committee (NZVCC) in the case of the universities, and either the newly-established Qualifications Authority (NZQA) or one of the recognized inter-institutional bodies with delegated authority for all other tertiary educational providers. The institution that proposed to offer a new study program had to outline it in considerable detail, list all contributing academic and technical staff as well as their qualifications, provide a detailed breakdown of the resources available to staff and students, and, in the case of a degree program, summarize the research activities of academic staff and declare the research support normally available to them within the institution. In brief, the process involved a mixture of academic approval and institutional accreditation. Permission to offer a new study program was usually subject to satisfactory arrangements being put in place for internal review and external quality audit. I found great professional satisfaction in assisting the New Zealand Institute of Surveyors develop unit standards for a range of surveying qualifications, and in 1996 that work was recognized by my election as Honorary Member of the Institute.

New Zealand academics remember the years since 1989 in different ways. My strongest memories relate to the quality movement, external review, and academic audit. In 1996 the NZVCC agreed to fund a stand alone Academic Audit Unit (AAU), and I was appointed to the roster of registered auditors after completing a training program. I had previously been engaged by NZQA to recommend approval of new study programs and accreditation of providers under its control, and was already closely involved with external reviews of degree programs in universities across New Zealand. Later I was a member or chairperson of three panels set up by the AAU to conduct academic audits of individual universities, and I served as Deputy to the Director in 2005. I have also been a member of twelve panels set up by NZQA to periodically audit the work of three tertiary educational bodies with delegated powers of course approval.

All of those activities provided me with a deep insight into New Zealand's system of tertiary education and they brought me into regular contact with parliamentarians, government officials, and members of industrial groups. They were also rooted in work I had done while a member of the Tertiary Action Group (TAG), a body set up in 1996 by NZQA to develop definitions for the legislated suite of named tertiary qualifications and to advise the Minister of

Education on procedures for quality assurance and credit transfer between tertiary institutions. TAG drew its members from all levels of the tertiary sector, industrial and administrative organizations, unions, and government agencies. It reported to the Minister fifteen months after its first meeting, and its report has helped shape the suite of general, professional, and vocational qualifications now available to tertiary students in New Zealand. It also paved the way for formal recognition of prior learning, increased participation by ethnic groups and older people in tertiary education, and resulted in a geographically mobile student body. In the course of that work I frequently made contact with individuals whom I came to think of as 'invisible geographers': geography graduates who had made productive careers in administration, local government, private industry, and the civil service, and who saw no reason to describe themselves in public as 'geographers'.

The universities were often resentful of involvement by outside organizations such as TAG but they appreciated that government was determined to receive value for the public money spent on education. 'Accountability', 'outputs', 'performance', 'quality', 'responsibility', and 'risk' quickly became six of the more commonly used words across the tertiary sector.

Fifteen years of increasingly overt governmental presence in tertiary education have produced a mixture of good things and bad. Staff and students came to understand that if an academic program does not attract sufficient numbers to cover costs then it risks losing institutional support. Amongst the consequences of that have been the down-grading of some long established academic disciplines and a shift away from the notion of a small number of core disciplines central to a university education. Whenever the occasion allowed, I would argue that each student coming directly to university from high school should have sound English language skills, a reasonable knowledge of basic mathematical operations, some training in a science subject and in a humanities discipline, and a good knowledge of one or two elective subjects. I would still like to see a prescribed common core of subjects for all undergraduate degree candidates – my short list is English, mathematics, introductory science, and a second language – but that remains a distant goal.

Another change that followed my move to the University of Otago was responsibility for more postgraduate research students each year than I had been used to at McGill University. In New Zealand, the 1980s and '90s were years of rapid growth in student numbers and declining staff resources, and I found myself supervising research topics to the edge of my knowledge and experience: resource planning, environmental management, development studies, fluvial geomorphology, and rural studies, to name five. That would not have struck George Jobberns and his generation as noteworthy, but it took me away from my research field of biogeography. In retrospect it was a mistake, even though I remained Associate Editor of the *Journal of Biogeography* for two decades from 1982 and as such was able to encourage many fine young researchers to submit manuscripts for publication. It has been a privilege, however, to serve as President of the New Zealand Geographical Society and to be closely involved with changes that should set that organization on a sound course in an increasingly difficult environment for professional bodies. But perhaps the greatest pleasure of all has come from seeing so many of my graduate students move on to important employment after graduation. As an Otago colleague and a most productive researcher once told me, a significant part of academics' work involves training our successors.

> *And then he thinks he knows*
> *The hills where his life rose,*
> *And the sea where it goes. Matthew Arnold (1822-1888), 'The Buried Life'*

I find the world of the first two generations of European settlers in New Zealand profoundly interesting, and am currently investigating what and how country folk learned about weather patterns, climate, and hydrology in the former tussock grasslands of both main islands. Not for nothing has the weather long been a favorite topic of conversation amongst rural people. Even in drier parts of New Zealand where water for irrigation and use by livestock is available, weather systems affect farm operations and have led to the installation of built features designed to lessen their ill-effects. I am trying to identify which environmental forces required an immediate response from the first two generations of settlers, and to document how people made the shift from environmental learning to environmental modification. As an approach to environmental history it draws upon the writing of Simon Sharma (1995), steers away from great men and official institutions, and seeks to place the ordinary person in center stage. It is intellectually risky, highly dependent upon access to and reasonable interpretations of unpublished material and oral history, a fusion of environmental studies and social history, and rooted in an ecologist's understanding of the biosphere. I hope it will lead me towards a deeper understanding of the mutuality of people and environment in a small but profoundly interesting part of the world.

## ACKNOWLEDGEMENTS

My research supervisors, Professors Jane Soons and Donald Walker, the graduate students whose research I supervised in Canada, Kenya, South Africa, and New Zealand, fellow students and colleagues in six universities, and the people with whom I served on university committees and academic audit panels, encouraged and informed me more than they know, and I am grateful to them. Drs Garth Cant and Alexander Wearing read a draft of this chapter and I acknowledge their many helpful comments.

## REFERENCES

Anderson, E. 1948 ' Hybridisation of the habitat' *Evolution* 1, 1-9

Ashby, W. R. 1952 *Design for a Brain* ( London: Chapman & Hall)

Aurousseau, M. (ed) 1968 *The Letters of F.W. Ludwig Leichhardt* (London: Cambridge University Press)

Bertalanffy, L von. 1960 ' Principles and theory of growth' Chapter 2 in Nowinski, W. W. (ed.) *Fundamental Aspects of Normal and Malignant Growth* (Amsterdam: Elsevier)

Blixen, K. 1964 *Out of Africa* (London: Jonathan Cape)

Boyko, H.1947 'On the role of plants as quantitative climate indicators and the geo-ecological law of distribution' *Journal of Ecology* 35, 138-157

Clark, A H. 1949 *The Invasion of New Zealand by People, Plants and Animals: the South Island* ( New Brunswick, NJ: Rutgers University Press)

Guthrie-Smith, H. 1922 *Tutira, the Story of a New Zealand Sheep Station* ( Edinburgh: Blackwood).

Hack, J T and Goodlett, J C. 1960 'Geomorphology and Forest Ecology of a Mountain Region in the Central Appalachians' *Geological Survey Professional Paper 347* ( Washington: United States Government Printing Office).

Horton, R. E. 1945 'Erosional development of streams and their drainage basins: hydrophysical approach to quantitative morphology' *Bulletin of the Geological Society of America* 56, 275-370

Leopold, A. 1949 *A Sand County Almanac, and Sketches from Here and There* ( New York: Oxford University Press)

Levyns, M R. 1950 'The relations of the Cape and Karoo floras near Ladismith, Cape Town' *Transactions of the Royal Society of South Africa* 32, 235-246

Lindeman, R L. 1942 'The tropho-dynamic aspect of ecology' *Ecology* 23, 399-418

MacLennan, H. 1961 *The Watch that Ends the Night* (Toronto: The New American Library of Canada)

Moroney, M J. 1962 *Facts from Figures* ( Harmondsworth:Penguin Books)

Morowitz, H J. 1968 *Energy Flow in Biology: Biological Organization as a Problem in Thermal Physics* ( New York: Academic Press).

Palmer, E. 1966 *The Plains of Camdeboo* ( London: Collins)

Pelikan, J. 1992 *The Idea of the University. A Reexamination (*New Haven:Yale University Press)

Schama, S. 1995 *Landscape and Memory* (Toronto: Random House)

Tuan, Yi-fu. 1977 *Space and Place: the Perspective of Experience* (Minneapolis: University of Minnesota Press)

Weiner, N. 1948 *Cybernetics* ( New York: John Wiley & Sons)

# NORTHERN REFLECTIONS

## Leslie J. King

I AM ASKED sometimes by friends who have sought refuge from the miseries of the Canadian winter by visiting New Zealand, 'why did you ever leave such a wonderful country?' Hard-pressed to give a convincing answer when the snow is knee-deep around me, my house furnace is burning expensive fuel-oil at an alarming rate and the zipper is stuck on my cumbersome insulated jacket, I usually mumble something about career opportunities and then seek to divert and impress my inquisitors with my knowledge of New Zealand geography by quizzing them on where they went and what they saw. Seldom do they press me further on the details of those career opportunities. But their questions have prompted the reflections that are the subject of this essay.

## *School days in Christchurch*

It was a career in university work that eventually led me away from New Zealand and my earliest steps along that path were taken as a young child growing up in Christchurch, New Zealand, in the 1930s and 40s. We lived for most of my childhood in Riccarton, then a small borough located west of the main city of Christchurch and separated from it by the broad expanse of Hagley Park. The community was typical of the city and indeed of much of the country in its white Anglo-Saxon character. We learned about the Maoris, the first inhabitants of the country, but those remaining in the area lived in isolated communities mainly on the nearby Banks Peninsula and it was not until high school that I ever met one. Ironically, the primary school I attended had a composite Maori name,Wharenui, meaning something like 'large house'.

As youngsters we were aware of few of the hardships that our parents had to endure. Learned commentators later would see us as children of the welfare state, nurtured and protected from the 'cradle to the grave', but such assurances would have meant little to my father, a fourth-generation descendant of a laborer from Paddington, London, England, who had emigrated to Christchurch in 1859. Dad had to struggle through those difficult years of the early 1930s as a laborer on various public works projects in order to provide the support for us. Then later in the decade as he was getting on his feet, leasing and running a small garden store, the war broke out and his drafting into the army, but fortunately not for overseas combat, meant that the business had to be sold. After the war, he would return to the same line of business but as a salesman for Yates Seeds, a company that he remained with until his retirement.

The war in the Pacific posed a real threat to New Zealand in the early 1940s and we were reminded of that fact by the underground air-raid shelters built on the school-grounds and the drills that paraded us into them from time to time. And the imprisonment of a close uncle in the Egyptian campaign, heightened my awareness of the unusual times. But otherwise life seemed to us quite normal; we walked or cycled to school, played cricket and rugby, and enjoyed weekend visits sometimes to the local picture theater or to one of the nearby beaches.

Neither of my parents had completed high school, probably because they both lost their own fathers while very young and had to go to work to assist in supporting their families. But like so many parents with similar backgrounds they were determined that their own children would have the education they had been denied. Their pressure and direction on us in those early years were firm but never oppressive. Homework had to be completed, sometimes with whatever help they could give, report cards were reviewed critically and explanations sought for any less than stellar marks. I know they were immensely proud when in three successive years, I, my brother and my elder sister won the 'dux' awards at the Wharenui school.

With primary school completed, I enrolled at the Christchurch Boys' High School, a school steeped in tradition, much but not all of it fashioned on the rugby field. School began each day with 'assembly' presided over by the headmaster, during which there were announcements, a prayer and the singing of one or more hymns, 'Jerusalem' often being the choice. Our education was a liberal one: we studied English literature, French, general science, geography, history and mathematics. Latin was offered but there was no requirement that we take it, a fact which on occasions later in life, I regretted. My interest in geography as a subject was stimulated by a corps of enthusiastic teachers of the subject and I studied it in all five years. We learned a mix of regional and systematic topics that focused principally, though not exclusively, on New Zealand. The classroom teachings were reinforced by field-trips and week-long excursions to the Mt Cook region.

At the end of the third year, we had to sit the national School Certificate exam in five subjects including English, and then with that hurdle cleared, prepare for the University Entrance exam a year later. A pass in that examination could be earned as an 'accredited' one based on satisfactory performance over the year and I was fortunate enough to achieve this. The fifth and final year at high school, in the 'upper sixth', was spent studying English, maths, history and geography.

## Varsity years

At the beginning of 1952 I entered the Canterbury University College in Christchurch, one of the four constituent colleges of the then University of New Zealand. For my father, I learned later, it was the realization of a dream. For me, at the time, it offered the prospect of a path to a career in teaching, and my obtaining of a 'post-primary teaching' bursary gave me the means to meet the costs of books and so on. In those wonderful days, tuition fees were unheard of. I lived at home during my university years and summer work at the local wool-stores provided me with the money to pay 'board' to my parents throughout the year, a practice that later in life I could never get my own sons to understand, let alone adopt.

My years at Canterbury College were interesting and enjoyable ones. Located just west of the city's center on one of the four avenues that bounded the original city, it was by today's standards a small college with only a few thousand students enrolled principally in the arts and sciences, and with accounting and engineering as the only professional disciplines. A good library was located alongside the quadrangle, surrounded by other Gothic stone buildings, with the students' center but a short walk away. Some of my fellow students undoubtedly knew, but I did not until years later, that Ernest Rutherford and Karl Popper had walked those same corridors.

The Geography department was housed in less august quarters, a rambling pre-fabricated 'temporary' building at the eastern end of the campus. It had many shortcomings but there was a strong sense of place about it for those of us who studied within its walls.

The B.A. program was then a three-year one, with no provision for an honors option or year. It required the satisfactory completion of nine subject units. I registered with the Geography Department and I recall my first meeting with George Jobberns, the Professor and Head, at which he planned my first year of study—English (which was required), economics, geography, and history. With those completed, I then did political science and both geography and history, stages II, in my second year, and geography and history, stages III, in my third and final year.

The geography courses involved a mix of regional and systematic subjects that reflected the interests and expertise of the teaching staff. The regional geographies of the U.K., Europe, the Pacific Islands and New Zealand were well represented at various points in the program; Africa, Asia and Latin America received scant, if any attention. Geomorphology, biogeography, economic, urban and historical geography were the stronger of the systematic fields. Climatology was taught by visiting professors and I recall being lectured on the subject by Professors Lamb from California and McIntosh from Nebraska. There was certainly no requirement for any training in quantitative skills and I cannot think of an occasion when we might even have been presented with an equation. That was true, I suppose, of most if not all geography departments of the day.

Others have written about the methodological and ideological debates that engaged the Auckland and Wellington geography departments in those years. The Canterbury department that I remember was free of such entanglements. We never had to do courses or seminars on the 'nature of geography' and if the lectures and writings of some of the staff in the department were guided or tinted by the arguments of one school or another, they never sought to press conversion upon us. We talked about theory especially in Jobberns' geomorphology course, the Davis versus Penck controversy, but the focus was always on the real-world subject matter and not on abstract arguments about what geography is or is not.

With the B.A. in hand in 1957, I faced the choice of seeking entry into the M.A. degree program in either history or geography. My decision was determined largely by the characters of the two professors involved. In history there was Neville Phillips, aloof and introverted, an authority on Edmund Burke and later, the Vice-Chancellor of Canterbury University. The polished nature of his lectures I still recall. Each one developed a theme or thesis and had a completeness and force about it that we struggled to emulate in our frequently assigned essays. His lecturing was an art and a way of teaching that we seem to have abandoned and even denigrated in too many of our university courses today. George Jobberns, the geography Professor, was a quite different character. Warm and outgoing, an expert on coastal terraces, a passionate advocate of developing an 'eye for country', he relied upon more of a Socratic method to get his arguments across. Only later did I come to appreciate the role that he was playing then in developing public awareness of environmental issues such as soil erosion and conservation. For me at the time he was a friendly and encouraging mentor whose conversation was punctuated with warm smiles, an occasional chuckle and the addressing of me as 'laddie'. Whether I could have gained admission to the history M.A. program was never tested; I chose geography and spent the next two years completing the four examination papers and the thesis required for the degree.

The supervisor of my thesis on the agricultural lime industry of the South Island was Leigh Pownall, formerly a teacher at the Christchurch Boys' High School, but now a Senior Lecturer in the department. He proposed the topic to me, arguing that the industry had such a dramatic impact upon the visual landscape that it warranted study. Pownall had spent a year at the University of Wisconsin and at the time was completing his magnum opus on the history, functions and land-use patterns of New Zealand cities for the Ph.D. from the University of New Zealand. He was a memorable character, a very good teacher, polished and articulate in his relations with people and, in my view, deserving of greater acknowledgment than he has received as an important figure in the development of New Zealand geography. Had one pressed him at the time, I think he would have come down on the side of Hartshorne's 'areal differentiation' view of geography that he would have been exposed to at Wisconsin. But later he showed considerable interest in the spatial analysis and quantitative work that Hartshorne spurned and his paper on low-value housing in two New Zealand cities (Pownall 1960), included two scatter-diagrams, a short step away from a more formal statistical analysis.

Upon completion of the Masters degree I was pointed in the direction of a career in high school teaching and in 1956 I joined with other recruits in spending a year at a newly opened teachers' college for post-primary school teachers. It was a year of highs and lows. Its best outcome for me was that I met there, Doreen, who had completed her studies in physical education at Otago— we married later in 1960 and continue to enjoy a wonderful life together. The low-points, not only for me but I am sure more so for the students involved, were the compulsory teaching training periods that I had to spend out at different high schools. Many years later, I obtained a copy of the reports on my performance in those visits and the phrase 'capable when interested' in one of them seemed to me to be quite generous, given my recollection of the experience.

I began to look for options and especially at the prospect of going overseas to do further study. Britain seemed far away not only in distance but in academic terms. My Masters degree standing had been 'upper second' and I doubted that any of the British trained lecturers in the department would be prepared to go to bat for me on such grounds. In late 1956 or early 1957 I attended a meeting in Dunedin of the Australian and New Zealand Association for the Advancement of Science and among the geographers there were Craig Duncan and Keith Thompson, both of whom had recently completed their Ph.Ds in the U.S., Craig at Ohio State and Keith at Washington in Seattle. They recommended that I follow in their footsteps. Ellis Thorpe from Armidale was there too and he kindly suggested that I think about joining his department as a 'demonstrator'. The U.S. won out after Pownall drew my attention to the Fulbright program; I applied for one of their travel awards and was successful. The prospect of going to America was now an exciting reality but to which university was the question.

I had decided that I wanted to pursue further studies in economic geography but I was not committed to any particular field of specialization or to any department. I have described elsewhere the factors that accounted for my ending up in Iowa (King 1979 ). Before I left New Zealand I had one hurdle to clear, that of the commitment I had made to spend a year teaching in a high school for each year of the teaching bursary support that I had received. My request to have the requirement waived was unprecedented apparently and it took a special visit and presentation by George Jobberns to the Education Department in Wellington to win me the approval. I am forever indebted to him for that intervention; I am pleased that I later had the chance to tell him that and I believe he felt it had been worthwhile.

## Amid the alien corn

The sea voyage from Auckland to Panama City via Pitcairn Island, followed by a flight to Miami and then a rail trip to Iowa City via Chicago, was the field-trip 'extraordinaire' for a 23 year-old geographer from Canterbury. Arrival on the campus at Iowa City and my first glimpses of its muddy river, the fortress-like brick dormitory in which I was to reside and the cramped Geography quarters in an old armory building, dampened my excitement somewhat but not entirely. It was only two or three weeks later that the flame came close to being extinguished. I was hospitalized with a strep throat and one of my fellow students visited and brought with him a copy of the book that was to be the subject of a joint geography-economics seminar on location theory in which I had enrolled. The book was Isard's *Location and Space Economy*, published the previous year, 1956. I leafed through it and when I came to the penultimate chapter on a mathematical formulation my spirits fell and my temperature must have soared. There were equations galore that made no sense at all to me and I began to despair over whether I had made the right choice. In the following weeks, however, many if not all of my fears were allayed. Most of the participants in the seminar, the economists included, proved to be equally apprehensive of the mathematics and whether by scheduling design or accident we never got that far in the book.

The head of the Iowa department was Harold McCarty, 'Mac' to all of his friends and colleagues. Trained as an economist, he had been the founding Professor of the Geography Department and by 1957 he was supervising only one or two students. His research work at the time, co-directed with his colleague Neil Salisbury, was concerned with the ability of humans to make accurate comparisons of isopleth maps that differed according to the intervals and color schemes used. This was not the economic geography that I had expected to work on under his guidance and there was no-one else in the department to whom I could turn. In that first year I often felt both frustrated and disappointed and those feelings were compounded by the stress of being required to register for statistics courses that introduced me to forms of analysis that I had never used before and for which I could see no likely future use. But all that changed when Edwin Thomas arrived in the department in 1958.

I had first encountered Ed in the fall of 1957 when along with McCarty and others I attended the meeting of the West Lakes Geographers at Northwestern University in Evanston. Ed was a panel discussant along with Harold Mayer on some subject having to do with urban planning. Their exchange was a portent of things to come in the years ahead in human geography. The elder Harold, drawing on his wealth of practical experience and knowledge, argued for the importance of the decisions made in the smoke-filled back rooms as a key to understanding. Ed, brash and assertive and armed with his battery of statistical techniques, was dismissive of such qualitative approaches and championed the cause of quantitative analysis. I do not recall that I was swayed one way or the other but it was certainly Ed's cause and not Harold's that was to shape my subsequent career. It was at that same meeting that I first met Bob Smith from Australia who was then studying at Northwestern.

While at Northwestern, Ed had known Bill Garrison who had since moved to the University of Washington. There he gathered together a group of very talented doctoral degree students, including most notably Berry, Bunge, Dacey, Marble, Morrill, Nystuen and Tobler, all of whom would later rise to positions of prominence within the discipline. In the late 1950s that group was exploring various avenues of quantitative analysis of geographic issues and disseminating their ideas by way of a discussion paper series. Ed Thomas was on their mailing list and the Washington papers soon became the subject matters for the seminars which he conducted at Iowa. I was involved in those seminars and soon came to look upon Ed as my supervisor.

Though other scholars such as Dickinson in the U.K. and Ullman and Harris in the U.S. had already given some prominence to the writings of the German geographer Walter Christaller, it was Garrison's group that placed his 'central place theory' front and centre in their quest to emphasize theoretical and quantitative work in human geography. Questions about the number, size, spacing and the functional complexity of urban places in a region were amenable to quantitative analysis and these lines of study were taken up by geographers around the world. Ed and I were among them. Ed was fascinated with what now seems to be an abstruse, some might even say trivial question, that of determining what constitutes 'same size' among a set of settlements. His answer was based in probability theory and suggested that for any particular sized place and a prescribed level of statistical confidence, there was a range in population size that could be considered the 'same' (Thomas 1961). I used his definition of same size in my doctoral thesis on the spacing of urban settlements in the United States, a study that was really an exercise in multivariate statistical analysis at a time when 'canned' computer programs were unavailable and the calculations demanded many late-night hours on the university's IBM 650 computer.

The two years that I spent at Iowa working with Ed Thomas provided me with credentials that were valuable in my subsequent career. The topics that we studied then seem now to be unimportant but in those days they had credibility. Ed, however, soon gave up on them; he moved from Iowa to Arizona and then back to the Chicago area and out of the mainstream of academic geography. Many years later, in 1988, I had a chance encounter with him in a deserted dining-hall at the East China Normal University in Shanghai where he was consulting on a remote-sensing project. He talked then mainly about his super-marathon running.

## A return to Canterbury

In retrospect, the year 1960 was a good one for me although at the time it seemed as though all my plans were coming apart. As a Fulbright scholar I was faced with the requirement that I leave the U.S. for at least two years once my program of study was completed. There was a position open at McMaster University in Hamilton, Canada, and I was invited up for an interview. It was on a cold winter day but the interview went well and I especially enjoyed talking about statistical analysis with Derek Ford, a geomorphologist newly appointed from Oxford. Confident that the position was mine, I made plans with Doreen, who was then completing a Masters degree at the University of Illinois, for us to be married in the University of Iowa chapel in the summer prior to heading north to Canada. A wedding dress was purchased in Chicago, a cake was mailed over in a metal container from Doreen's mother in Dunedin and a best man was chosen. Then a cold front swept down from the north, followed soon by a warming and considerable turbulence. First, a short formal letter from Hamilton informed me that I had been unsuccessful in my application; a week later a telegram arrived from Pownall, now the Professor at Canterbury, offering me a lectureship starting as soon as I could return. Doreen and I were both relieved and excited by the prospect of returning home. Reluctantly, we abandoned the plans for the Iowa wedding, reasoning that our families would be well-pleased to be party to the ceremony in New Zealand. The wedding-dress was packed carefully into the luggage, the cake made its second trip across the Pacific and my brother was pressed into service as the best man at our wedding in Dunedin in October of that year.

The Canterbury department that I joined in late 1960 was not too different from that from which I had graduated a few years earlier. Pownall had succeeded Jobberns as the Professor and head of department but his tenure in that position was to be a short one—in 1961 he was appointed Vice Chancellor of Canterbury University, one of the four separate universities that replaced the old University of New Zealand. Barry Johnston and Murray McCaskill were now my senior colleagues; Bill Packard had left for a post in Australia and Jane Soons, a geomorphologist from the U.K. had joined the staff. Then early in 1961 two other lecturers were appointed— John Rayner, a climatologist who had completed his M.Sc. at McGill, and Reg Golledge, an economic geographer with a M.A. degree from Armidale, Australia. My association with these two men was to develop and strengthen greatly in the years that followed, our careers intersected more than once and our families became good friends. They will smile when they read my confession that the terms of their appointments in 1961, which called for them to receive salaries not too different from my own, caused me some annoyance, given that they had then both only recently completed their masters degrees.

The two years spent back at Canterbury were enjoyable ones. Relations within the department were warm and friendly, a legacy of the Jobberns era, and there were some bright young post-graduate students including Bill Clark, Roger McClean, Peter Hoskins and Peter Holland, all of whom were about to go overseas for doctoral degree studies, who were interested in learning about quantitative techniques. There was good support for research and on the applied level a group of us led by Barry Johnston did much of the analysis and preparation of a transportation study for the city of Christchurch. Colleagues within the department were very supportive of my proposal that Harold McCarty from Iowa be invited as a Visiting Professor and he and his wife Vivian arrived early in 1962. His visit was a highly successful one, further enhancing the tradition of U.S. visitors to the department that had begun in 1945 with Andrew Clark and which is ongoing today. During his visit, Mac persuaded Reg Golledge to go to Iowa for doctoral studies and I recall that the three of us were reunited during the 1963 AAG meeting in Denver when Reg was en route to Iowa City.

## A sojourn at McGill

Early in 1962 I received a letter from Ken Hare, the Professor at McGill, asking me whether I would be interested in a position there. It did not take Doreen and I long to decide. We were very happy living in Christchurch with family members nearby and a widening circle of good friends at the university. But the opportunity of getting back into the North American academic arena by way of the prestigious institution of McGill was too strong a pull and I accepted Hare's offer.

When Pownall had offered me the Canterbury job two years earlier, it seemed that he had no sooner signed the letter than he moved upstairs to the Vice Chancellor's office. My experience at McGill was similar: by the time I arrived there in September 1962, Hare had moved out of the department and into the position of Dean of Arts and Science. Trevor Lloyd, a cultural geographer, had succeeded him as chair.

Montreal in the early 1960s was an exciting city. The cultural transformation of Quebec was underway with the shackles of the church on its society being thrown off and with the emergence in the political realm of the separatist movement. But there was no sense of excitement or yearning for change reflected in the life of McGill's Geography Department. A strong group of physical geographers encountered little opposition in their machinations from a rump of human geographers bent on spending as much time as possible in the Caribbean. No-one was openly opposed to what I was promoting in spatial analysis and quantitative work, they were just indifferent. But there were some good students who were interested, Bryn Greer-Wootten, Janet Henshall and Chris Kissling being notable in this respect, and Fritz Muller, the glaciologist in the department, became a good friend with whom I had many interesting conversations about what was happening in geography. Some years later when Fritz took up the chair of geography at the ETH in Zurich, he invited me to spend the spring term in his department and offer a seminar (in English fortunately) on urban models. Memories of those four months in 1972 that Doreen and I and our two young sons spent in Zurich are still very warm ones.

One event of those McGill days that I do recall well was the 1963 annual meeting of the Canadian Association of Geographers held at Laval University in Quebec City. Ian Burton from Toronto and I were invited to speak in a special session on quantitative methods in geography, chaired by Ken Hare. It is memorable because when Ian published his paper later that year in *The Canadian Geographer* he coined the term 'quantitative revolution' that continues today to be the subject of discussions within the discipline.

I have other good memories of McGill. The summer school run by the Geography department at Stanstead College is one of them. There in a delightful setting on the Canada-U.S. border we taught in the morning and then relaxed for the rest of the day, often entertaining distinguished visitors. The McGill faculty club was another strong attraction. Though it was steeped then in old-world traditions that excluded women from certain of the dining areas, it provided nevertheless a very comfortable forum for lunchtime conversations with colleagues from all disciplines and for social events involving the faculty. My election as a representative of the junior faculty to the McGill Senate and service on a committee charged with considering possible uses for the Mont St. Hilaire estate that had been willed to the University, gave me my first taste of university administration and I enjoyed it.

It was in 1964 that I first mapped out plans for a book on statistical analysis and I still have the publication agreement that I signed with the representative of Prentice-Hall. It called, I note, for the manuscript to be delivered by September 1st, 1965, a target which I missed by several years but fortunately they still published the book. I dedicated it to Jobby and Mac and I have a cutting from the Christchurch paper in which Jobby is being interviewed on the occasion of his celebrated appointment as an honorary Fellow of the Royal Geographical Society. He cites my book saying, 'I just can't keep up with some of the latest developments in geography. I'm not very good at sums. I just can't understand most of it.' Perhaps as might have been expected, the geography that Jobby understood has proven to be more lasting than those so-called 'latest developments.'

## *Hello Columbus*

By early 1964 I had decided to join Ned Taaffe at Ohio State. His plans for the revitalization of that department were ambitious and interesting ones and along with the terms of appointment that he offered, they effectively trumped the other leads that had been made to me. That summer was spent at Berkeley attending a six-week program on regional science, supported by the National Science Foundation, and it was there that I first met Gunnar Ollson. His musings then on the gravity model, voiced as we picnicked among the Napa valley wineries, seemed quite comprehensible but in later years their philosophical dressings confounded me. We remain good friends. After the Berkeley session we traveled back to Northwestern for a seminar on spatial statistics led by Duane Marble and Michael Dacey. David Harvey was there, studying along with the rest of us the properties of various probability distributions. That was the start of a friendship with him that Doreen and I enjoyed over the next decade but in the seventies we drifted apart and it was somewhat ironic that three decades or so later, he served as a reader on my son Loren's Ph.D thesis in political science at M.I.T.

Our six years in Columbus, Ohio, were full and enjoyable ones. On the home front, we had the joy of having our two sons born there, the experience of buying our first house and the challenge of coping with the first of what has proven to be a succession of large disobedient dogs. The university experience proved to be more rewarding than I could ever have hoped for. Ned Taaffe was an exceptional leader and colleague. A man of broad intellect who could converse wisely on the arts, science and politics, he had a strong vision of geography's place in the academy and good insights into the workings of the university. He attracted to the department a group of bright, ambitious young scholars who were supportive of his belief in geography as spatial analysis and he encouraged, by personal example, a commitment to life-long learning of new approaches and techniques. There was a lively intellectual fervor in the department that he fostered and which persisted beyond his retirement. I derived particular enjoyment from my supervision of graduate students such as Stan Brunn, Doug Jeffrey and Yorgos Papageorgiou and from the joint research that I published with Emilio Casetti. We sought to model the movement of economic fluctuations through a system of cities but our ability to test such models was hindered by the lack of suitable disaggregated data and we ended up relying upon unemployment numbers for metropolitan areas, a weak surrogate for the level of economic activity.

There were certain projects on which Ned Taaffe and I worked closely together. One involved the continuation of the summer institutes on quantitative methods that he had begun at Northwestern. We obtained support from the National Science Foundation for a second such institute in Columbus in 1969. The following year, we offered a similar summer program, again supported by the National Science Foundation, on urban models. I think these institutes did play a significant role in diffusing knowledge about the application of quantitative techniques in human geography and spatial analysis to geography departments in North America. Whether they were as effective and as long-lasting in their effects as the Madingley Lectures, devised and run by Peter Haggett and Dick Chorley for high-school teachers of geography in the U.K., would make for an interesting comparison. I had the pleasure of participating in the Madingley program in August, 1967 and it impressed me as a very well-organized and stimulating experience.

Along with Bob Smith who was then at Wisconsin, Ned and I co-authored a collection of readings on the location of economic activity. The book, published in 1968, brought together a series of papers that presented statements of location theory on the one hand and applications on the other. It was no best seller but it did wave the banner for spatial analysis and theory. Another project involved Taaffe and I in the writing of a unit on urban settlements for the High School Geography Project which was launched by the Association of American Geographers with support from the National Science Foundation. We sought to bring together the work that had been done on urban centers as central places and as nodes in transportation networks and flow patterns. We thought our synthesis was a good one but that judgment was not shared by the project leaders and the teachers involved in the trials. The unit ended up being reworked by others and in its final form was barely recognizable by us. My earlier miserable experiences as a teacher trainee in Christchurch probably should have made me more cautious about getting involved in such a project but career ambition won out then over concern for student welfare.

More enduring success accompanied another joint venture, the launching of the new journal, *Geographical Analysis.* There was an on-going discussion at the time about the desirability of having a journal devoted to work on theoretical and quantitative geography, a discussion fueled in part by the experiences of some in having papers rejected by the existing journals. At Michigan, John Nystuen and Waldo Tobler had a strong discussion papers series established but it was not a refereed journal and there seemed little prospect that they could obtain the resources to support its upgrading. Nor could any other group offer a better prospect. We at Ohio State, however, had a fortunate mix of factors working in our favor. The departments of both geography and economics were located then in the College of Commerce that was headed by Dean McCoy, an amiable but shrewd administrator. He had been sympathetic to the demands of both department chairs that they be given the resources to upgrade their faculty complements and was supportive of their ambitions to raise their departments' national profiles. Karl Brunner in economics had a plan to launch a new journal of *Money, Credit and Banking* and we came up with a corresponding one for *Geographical Analysis.* The Ohio State University Press, that already published a journal in education, was anxious to expand its journal offerings and was prepared to publish and subsidize both new journals. With this assurance, the Dean provided the support for the editorial offices and the two new journals were launched in 1969. I served as the editor for the first five years before handing the task over to Reg Golledge.

Reg had been recruited to Ohio State from the University of British Columbia where he had gone after completing his Iowa Ph.D. His arrival in Columbus had been preceded a year or so earlier by that of John Rayner from Canterbury. I had proposed John as the perfect candidate for a joint appointment which the university's Polar Institute wished to make with geography. As it turned out, the fit of John within that Institute was not a good one, due to no fault of his, and his appointment eventually was transferred to geography. With Reg's arrival, the three of us were again colleagues in the same department and we remained so until I left for Canada in 1970. Reg would leave for Santa Barbara, California, a few years later while John stayed on at Ohio State, assuming the chairmanship when Taaffe retired, and serving superbly in that role for twelve years.

## McMaster finally

Canada beckoned me in the fall of 1969 and the inquiry came from McMaster University, the institution that had spurned me in 1960. The geography department there had been under the leadership of Frank Hannell for almost three years and was looking to make a change. Hannell, a climatologist, had come from Bristol in 1967 and had been extremely successful over a short period in building up the department in terms of its faculty complement and operating funds. But his style of command was that of an army sergeant-major and that did not sit well with his junior colleagues, many of whom were also from England. They had persuaded the administration that a change was needed and invited me to stand as a candidate. Their invitation was timely given that Doreen and I were becoming increasingly frustrated by what was happening in the U.S. both in its internal affairs and its foreign policy and we were attracted to the idea of being able to raise our young sons in Canada. My interview went well and this time around I was successful. I took up my new appointment on July 1st, 1970, a few months after having witnessed the National Guard troops close down the Ohio State campus, a prelude to the tragedy at Kent State. It seemed to be a good time to be leaving.

McMaster with its ten thousand undergraduates and fifteen hundred graduate students was a small college in comparison to Ohio State with its fifty thousand or so students. It had been founded in the late nineteenth century as a Baptist college in Toronto and had moved to Hamilton in 1930. Two decades later it shed its religious affiliation and became a Provincially funded institution. Under the leadership of Harry Thode, a physical chemist, it had established itself as one of the top six or so universities in Canada in its commitment to research and graduate education.

Geography had first been given recognition in the university with the appointment of Wreford Watson as a lecturer in 1939[8] and a department had been established in 1946. It was located in the Faculty of Science but had representation also in Social Sciences. Its faculty included several outstanding physical geographers whose research was well funded by external agencies and highly regarded in the Faculty and they gave me valuable support in my recruitment efforts aimed at building up strength in economic and urban geography. I had

---

8    Contrary to what is sometimes written, Watson did not come to Canada for the purpose of doing doctoral studies with Griffith Taylor at Toronto. He was recruited directly by McMaster and appointed as Lecturer in geography with responsibility also for anthropology. In his early years at McMaster, with the aid of a small Carnegie grant he completed a study of the Niagara Peninsula that was submitted to the University of Toronto for the Ph.D. The degree was awarded in 1945.

persuaded Yorgos Papageorgiou to accompany me from Ohio State and within a couple of years Mike Webber joined us. These two became the leaders of a group that established the department's reputation as one of the stronger centers on the continent for theoretical and quantitative work in economic and urban geography. I think, on reflection, that Papageorgiou's research on the land use structure of the city, Webber's on economic development and that of Les Curry in nearby Toronto, with whom we interacted, on the random spatial economy, came closer than any other published work of the time to fulfilling the ideal of a theoretical geography that we had in mind when we launched *Geographical Analysis*. Others, I know, will have different assessments and recollections on this point.

The McMaster department was a very pleasant environment in which to work. Our location within the Faculty of Science meant that we had funds for equipment, travel and field-trips that would have been denied us had we been in Social Sciences, the Faculty in which most of our undergraduate students were registered. Our undergraduate programs were well supported, reflecting in part the fact that geography was a strong high school subject in Ontario, and our graduate programs attracted very good students, including some from the U.K. and Australia and New Zealand. Many of them now hold prominent positions in universities in Canada and abroad.

## On the slippery slope of administration

I survived the trials and tribulations of my first three years as chairman and won the backing of my colleagues for reappointment. But no sooner had that been confirmed than I was offered the position of Dean of Graduate Studies. McMaster at that time was proud of its standing within Canada as a leading center for research and graduate studies and remains so today, but in contrast to the present situation the budget for all graduate student teaching assistantships and scholarships then was in the hands of the Graduate Dean which gave the position considerable power and authority.

I spent five years as Dean overseeing the development of new graduate programs and the assessment of existing ones, serving on appointments, tenure and promotions committees, fashioning submissions to numerous committees and agencies and seeking to balance the demands of departments and students alike for more money.

In the mid 1970s, prompted in large part by arguments about the need for greater differentiation of roles among its fifteen universities, Ontario embarked upon a program of province-wide assessments of the quality of all graduate programs, discipline by discipline. I was pleased when our geography program received endorsement as one of the stronger ones. Ironically, it was a successful proposal by Queen's University that it begin doctoral work in geography that contributed to the erosion and eventual abandonment of the assessment program. Queen's had been told that its doctoral program in chemistry was weak and should be shut down. The university responded indignantly that it made no sense to close down a program that was integral to its other work in science while being given permission to start one in geography. That led to the addition of a 'consequent appraisal' mechanism that essentially gave a university the opportunity to correct any weaknesses revealed in an assessment. Hence, hardly any existing graduate programs were closed and once the first round of assessments was completed this attempt at province-wide strategic planning withered away.

In 1978 I was reappointed for a second five-year term with the first year off on leave in Australia and England. Two events during that leave I recall very well. The first occurred when along with my family I was driving from Sydney, where I was based in Barry Garner's department at the University of New South Wales, to Adelaide where Murray McCaskill had invited me to give a presentation in his department at Flinders University. In a small place called Merino, I phoned Murray to give him our arrival time and he said that a chap named Bourns from Canada had been trying to reach me. Art Bourns was then McMaster's President and when I eventually contacted him he said that they wanted me to take on the position of Vice-President (Academic) when I returned. The tyranny of distance prevailed—down there in Merino it seemed like a good idea and I accepted.

The second event was at Cambridge where I visited for the first few months of 1979. Andy Cliff, of spatial statistics fame, kindly invited me to dinner at his college, Christ's. We dined in the Master's lodge. I was seated on the Master's right with Andy beside me and across the table was an American guest with his host, a crusty Fellow in English. That week, David Stoddart, one of Andy's geography colleagues, had been mentioned in the Queen's Honours list, I think with an O.B.E. At one point during the dinner, Andy, seeking to make conversation, said across the table, 'did you see that Stoddart received an O.B.E?' The English Fellow merely grunted, 'oh really, I'm afraid I never read that far down the list!' We retired for coffee and port.

I spent ten years as Vice-President (Academic) at McMaster and in retrospect it seems like it was one committee after another—'member ex officio' was my second name. In fact, there were many enjoyable features of the position. To begin with, simply being chosen by a search committee of one's colleagues to take on such a senior post gives one considerable satisfaction; their expression of confidence in your ability and judgment is not easily spurned if you have, as I know I did, strong self-confidence in your ability to do the job. The subsequent experience of working with colleagues in all of the different faculties of the university and of developing an awareness of their diverse research and teaching interests remains for me a source of rich memories.

The funding of post-secondary education in Canada is a Provincial responsibility and although various forms of federal programs have been in place over the years to provide for transfer payments from Ottawa to the provinces for higher education, there have been no accompanying requirements that the provinces use those funds only for that purpose. Ontario often has found other uses for the money and as a consequence its universities survive on government grants that are among the stingiest provided by any jurisdiction in North America. Notwithstanding repeated submissions and commission reports, they are only a little better in relative terms today. Financial and budget matters therefore, always loomed large in McMaster's affairs and I found it fascinating to sit as a member of the finance committee of the Board of Governors, that involved at the time some of the leaders of Canadian industry, and participate in their discussions of the university's budget, its investments, its pension and health plans. My role was to champion the needs of the academic programs which meant that compromises always had to be achieved with the competing demands of physical plant, student services and so on.

The launching of major new academic programs in such circumstances was a special challenge but we had our successes. My proudest achievement was in overseeing and assisting in the development of the Arts and Science program, a specially tailored honors undergraduate program that provides an education in the arts, sciences and mathematics for highly qualified students. It admitted its first students in 1981 and is flourishing today (Jenkins et al. 2004).

There were other academic endeavors that also brought enjoyment. One in particular was McMaster's agreements and exchanges with Chinese universities. I had first been to China in July 1976 when I joined a group of Hamilton school-teachers, mainly geographers, and three colleagues from the university on a two-week visit that took in Beijing, Shijiazhuang, Tientsin and Shanghai. It was an eye-opening and unforgettable experience. In Shijiazhuang we visited the Norman Bethune Memorial Hospital, named in honor of the Canadian surgeon who died in 1939 serving with Mao's Red Army. From there we traveled back through Beijing and on to the port city of Tientsin where we had time to wander around the streets of the old nineteenth-century British section of the town. We were fascinated by the high density of families living in the Victorian style homes but tragically, two weeks later on July 28th , those same homes became death-traps when the city was devastated by the Tangshan earthquake and close to a quarter of a million residents perished. The contact made with Chinese geographers during the trip was broadened in 1983 when we hosted at McMaster a conference marking the first official visit to Canada of a delegation of geographers from the People's Republic of China. Professor Chuan-jun Wu of the Beijing Institute of Geography led the delegation (Gentilcore 1983).

In 1985, fifty or so senior administrators from twenty-two universities that were under the auspices of the Chinese Ministry of Metallurgical Industry and the Beijing Higher Education Bureau spent a month at McMaster learning about Canadian universities and our institution in particular. I spoke to them about how our teaching staff were appointed, promoted and tenured, subjects that were summarized under the title 'Management of Teachers' in the book that the

Chinese later published (Wang 1988). That descriptive title would not have sat well with my colleagues in our Faculty Association but I doubt that they ever saw the book. As a follow-up to the seminar, we were invited to visit China the following year to see how their universities operated. It was planned that Doreen and I would accompany our President and his wife on such a visit in August, 1986, but at the last moment they pulled out and Doreen and I made the trip alone. We had a wonderful time, enjoying all the 'perks' that had been arranged for our President—the best of hotel rooms, an interpreter-guide with us all the time, tours in Guilin, through the Three Gorges on the Yangtze River, in Xian and in Beijing. In the capital city, we even had a chauffeured, new Mercedes to drive us from our hotel in the western hills to various places. A banquet hosted by the Minister at which there was an extended round of toasts with glasses of 'mao-tai' was the closing event on our itinerary.

In 1988 I was back in China giving the opening remarks to a conference on urbanization in Nanjing, accepting an appointment as an advisory professor in the Geography Department at East China Normal State University in Shanghai, and acting on behalf of the Canadian Association of Geographers in making the presentation of a special Honors Award to Prof Chun-fen Lee of that university. Lee was the recipient of the first Ph.D. in geography in Canada, graduating with the degree from Griffith Taylor's department at Toronto in 1943. The presentation ceremony, a most pleasant occasion, was held at the Canadian Consulate.

Three years later, I revisited China as McMaster's representative on a three-person delegation sponsored by the Chinese Ministry of Metallurgical Industry. A year or so earlier they had sent a group of iron and steel executives to Hamilton and McMaster to study steel-making. Now they wished to have us visit on the occasion of their publication of a book on their findings. The two-week trip took us along part of the old silk-route, beginning in Lanzhou and ending in Urumqi. On the way we spent two days in Jiajuguan where the book-launching forum was held and where we visited the fort at the western end of the Great Wall, stayed a night in a company guest-house at an iron-ore mine 2700 metres up in the Qtian Shan mountains, and gazed with wonder on the Buddhist temples and grottos in Dunhuang. The visits to dusty, rubbish-strewn local steel mills that were for me a too-frequent item on the itinerary, did not detract from the overall pleasure and enjoyment of the trip.

My years spent as vice-president also had their less pleasant sides. A week-long occupation of my office in 1981 by students after the University had resolved to bar students from sitting on departmental tenure and promotions committees taxed my patience but fortunately left my sherry decanter untouched. Far more trying were those occasions when I had to sit as a member of the administration team in salary negotiations with the faculty. Although all of the Ontario universities are government funded they are autonomous in such matters as the setting of salary and benefit levels for their employees. However, a uniformity of approach has come to prevail and in all but three or four of the universities there are unions of the teaching staff that are formally recognized under the Ontario Labor Relations Act. Hence there is considerable sharing of salary information and a common cause in many issues of negotiation. Those universities without formal faculty unions, and McMaster is one of them, nevertheless have in place negotiated agreements that are essentially union contracts in all but name only. Ours calls for three administrators to negotiate salary and benefits and other terms of employment with three representatives of the Faculty Association and for all ten years that I was Vice–President I served as the leader of the administrative team. I was joined at the table by the Vice-President (Administration) and a Faculty Dean.

Collegial relations can dissolve quickly in such situations and the language and posturing of industrial relations soon become the order of the day. The scorn and suspicion of faculty colleagues were on occasion mirrored by those of the Board members to whom I had to report. For two years during my tenure, the Board's finance committee was chaired by an irascible local industrialist, now deceased, who insisted that I call him at his winter home in Florida to give daily reports on the salary negotiations. On one occasion when we finally reached an agreement, he referred to me in a meeting of the finance committee as 'give-away King' and though his remark was treated jokingly, the chairman of the Board saw fit to apologize to me later for the comment. At some other universities, the salary negotiations are placed in the hands of so-called 'professionals' from the personnel office but we resisted those pressures, believing that academic administrators should be in charge of all negotiations having to do with the teaching staff— a hanging on to collegiality by the finger-tips, some would say.

## Return to the classroom

My involvement in administration ended in 1989 after a period of sixteen years. I was a candidate that year for the Presidency and was disappointed at the time when the selection committee went outside and recommended the appointment of the University's first woman President. Friends sought to console me with comments about a feminist lobby but I knew it was not that simple. I had trodden on too many toes over the years, dented too many egos and been a member of an administration that had lost the confidence and support of too many faculty members. Perhaps, had I really wanted to be a university President I should have moved earlier and stepped up the ladder as I did so. But I never had a strong desire or incentive to leave McMaster and Hamilton. Doreen and I have always been happy in the university and local community and our two sons have grown up very well here. It was an occasion of special pride for us when in 1992 our elder son Loren won one of the first Canadian Fulbright awards that took him to M.I.T., some 35 years after I had gone to Iowa under the same program.

In 1990 I returned to the Geography Department, content to do extra teaching to compensate for the fact that I had no interest in trying to resurrect a funded research program. The urban and economic geography that I had been interested in no longer attracted many graduate students to the department and qualitative studies in health geography were now the preferred option. In the years before my mandatory retirement in 1999 I joined with my human geography colleagues in trying to make sense out of the administration's proposal to merge geography and geology, but the union was forced on us anyway. I have written about this elsewhere ( King 2001). I did draw considerable enjoyment in those same years from writing the centenary history of the Hamilton Golf and Country Club which I had joined away back in 1970 and which has been a significant 'fringe benefit' to our life in Hamilton. At the urging of some colleagues, I even threw my lot in with the Faculty Association, my former adversaries, and one year sat on their side of the table in negotiations with my successors in the administration. It was not a good experience and along with most members of the association, I was happy when it was over.

In 2003 and 2006 I had the pleasure of renewing my acquaintance with New Zealand geography by way of serving on the Social Sciences panel of the Performance Based Research Funding assessment program administered by the country's Tertiary Education Commission. Though I came to believe, as did others, that the program is an unnecessarily complex and expensive way of establishing the quality rankings required as the basis for allocating research funds to the various tertiary education institutions, it was pleasing to see how well the human geographers fared alongside their social science colleagues. In the 2003 results human geography ranked eighth in overall quality (adjusted for full-time staff equivalents) among all of the forty-one subjects covered and only anthropology and archaeology, and psychology outranked it among the social sciences. The 2006 survey produced equally impressive results.

An episode in the 2006 exercise reminded me of how human geography has changed. I was asked to assess an economist's research portfolio that had been cross-referred from the Business panel. The individual described his field as that of the 'new economic geography' and his publications addressed issues related to those that interested us back in the 1960s. I asked my two geography colleagues on the panel, one of whom was from the same university and a former chair of the geography department there, whether they knew of the individual's work. 'Never heard of him' was the reply, and they showed no interest in learning about his work.

I should not have been surprised. Geography, like all subjects, has its shifting emphases and changing currents of thought and it was, after all, one such change that gave me my opportunities back in the 1960s and enabled me to have an enjoyable career.

REFERENCES

Gentilcore, R. L. ed. 1983 'China in Canada: A dialogue on resources and development' *Conference Proceedings* (Hamilton: McMaster University)

Jenkins, H., Ferrier, B. and Ross, M. eds. 2004 *Combining two cultures. McMaster University's Arts and Science programme: A case study* ( Lanham, Md.: University Press of America)

King. L. J. 1979 'Areal associations and regressions' *Annals, The Association of American Geography* 69 (1), 124-128

King, L. J. 2001 'On the relations of geography and geology: a Canadian perspective on Halford Mackinder's judgement' *Proceedings, NZGS/IAG Conference,* Dunedin, 81-87

Thomas, E. N. 1961 'Toward an expanded central place model' *Geographical Review* 51, 400-411

Wang, Z. 1988 *Higher educational management in Canada* ( Beijing: Northeast University of Technology Press)

# JOURNEYS THROUGH TIME AND PLACE

## Malcolm I. Logan

WRITING A BRIEF memoir of one's journey through time is a way of reducing the chaos of experience to some kind of order, and to live again the follies, successes, failures and exaggerations of the past. But memory is like a long broken night: fragments remain fragments and the complete story often escapes forever. So a memoir is nothing but a set of personal recollections about achievements and failures, the influence of others and those you may have influenced or written about without guilt or regret.

My family came from the highlands of Scotland in the 1860s and found their way to the pastoral frontier at that time, settling in the tiny village of Bunnan, half way between Scone and Merriwa in the upper Hunter Valley of New South Wales. They had virtually no skills and no money and, being good Presbyterians, were content to serve out their lives as drovers, shearing shed rouseabouts, burr-cutters, fence-menders and anything else on offer from the surrounding huge properties that wealthy individuals or companies had carved out of the land. They never acquired any land and, except for two brothers, none ever left the Hunter Valley. The only entrepreneurial decision made was, for reasons never explained to me, to open a small wine shop in a corner of the house.

It appears that at some stage a decision was made that one brother, my Uncle Jack, should join the 416,000 Australians who volunteered in the first world war; that mad, awful struggle but a kind of Homeric event for so many young people. It was not long before he joined the ranks of the 45,000 Australians who were killed and became one of the ghosts who crowd that dreadful landscape. I have often pondered why he went. Maybe it was the duty he owed his king, maybe it was an adventure too grand to miss. I have no recollection of anyone in the family ever talking about him but many years later on a visit to the battlefields of northern France I spotted his name, Logan John Private, on the enormous Commonwealth war memorial listing those known to have died in the mud and blood of the Somme.

It was also decided that a much younger brother, my father, should become a school teacher and for the rest of his working life he taught in what were known as one-teacher schools in small villages around inland northern New South Wales, where I too spent all my early years. When I was 13 he moved to a village 12 kilometers outside Tamworth which enabled me to commute daily by bicycle to Tamworth High School, where I was to spend another five years.

Growing up in the Australian bush at such a determining period of life left indelible marks that influenced one's perceptions and behavior throughout the journey that was to follow. The overwhelming impression was of almost endless space, interrupted occasionally by dry and dusty, isolated country towns that all looked alike: arid, flat, empty landscapes captured best in the paintings by the artists Fred Williams and Russell Drysdale. For the people who lived there daily life was about coping with loneliness, isolation and a pretty harsh environment, often with prolonged droughts, bushfires and plagues of locusts, problems that called for mutual support and friendship, where the collective could be more important than the individual.

There is a long held view that the bush is the crucible of the nation's spirit, of its imagination and its binding values. It is the place where the legends were born and so was mateship. Certainly the iconic national character and popular, but not necessarily accurate perceptions of our way of life, have been associated with the bush: the collective ethos; a somewhat fatalistic rather than optimistic outlook on life; a skeptical, tough, laconic character; a willingness to lend a hand when the going got tough and a strong sense of equality. On the dark side there was a rarely-spoken about but intense dislike of people with different colored skins, especially indigenous Australians and people of Asian background. These kinds of values were held by people in my early life. The point should be made, however, that over time even Australia's more benevolent values have given way to a kind of rampant individualism, greater inequality, more overt racism and an absence of generosity. The great bush is no longer a challenge but a place to scream through in four wheel-drive vehicles. Empty roads, long distances and cruise control generate a wonderful state of mindlessness, with pleasure coming from not having to think.

## High School and University Years

Tamworth High School, during my five years, lived up to its reputation as one of the best public (government) high schools in rural New South Wales. I remember most clearly an excellent geography teacher, Colin Sullivan, and he, probably more than anyone, was responsible for my life-long interest in the subject. He would draw maps covering the entire blackboard showing in vivid colors distribution patterns of corn and cotton, and almost anything else. His maps simplified everything and told a story that would otherwise take many pages to tell. In hindsight, they resembled the kinds of mental maps that characterize so much contemporary aboriginal art. Occasionally, he passed around the class aerial photographs of urban places from different countries, and suddenly a new world of interest in shapes and patterns opened up. The syllabus we followed for five years was a mix of physical, human and regional geography, the former being the least interesting maybe because there was so little variation in the immediate physical landscape.

My strong recollection of these school years is that although rugby league and cricket were important, scholarly work was taken very seriously. At school assemblies the sporting heroes were duly recognized but so too were significant academic achievements, and failures. Our lives revolved around half-yearly and yearly examinations, all very formal and quite rigorous, with results being posted alongside names ranked in descending order for each subject on school notice boards, and a report with teachers' comments being sent home.

During these school years, as well as geography I studied English, French, European history, maths, chemistry and physics. The final two years were a preparation for a state-wide examination, known at that time as the Leaving Certificate, which served also as a university entrance examination, and for which additional work could be done at what was known as honors level. I chose history and geography which were to become my enduring areas of academic interest. The results of this examination were published in detail on the front page of the local newspaper.

I cannot recall any serious discussion with my father or anyone else about what I might do after completing high school but there was always a kind of understanding that as teaching had turned out to be a good safe career for him, lifting him out of Bunnan and an economic depression, so too it was appropriate for me. There was never any deliberate decision on my part that teaching was something I really wanted to do; rather it was something I drifted in to. So I applied for, and won, a teachers' college scholarship which was to sustain me for the next five years at university and teachers' college. The scholarship was essential but it carried some constraints, the main one being a bonding arrangement whereby a commitment had to be made to teach in government schools until the value of the scholarship had been paid off. In fairness, it should be said these scholarships made it possible for thousands of students to enter university and that, in practice, the bonding was never taken too seriously.

The nearest university was New England University College just outside Armidale, a college of the University of Sydney which formally awarded the degrees; in 1954 the college became a university in its own right. When I arrived the college offered degrees in arts and science only, and consisted of two buildings on a bleak hillside plus the original homestead, 'Booloominbah', a gift from the Wright family, wealthy graziers in northern New South Wales. Apart from this gift the Wrights are best remembered through the fine poetry of their daughter Judith Wright, whose literary sensibilities always sat uncomfortably with the mores of the landed gentry.

In the late 1940s there were about 400 students living in small hostels scattered around the town. Cold and dreary it was completely disconnected from the university. On a visit to the place forty-five years later I was surprised at how little had changed; a few more buildings at the university but not much more.

I have two enduring memories of my student days at New England. At that time Ellis Thorpe was the sole teacher of geography and, inevitably, we got to know one another very well. He was never an inspiring lecturer but to many of us who had suddenly arrived in a rather strange environment, he was a warm and welcoming friend, someone with whom it was possible to talk easily, to have a glass and even play the odd game of golf. Ellis was a product of the University of Sydney's Geography Department and as our examinations were set and marked in Sydney, his link with Macdonald Holmes, the only professor of geography in the country, were of critical importance. An ex-serviceman with only a first degree like his friend, Jack Devery at Sydney, Ellis was completely non-threatening to Holmes and was one of the very few who could interact with him.

As well, universities in the late 1940s had two types of students, young school leavers and much older ex-servicemen, some having fought in New Guinea and the Pacific islands. The latter group, having fought for a better world, were determined to keep up the struggle in civilian life. Many of them became articulate and well-organized student activists engaged in political debate both on the campus and at the national scale. The Labour Club was the centerpiece of the small university community and while the debates were fierce, they were always civil and never degenerated to the kinds of violence that characterized student politics in later years. Fiery speeches on social justice by such visiting firemen as Ian Turner and Noel Ebbels from the University of Melbourne had a lasting impact on young minds.

Australian universities are modeled on the Scottish system where only very few students proceed to a fourth year, known as the honors year. The decision is based on results in the first three years, and I had a choice of geography, history or English. I chose geography probably because of advice from Ellis Thorpe, but also because of the growing realization that geography was a very broad church indeed and there appeared to be no end to the things that came under its roof; geography was what geographers did. This necessitated a move to the University of Sydney, where at the age of 20 I first encountered 'the big smoke' and entered the honors class with three others, each of us under the supervision of Macdonald Holmes. He was an unusual man as was the entire department.

The Geography department at Sydney had been founded in 1921 with the appointment of Griffith Taylor as its head with the title of associate professor and it was not until 1946, long after Taylor had left the shores that a full professorship was created. I got to know and like Taylor in his later years when he returned from Canada but I feel many of the problems in the Sydney department and, indeed in Australian geography more generally, were due to the strange circumstances in which he left the University. In his university years Taylor studied science, mining engineering and geology, and became an enthusiast for field research in palaeontology and physiography. He won acclaim as a member of the scientific team on Captain Scott's 1910-1912 expedition to the Antarctic, was feted by the Royal Geographical Society, and took up academic life at age 40 when the nation was in the midst of an intense debate on the limits to population growth and the so-called White Australia Policy. From his new position Taylor jumped right into the debate claiming that there were severe environmental limits to growth, ridiculing those who argued otherwise and consigning the 'Australia Unlimited' rhetoric to oblivion. It was all too much for the university which steadfastly refused him a full chair and Taylor departed in 1928 amidst extremely bad feelings to the University of Chicago and later the University of Toronto. It was not until a quarter of a century later that the University of Sydney could bring itself to establish a full chair in geography, and all other universities in the nation delayed the teaching of the subject until much later. This was the academic environment in which Macdonald Holmes found himself.

The honors year consisted entirely of writing a thesis on a topic approved by Holmes. He would meet with us about once each week to see if we had discovered our 'problem', discuss personalities, and his considerable power in determining senior appointments in both Australia and New Zealand. This was a very frustrating time and we sought support from others in the department: Jack Devery and John Andrews, later to found a department at the University of Melbourne, were helpful; others such as David Simonett, then a demonstrator, were distant and not all that helpful.

After some six weeks of isolation one of my colleagues dropped out, and only three of us were left in the big class room with 'Honours year' written on the door. It was time to make a move. I recalled an earlier conversation with Holmes where he had referred to the Murray Valley as important in the water policy debate that Australia feels the need to have from time to time. He himself had written a book on the Murray which did address important public policy issues on irrigation, agriculture and the federal system. So my 'problem' became sub-regional differentiation in the Murray Valley, which won his instant approval. This decision extricated me from the department, and onto buses that connected all parts of the valley and into landscapes and towns which I had never seen before. It also opened doors to government departments with libraries full of records and data. Quite suddenly what had started so badly became a kind of personal adventure with virtually no supervision but with lots of fun, out of which I produced a thesis that was awarded first-class honors. I remember thinking at the time this was a worthy achievement especially as I had done all the work by myself; there were no words of encouragement from the department. On reflection the positive outcomes were an opportunity to read the literature in a very good library, and an appreciation of the frustrations and pleasures of independent research.

## School Teaching

By this time, largely by default, I was well on my way to a teaching career; all that remained was the completion of a one year diploma in education at Sydney Teachers' College, located just down the road from the Geography department. Intellectually this was an inordinately useless year. From a professional viewpoint the most useful outcome came from two spells of practice teaching where one experienced for the first time the challenge of trying to teach young people who really did not want to learn. Standing in front of such a class can be a matter of survival as much as anything else but all good teachers learn how to survive and move on to reap the rewards that come from this very worthy profession. It was here where I met Toni, my future wife, who became a successful primary teacher and later a university teacher in urban and regional planning, despite the dislocations caused by moving around the world with me.

My first teaching job was at Forbes Intermediate High School. Forbes, an old gold-mining town of about 2000 population, was located on the western plains of New South Wales about half way between Sydney and Broken Hill. I was to remain there for two years. It was tough going and at times I felt I had fallen into a pocket out of life and out of time. The town's redeeming feature was a number of fine old public buildings: several banks, a courthouse, hospital, post office, and numerous churches, all built at a time when there was a pride in public investment in rural Australia. Now, exactly as Christaller said, most are closed and derelict or subdivided into estate agents, beauty salons or fast food places. The people have departed, the functions have disappeared but the buildings are left behind, a combination of circumstances that is repeated all over rural Australia.

Twenty people, all young, taught at the school, no one there by choice. Likewise the students were there because schooling to age 15 was compulsory. Life was at best desultory and it did not take long to understand why country towns like Forbes had a pub on almost every corner. They were the focal points of failure, places where people completely undisturbed by ambition could gather comfortably. I had two lucky breaks in the cloud at Forbes. In my first year I taught a small Leaving Certificate geography class and one student topped the state; I always thought it rather strange that I should get more credit for this than the student or the school but I did not complain. The clouds lifted again when the geography/economics inspector, one Frank Brown, took me aside during his annual visit and said he thought they could do 'something better' for me than Forbes.

The 'something better' was Armidale where the schools provided what were known as demonstration lessons for students at the local teacher's college where they were training to be high and primary school teachers. So Toni taught in the primary school and I in the high school. Life the second time around in Armidale was more challenging and more rewarding. Toni completed a degree at New England and I did a number of courses in economics, and the high school had something of an intellectual air about it with quite distinguished teachers and some very good students It was here where I first met Bob Smith, then a student at New England, the beginning of a long friendship during which our careers from time to time were to run parallel to each other. No academic colleague was to play a more constructive and helpful role in the rest of my career than Bob.

I cannot recall whether I applied or not, but after two years at Armidale I moved to a lectureship in geography at Sydney Teachers' College. This was a more interesting institution than it appeared: while research activity as such never figured that prominently it was always embodied in the teaching programs and there was a strong academic underpinning of decision-making. Compared with numerous university departments I was to encounter in later life, there was an appealing discipline and commitment to the job here. The students, too, were of particularly high quality, many pursuing careers in physical education, infants' and primary school education at a time when there was considerable prestige associated with the profession. I think I learnt far more about how to teach by observing these students in classroom situations than I ever gained in my own Diploma year. It was also an opportunity to take a bigger view on life and to contemplate seriously a career in the academy. Despite moving away from it physically for five years I had always kept in touch with the university through personal relationships or through the activities of the New South Wales Geographical Society, and with the passage of some time and greater experience of life more generally I considered myself now better equipped for an academic career.

## *The University of Sydney Experience*

After two years at the college I applied for and was appointed to a tenured lectureship at the University of Sydney, and, later, to a senior lectureship. I was rather surprised at this because Macdonald Holmes, with whom I never had a particularly close relationship was still in the saddle playing very much the role of a god professor, overseeing all appointments, promotions, courses and even student grades. By this time Oskar Spate had been appointed to the Australian National University (ANU) but Canberra was a distant place and Holmes by reason of longevity, the standing of Australia's oldest geography department and the oldest university in its premier city, remained a highly influential figure. Despite this he rarely interfered in the daily life of the department and individuals developed their own courses independently as I did with enthusiasm in economic geography and urban geography. With a colleague, Denis Jeans, I published my first two papers based on an elementary statistical analysis of population movements in the Sydney metropolitan area. Research had suddenly become exciting and there was a strong stimulus coming from geographers in the US, especially from Australians and New Zealanders who had moved there such as Les King and Reg Golledge. I corresponded frequently with Harold Mayer who continued to take an interest in my work even after we migrated to the United States.

Although the department was riddled with politics and the university even more so and everyone worked in a highly individual way, the atmosphere was conducive to constructive work. We shared the same building with the department of urban and regional planning where there were a number of ex-British planners with interesting ideas about Australian cities, and urban public policy became an important research focus. Some of the ideas generated in this research were important contributions to the gathering national debate on urban and regional policies. The university generally attracted many of the high-achieving school leavers in the state and the standard of teaching was high, something that became more apparent to me later when I was to teach American undergraduates. The quality of work produced in the honors year was sometimes of a Masters' degree level. A number of graduates went on to successful academic careers, including Maurie Daly, Terry Beed and Bruce Thom.

As so often happens in university departments, new appointments can bring new ideas and new skills, but they can also change previous patterns of interaction and departmental conviviality. This occurred with the appointment of two former public servants, John Rutherford and Trevor Langford-Smith, each with a PhD from the ANU. John Rutherford was a very competent agricultural economist who tried to incorporate the rigor of economics in all his teaching. Together with Geoff Missen, a former colleague at the teachers college, and now teaching at the University of Melbourne, we produced *New Viewpoints in Economic Geography*, which attempted to change the way students approached the study of geography, away from the uniqueness of places to the economic processes that underpin spatial development. The book was quite influential in both schools and the university. Despite this success the department became more divided and a rather free-wheeling environment gave way to growing disenchantment. The arrival of a new professor, George Dury from Britain, was welcomed by all.

George had his idiosyncrasies but was an outstanding geomorphologist, a strong advocate of research and had a good understanding of trends in human geography. He took a personal interest in my research and encouraged me to complete a PhD while teaching full-time, a not uncommon practice in Australian universities at that time. I studied location patterns in manufacturing industry in Sydney, wrote the usual long dissertation which was examined favorably by Max Neutze and Peter Scott. The department performed well under Dury: links with schools and the local geographical society were firmly established, regular staff-student research seminars were introduced and Dury himself taught a particularly interesting course on statistical methods applicable to both human and physical geography. The prestige of the department was lifted after many years of decline, and some stimulating interaction developed with other parts of what was an intellectually well-endowed university.

The University of Sydney was at that time a very political institution where judgments were not always based on sound academic principles, and it was not unusual for the academic staff to be completely divided on issues of almost any kind that emerged anywhere in the institution. Almost inevitably because of the tribal nature of the place one was drawn into a kind of academic warfare which became singularly debilitating and time-consuming. The decision-making structures simply did not function properly. Deans who had little real authority were elected, not appointed, and were therefore accountable to their departmental colleagues; the Vice-Chancellor was virtually invisible. The university senate, the most senior academic decision-making body, was obsessed with applying rules and regulations that had been developed over the past century to matters that came before it, all in the name of maintaining standards. The result was a systematic blocking of many worthwhile initiatives developed by individual scholars or by departments. Instead of encouraging intellectual enquiry the administrative structure was actually stifling, if not killing it.

On reflection, it is difficult to imagine a better place to observe the follies, the successes and tragedies of academic life than in Australia's oldest university. At the time I was there, they were all dreadfully exposed in the great sandstone institution that from the earliest colonial times brooded over the life of Sydney and produced the professionals the place needed. Its motto, 'sidere mens eadem mutato', loosely translated as 'the same spirit under a different sky' summed up its colonial Oxbridge origins and its contemporary aspirations. My enduring memory of it was its capacity to go into process mode and block reform and even to destroy its mission. Personally, I had the highest regard for many who pursued their academic careers within its walls but I also caught glimpses of the operations of the 'punishers' or 'straighteners' in the academy, those who intrigue and plot so effectively against new ideas and change.

In the late 1960s after I had been at Sydney for ten years, I renewed my friendship with Bob Smith who by that time had a tenured position at the University of Wisconsin in Madison. At that time, to Australian geographers Madison was certainly the best known geography department in North America; everyone had heard of Finch, Trewartha and Hartshorne. I believe Bob was then on a sabbatical and spent some of it in the Sydney department where his enthusiasm for the North American scene was contagious. Both Toni and I had become somewhat jaded with life in Australia, and although my decade had been academically successful, I became conscious of the view that success is never complete, rather it is a kind of moving on. Bob encouraged me to spend a six months sabbatical at Wisconsin in the first half of 1966, and this was to prove to be the break in the clouds that both Toni and I needed at that time.

## The Wisconsin Years

We arrived in Madison in mid-winter. Although on a sabbatical I taught two courses and participated fully in the life of the department. In many respects it was an exhilarating time: a warm welcome from generous colleagues almost without exception, a frankness and willingness to discuss issues that I had not encountered before, an opportunity to observe a great university that was outside the British model and, despite the dreadful cold, the pleasure of the midwest landscapes.

A visitor has a unique opportunity to learn how a department and university work, to discover the power brokers and to get an overall feel for the place. The first impressions I formed, and subsequently to be confirmed, were the decentralization of authority from the center to the department level and a remarkable absence of bureaucratic processes in virtually all decision-making.. The god-professor was gone and even salary increases were decided by the department. There were graduate students in large numbers who gave seminars, assisted in teaching some courses, and wrote short dissertations under close supervision, not in some dusty corner of a library. Ideas were shared far more easily probably because there was an entity designated as a graduate school, with a dean, who was clearly an important figure. But there was no sacrifice of the undergraduate base of the institution which was broad, inclusive and highly accessible to local students. In other words here was an institution with a quite different approach to teaching and research than I had experienced before, an approach that was to influence greatly all my thinking about the purpose and administrative structure of universities in the years ahead.

It became apparent that despite an outward show of democracy, there was a pretty clear hierarchy in place at the department level. It appeared to me that the dominant figures, Andrew Clark, Arthur Robinson ,and to a lesser extent Dick Hartshorne, had all made significant contributions to the discipline, but that their time was running out. It was difficult for younger people including Bill Clark, David Ward and, later, John Hudson to introduce new approaches that were now transforming the discipline elsewhere. I never sensed any direct pressure to keep out new ideas, rather that it was simply an aging department that had enjoyed great success and was now beginning to feel under pressure in the North American competitive environment. One of the most underrated persons was Fred Simoons, such a true believer in Carl Sauer's teachings that he always placed his mentor's photograph on the table in graduate seminars. But a conversation with Fred ranged across the whole breadth of contemporary geography and its place in the academy in general. He introduced me to the Annales school of French historiography, the work of Fernand Braudel, and to trends in German geography. He understood how quantitative methods were bringing greater analytical skills to the discipline and never saw them as a threat, maybe because his own research was so far removed.

A stay of six months also allowed observations of the broader American community. I never managed to reconcile the election by the voters of Wisconsin of Joe McCarthy on one hand with that of Gaylord Nelson who was advancing environmental protection ideas decades ahead of their time. Another odd feature was the parochialism of Madison despite the presence of a large minority of university people drawn from all over the United States and, indeed, the world, The two local newspapers had very little news coverage of events in the east or west coasts of the US. International travel and even travel over the short distance to Chicago was relatively rare among local people. To an Australian used to knowing about the rough and tumble of national affairs all this came as a surprise. So too did the dedication of the Wisconsin dairy farmers and tax-payers to this hugely expensive institution, founded originally as a land grant college but which was now drawing students and staff from many nations.

The second half of 1966 was spent at the London School of Economics where Peter Hall was teaching an interesting course on urban planning, and at the University of Belgrade in the former Yugoslavia. At that time the Yugoslav federation was functioning well but the signs of disintegration were becoming apparent. Being one of the newest and most fragile federal systems there was an abundance of data on economic and social indicators of the different regions and, with a Yugoslav colleague, I published the results of an analysis of their economic performance over time.

The following year back at Sydney was something of an interregnum. Bob Smith was a strong advocate of a return to Madison and when I received an offer of an Associate Professorship with tenure from Arthur Robinson we did not hesitate. The earlier experience had been both pleasant and academically beneficial. We could still see the United States as a great power that helped to create a world richer and more stable than any would have imagined possible. I look back at the events of that time with some amazement. The Wisconsin department arranged all immigration procedures with great efficiency; we sold up everything and arrived in Madison in 1968 once again in the middle of a dreadful winter, but this time clutching green cards. How simple the immigration process was then!

This time, no longer a visitor but a regular member of the faculty, and having migrated, circumstances should have been very different. But in fact they were much the same. I taught a large introductory course and ran a graduate student seminar and set about publishing some papers in American journals. I really appreciated the pleasure of working with a number of graduate students, each of whom I think came from other states, bringing with them a wide range of personal and professional experiences. We all learnt from each other, a quite different experience to supervising graduate students in the Australian university, a difference which remains to this day.

There was now time to take a closer look at the department which encouraged a hardening of some views I had formed previously. Clearly it had a distinguished past with some of the older members of the department being household names in world geography. Some, such as Dick Hartshorne and Andrew Clark continued to produce good ideas but in a rather isolated kind of way that no longer had an impact on the way the discipline was heading. Because it was a department that covered a lot of territory there were also cartographers, geomorphologists, climatologists and cultural geographers, each of whom pursued their own interests, interacting little with others. These two groups co-existed with a younger, more recently appointed set who were attuned to, if not heavily involved in, some of the quite revolutionary changes being introduced to the discipline. Perhaps this kind of division was inevitable in a department with a long history but I felt that from time to time its history was retarding its advance. The department needed a contemporary mission and a strong chairman but neither was to emerge; rather, personal antagonisms and unpleasantness raised their heads.

None of this is to say this was not a convivial place in which to work nor that this was not a particularly fine university. Some parts of the institution were quite outstanding. I found the graduate school and its dean singularly helpful in funding research and providing a whole range of opportunities. It was the dean who approached me to join the University Development Program being sponsored by the Rockefeller Foundation, which would involve one year at the University of Ibadan in Nigeria teaching courses on regional development and planning. I had no knowledge of West Africa but I had a strong interest in the spatial impact of economic development and this was an opportunity to examine it at first hand. Moreover Bob Smith had spent a year there and, as a result, had published some excellent work on periodic markets. This was a time when there was a lot of movement with job opportunities everywhere. So, together with about twenty others we left Madison in mid 1968 for Ibadan on what felt at the time like a great adventure.

En route we spent an important three months in Europe, mainly in Paris at the Maison des Sciences de l'Homme where Fernand Braudel was the chief administrator. He was a household name in France commenting frequently on national and international affairs. One could not help but be impressed by the breadth of his knowledge, his intellectual vigor, and the way he had combined history and geography in his writings. He considered the two disciplines intimately intertwined; his earliest work on the Mediterranean explores this interrelationship in great detail. There has always been little interaction between the Anglo- and Francophile academic worlds. The Annales school, for example, was launched in France as early as 1946 but it made little impact on the academy outside of France. Braudel himself put this down to a preoccupation by British historians in particular with the stories of great men and a lack of interest in the stories of everyday people. To him the stories of men and events were to be distrusted as brief fluctuations, and the only meaningful history dealt with the relationship of man with his environment, an almost timeless history with deep currents and slow movements. I found his views and his sheer enthusiasm so compelling that they were to influence most of my future research.

## Nigeria

The University of Ibadan, seventy miles north of Lagos had been sponsored by the University of London and, as a result, was a traditional type of Commonwealth university. It was staffed by Nigerians, mainly of the Yoruba tribe and by a large, but declining number of British expatriates. The Rockefeller enterprise was extensive and very well-resourced, concentrating on agriculture, veterinary and medical sciences, and to a lesser extent the social sciences. The geography department was an active participant in this program and others which gave it a constant flow of visiting 'firemen'.

The dominant figure was Akin Mabogunje who was not only well connected to the North American academy but also to the major aid agencies including USAID, UNDP and the World Bank. His academic work was widely respected, he understood West Africa and its tribal/political system, and was influential in government circles as well as in the university system. On the other hand the head of the department, Michael Barber, a somewhat eccentric Englishman, never appeared to have much influence. Daily life in Ibadan was such an assault on the senses that it was virtually impossible to separate academic work from life on the street, characterized by poverty, disease, over-crowding, constant traffic jams and general chaos. It is difficult to describe the ordeal of the four hour drive from Lagos with its 13 million people to the airport 20 kilometers distant with constant demands for 'dash' from armed robbers as the cars are caught in gridlock.

It took a year to become familiar with Nigeria so we extended our stay for another year. Rockefeller was an excellent employer and, despite all the problems of living in a large indigenous city which had just come out of a civil war, we were comfortable. And I had some interesting work underway in which I was attempting to understand the impact of the short period of British rule during which they cobbled together some 250 ethnic groups into the entity called Nigeria essentially to serve London's economic interests. Academic life was soon interrupted by a student revolt on the campus, a quite remarkable experience which saw the vice-chancellor's office trashed in a matter of minutes, and a violent confrontation between students and armed police during which a number of students were killed. Only the threat of local market women to march on the campus to sort things out brought calm but by this time many students had returned to their villages. The lasting impression of Nigeria was of a country struggling with the implementation of a western-style democracy which has actually deepened the religious and ethnic divisions rather than healed them. Devoid of appropriate infrastructure, the corruption and anarchy that permeated Nigeria at that time made it, despite its huge oil wealth, arguably the largest failed state on the planet.

Quite unexpectedly, I received offers of chairs from two Australian universities, the University of New England, about which I knew a great deal, and Monash University in Melbourne, about which I knew very little except that it was new. These arrived at the time we were about to return to Madison and caused us to consider the future more carefully. There were some aspects of American foreign and domestic policies that were causing us some difficulty and, although sympathetic to the objectives, the violence of the anti-Vietnam war protests on US campuses had not been pleasant. Moreover, after the two years abroad I had drifted away from the department which was experiencing a good deal of dissension. And by now we had a young daughter to consider. So I went to Monash.

## The Monash Years

By the time of my arrival in 1969, Monash University, only ten years old, had already established an international reputation in some fields, notably medical research and south east Asia. The place had a liveliness and vigor that were absent from other Australian universities, including the University of Melbourne from which most of its senior staff had come. In short, it seemed to be an institution that was on the move and was still malleable, observations which turned out to be correct over time. It had a strong vice-chancellor, Louis Mathieson, who gave a direction to the place, and a management structure of non-elected but appointed deans of faculties and chairmen of departments which minimized bureaucratic processes in decision-making.

The geography department itself had some capable and committed people, such as Murray Wilson and Jim Whitelaw who had strong New Zealand connections. Importantly there were five vacancies to be filled within a year. I persuaded Bob Smith to return to be chairman for some years and together we made a number of appointments of young graduates whom we hoped would introduce new and stimulating courses. There are always successes and failures in this process but on balance I think we succeeded with the appointments of Chris Maher from Toronto, Kevin O'Connor from McMaster and Peter Kershaw from the ANU.

Undergraduate numbers were huge; I taught an introductory class of 350 at one stage. This was due primarily to the bridges which we built with secondary schools and our involvement in their final year external examination. But graduate student numbers were very small, a common characteristic of Australian universities to this day. Much later when I was vice-chancellor I made an attempt to address this problem by advocating the establishment of a graduate school, a proposal which was unsuccessful because it was seen as a threat to the power of deans. In the department we encouraged research by inviting a number of visitors for a semester to work with graduate students; Derek Diamond from LSE and Peter Haggett from Bristol made particularly important contributions. Over time we produced a number of graduates with PhDs who have followed very successful careers.

Given the small size of geography departments in Australia, and uncertainty in the wider academic community about what geographers actually do, it was important to concentrate research effort and to identify the department with a small number of fields. So at Monash the department concentrated on urban and regional development, third world development and related public policy issues. In physical geography the emphasis was on Australian biogeography. Over time the spatial impact of policies became more important, to some extent a reflection of growing community interest in cities and in engagement with south east Asia.

The election of a new Labour government in 1972 ushered in some quite extraordinary policies that were particularly relevant to geographers. For the first time an Australian government explicitly recognized that quality of life was determined by where one lived and not just by personal wealth. It established a new Department of Urban and Regional Development to devise a wide range of programs addressing infrastructure, housing, planning controls, land supply and access to services in cities. Many of the ideas that underpinned the new policies came from research findings by academics in a number of disciplines. I was a part-time head of the Strategy Division in DURD for a number of years and experienced the successes and frustrations of the implementation of the policies of a new department in a federal system. At about the same time, the Canadian government developed similar policy interests in its federal system which led to a sharing of experiences initiated by Harry Swain from Ottawa. Later he became head of an urban systems group at the International Institute for Applied Systems Analysis in Laxenburg just outside Vienna. I spent two months there and although we had some interesting seminars and working groups, we never fitted comfortably with the highly theoretical work being done by the Russians there.

We established a more productive link with the Urban Affairs division in the Environment Directorate at the OECD in Paris; indeed for some years Australians were the main contributors to the urban policy work there. Unfortunately, anything to do with urban policy was marginalized at OECD because its focus was on macroeconomic policy and some important urban work was never published. I was there on a number of occasions, the most productive being when John Zetter, formerly head of external relations at the Department of the Environment in the UK, was seconded to OECD. Under John's direction five examiners, of whom I was one, were appointed to study Japanese urban policy and that required five visits in two years to cities all over Japan. There was, in fact, no Japanese urban policy but we did produce a valuable report advocating the need for such a policy and what might be its components. This report never saw much daylight mainly because it drew attention to the deplorable quality of Japanese housing.

By this time I had pretty well drifted away from academic geography except for some work on those living on the margins in the informal sector in Malaysia and Indonesia. This inevitably had policy implications given the obsession of those in authority to get rid of them. The United Nations Center in Nagoya became an important meeting point for both officials and academics working on the development process in Asian countries. Fu-Chen Lo organized frequent conferences mostly in Nagoya ; participants apart from myself included Kamal Salih, R. P. Misra, Akin Mabogunje, Koichi Mera, Ben Higgins, John Friedman and Terry McGee. At this forum John Friedman expanded on his earlier work on growth pole theory by applying it to the role of Asian cities in economic and social development, important in a wider perspective because it helped to lift urban and regional planning from a preoccupation with design and planning controls. The work of the group was continued in Tokyo when Fu-Chen moved to the United Nations University. Some of the same participants were to comprise the core of an IGU working group on regional development.

From my perspective the most useful outcome of these deliberations was the book, *The Brittle Rim* (1989) which I co-authored with Maurie Daly, then a professor at the University of Sydney. I believe this was an important book, although the reviews did not always take this view. All the mainstream literature at that time referred to the 'Asian miracle' and assumed that the economic supremacy of Asian economies was just around the corner. But we had both witnessed the oil boom and its spectacular collapse in Nigeria and saw some parallels in east Asia. Our focus was on the inability of nation states such as Indonesia and Thailand to repay huge borrowings at high interest rates in foreign exchange negotiated in a boom when a severe economic downturn occurred. In pursuing this theme we were able to accurately predict what actually happened in the Asian crisis in a few years time. Paul Krugman, one of the few economists to comment about their misjudgments, modestly pointed out that he had been 90% wrong about Asia, but everybody else had been 150% wrong.

In 1986 I was appointed vice-chancellor of Monash University for a period of ten years which saw me through to my retirement from the university. This was never planned but I had moved away from the discipline and become more interested in public policy and in public institutions, especially in how to change them. I had learnt also that to be an effective agent for change you needed some altitude in your position. An appointment to a vice-chancellorship without having served an apprenticeship as a dean was probably unusual but I did not think about it at the time. An appointment from within certainly was unusual; it meant there was no honeymoon period but on the other hand I knew the place well.

One of the great problems in Australian universities was, and still is, their administrative structure, inherited from the British system and designed for very small institutions with a more collegiate system of governance. Fortunately, Monash operated on the basis of deans appointed in much the same way as a vice-chancellor and the committee of deans, which I chaired, was really the powerhouse of the university. This was a successful system except when the deans saw their territories being potentially diminished by the establishment of a graduate school, a mission on which I failed. Another problem is the role of the vice-chancellor who carries responsibility for all internal as well as external matters that relate to the university, clearly an impossible task. The great majority of Australian academics have little experience of how US universities actually work and the idea of a provost responsible for the internal life of the institution is quite foreign. Half-hearted attempts to overcome this problem by the appointment of deputy vice-chancellors with special responsibilities who report to the vice-chancellor simply do not work. I attempted this tactic with two deputies with disappointing results for them and for me.

At the time of my appointment the entire tertiary system, consisting of non-degree granting colleges of advanced education and universities, was in disarray, with the boundaries between the two becoming more blurred day-by-day. A new federal government minister, John Dawkins, whom I had known for some time through our mutual friend John Button, then minister for manufacturing and technology, moved with a good deal of enthusiasm and energy to change this system. He had a bigger view than most vice-chancellors and academics of the capacity of universities to contribute to national development, and was determined to break down the barriers around them, to end the sheltered workshop mentality for all time. Universities were, in a sense, microcosms of the Australian economy which was heavily protected by tariff walls and rigid financial exchange controls. To implement his reforms he needed direct access to the universities which for decades had sheltered behind commissions and councils made up often by people who had no sympathy with government policy. There was a clear expectation that all academics should engage in research, and there would no longer be any teaching-only tertiary institutions so the binary division separating colleges from universities had to go. More importantly, universities were to open their doors more widely and accept all qualified students irrespective of background; the result was a huge surge in student numbers with Monash expanding from 13,000 to 40,000 over five years, all funded relatively generously by the federal government.

Not surprisingly tensions ran high. Those who had been waiting for change for many years were as quick to emerge as those who saw reform as an attack on their freedoms, the kind of academics who pretend to cherish the past, are out of step with the present and dread the future. I was closely identified with many of the changes and experienced my share of the turbulence which rolled around universities for some years. As John Cain, a former premier of Victoria, and opponent of the reforms, expressed it in his book *Off Course* (2004), "Monash University's Mal Logan is seen by many as a key player...When Dawkins became minister in July 1987, Logan, vice-chancellor since late 1985, had settled in and knew his way about the system. He was smooth, with good political instincts and connections and he was regarded as reflecting Labour Party values and aspirations..."

The new external environment allowed some changes at Monash. Resources were allocated to deans of faculties in an open transparent way; the vice-chancellor's office was expanded, we developed a range of cultural outreach services, and we enrolled a large number of well qualified students from outside Australia. We were the first university to establish a vigorous orientation scheme for indigenous Australians and the first to engage actively with South East Asian countries. We established the Open Learning Agency (OLA) which gave mature students, especially women and those who wanted a second chance, open access to university degree programs delivered though television, radio, written material and, increasingly, by on-line learning. This initiative, so full of promise, has never fulfilled its potential largely because it was seen as a threat to courses already offered by those universities that we invited into the OLA consortium.

It is never easy to evaluate the effectiveness of radical reforms until many years have elapsed but we can say with some certainty that a major crisis in the system had been averted. At last there was a convincing model within which institutions and individuals could organize their lives and ambitions. All previous visions had lost relevance and there had been a retreat into confusion, uncertainty and anxiety. We now had a system, albeit with some uniformity, where research, student access and community service were of paramount importance, and where the university was more integrated into the nation's economic and cultural life.

Another outcome of the huge public investment in human capital in the Dawkins' years has been in the strong performance of the Australian economy over recent years, made possible also by the lowering of tariffs and the floating of the Australian dollar. Many of the thousands of additional students who were allowed into universities and enrolled in courses in information technology, the applied sciences, business and commerce have helped transform the economy. More recently, conservative governments supported by unimaginative vice-chancellors have reversed this trend. Now the powerful exclusionary instincts just under the surface in the academy have come to dominate university culture. By reducing the size of their intake and by imposing prohibitively expensive fees universities are preventing many well qualified students from entering; prestige comes from the number of applicants who are rejected, not by the quality of the institution.

Anyone in public life in Australia is almost inevitably drawn into various government initiatives. I was approached by the Victorian government to chair a review panel to advise on the feasibility of a very fast train service linking Sydney, Canberra and Melbourne. The application of a simple gravity model to the volume of movement by road and air between the two major cities made this an interesting enquiry. Interviews with environmentalists indicated no great problems and in a final report in 1990 we recommended the concept be pursued along the lines of the French TGV system. Not surprisingly, the whole idea proved too difficult for Canberra economists and politicians and the project lapsed.

At about the same time the government decided to develop a large parcel of derelict land around the Port of Melbourne, which would effectively almost double the size of the CBD. I served as a director of the Docklands Authority for its first five years. Our main concern during those years was to ensure the financial viability of the development; design and planning considerations, unfortunately, received little attention. As a result, the Docklands now features financially viable high rise apartment towers attractive to some residents because of their water views but which create a dull and dreary extension of Melbourne's otherwise attractive CBD.

While vice-chancellor I was able to continue my interest in south east Asia by taking graduation ceremonies regularly to Singapore, Kuala Lumpur and Hong Kong. I also served as a member of AUSPECC, the Australian National Committee for Pacific Economic Co-operation, a non-government body consisting of business leaders, bureaucrats and some academics with interests in building links with Asia. Each Pacific country had its own PECC which advised the official APEC secretariat on a range of matters including international migration, human resource development and educational needs. It was in this context I first met Bill Saywell, then president of Simon Fraser University, who was active in the Canadian PECC.

Retirement from Monash allowed a return to a sort of geography. A fascination with place, initiated in the Wisconsin years, never went away and it has been in many respects a great relief to explore the relationships between place and time in greater depth. To do this we were drawn almost inevitably to the Mediterranean because, as Braudel pointed out many years ago, that is where the interaction between history and geography is most apparent, and also where the landscapes are most exquisite. Some years earlier, being mindful of a potential gap coming up, Toni had commenced a book describing some of our earlier experiences traveling around the Mediterranean (Logan 2000). We were now able to use the house we had bought previously in the small village of Le Bar-Sur-Loup in the hills behind Nice, as a base from which to examine the Mediterranean world in more detail, a task which has taken us on numerous visits to mainland Greece, Crete, the Dalmatian coast, Sicily, Tunisia as well as southern Italy and France. In these and other places we have found much pleasure in seeking to unravel the many layers of history that underpin the contemporary landscapes, an exercise that encourages us to follow the sun half way around the world each year.

**REFERENCES**

Daly, M.T. And Logan, M. I. 1989 *The brittle rim: Finance, business and the Pacific region* ( London: Penguin)
Logan, T. and M. 2000 *Mediterranean journeys in time and place* ( Melbourne: Black Inc.)

# ACQUIRING GEOGRAPHIC KNOWLEDGE: RESEARCHING PLACE

## Terry McGee

*'And then suddenly, out of nowhere I was armed with all this detail.'*
ROBERT PLANT LED ZEPOSAURUS,'LED ZEPPLIN'

*'It is a time when people begin to hear an inner voice that says 'if not now, when....'*
GENE D. COHEN 'THE CREATIVE AGE'

IN THIS ESSAY I pursue the idea of how geographic knowledge is gained by living in, and carrying out research on places, particularly those places that are sharply contrasted in cultural terms with the place in which you were born and lived your formative years. The common theme of the memoirs in this volume is the fact that the writers shared formative experiences in the white settler colonies of Australia and New Zealand and then moved to other countries, in many cases for most of their academic lives. How this affected their geographic practice is an intriguing question, which each author pursues from their own perspective. I choose an approach which for me captures the central concern of my geographic life which is the pursuit of geographic knowledge through research. But I also recognize that research is carried out in particular places, in institutional settings and at times of one's life that influence the research. Research cannot be set apart from relationships with fellow investigators, colleagues, students, family and broader currents of change and fashion.

## The chronology of a geographic life

I begin with a brief chronology of my geographic experience. I was born in Cambridge, New Zealand in 1936. At that time it was a small country town in the Waikato, then a farming area that produced mainly dairy products, wool and fat lamb meat much of which were exported to England. My mother's family were farmers who had arrived in New Zealand in the 1850's and after carving a farm out of the bush in the Wairarapa had moved north to Hawkes Bay and eventually after the wars of the 1870's to Waikato. My father was a postal clerk whose own father had emigrated from Ireland in about 1912. The family was a large urban brood who for various reasons I never came to know well. I was later to learn that this urban-rural union of my father and mother had never sat very well with my mother's family who probably would have preferred a strong kauri-legged farmer of which there were many in the district.

I never knew my mother .She died of tuberculosis when I was three months old and for a time I was placed in Karitane, a famous New Zealand institution that provided care for children without adequate support. As the war approached and my father enlisted I was put in the care of my mother's aunt and was reared partly on the farm and partly in the town before moving to Auckland where my father settled after the war.

From this time I became an urbanite (although this was interspersed with long holidays at my uncle's farm in the Waikato). My great aunt took on the role of housekeeper and surrogate mother and with quiet stubborn determination encouraged me in my school and university education. Despite her limited educational background she embraced the idea of education. My father was not opposed to education but he regarded university education as unnecessary and seeking advancement beyond one's status. It was a place where the sons and daughters of the rich went as a matter of course. Much better to learn a trade which those of us who became university teachers later realized would have offered us much more income. He certainly was not convinced of the much vaunted egalitarianism that was a central element of New Zealand myth–making. Eventually, after a rather average performance in secondary school I managed, in the early nineteen fifties, to be accepted into Auckland University where I spent three years before moving to Victoria University in Wellington. My first love was not geography but history which was stimulated by the remarkable teaching of Willis Airey on Russia and Keith Sinclair, then one of the country's more prominent poets, who taught a richly-imaged history of New Zealand. The courses I took on geography were unexciting in comparison, too concerned with description and limited in ideas

I was fortunate that the generalist approach offered in undergraduate education in New Zealand universities at that time enabled me to pursue courses in history, political science, education and English as well as geography, and this provided me with an inter-disciplinary background that fostered a concern with process and cause and effect. This was to facilitate greatly my engagement with geography after I moved to Victoria University in 1956. There the courses were heavily dependent on interdisciplinary content and I found myself reading Marx, Mumford and Malinowski (and these names were just in the middle of long reading lists that accompanied each course), writings that were far more exciting than geography's Hartshorne that I had been imbibing in Auckland. All these ideas were siphoned through regional courses on the Pacific, Europe and Asia taught by Watters, Franklin and Buchanan. Of all these regions Asia excited me the most and Keith Buchanan had a fiery way (perhaps learnt from his Welsh ancestors) of kindling this enthusiasm. His lectures on Southeast Asia were highly politicized, dealing with the evils of colonialism, rapacious multinationals and the creation of socialist utopias such as Vietnam that had been brutally bifurcated by Cold War policy. His ideal was some form of soft socialism combined with Welsh Calvinism that I thought was something of a challenge to the Southeast Asian peasant. He was particularly vigorous in his discussion of the predatory effects of imperialism in creating poverty, inequality and underdevelopment. As a lapsed Calvinist and an ardent New Zealand nationalist, I was very sympathetic to his message.

At the time I never thought of a life as a university teacher but on the completion of my B.A I enrolled for an M.A in the Geography Department and began to have such thoughts. My hopes were encouraged in 1958 when I was appointed as a temporary Junior Lecturer ( I think this was the title) to teach Harvey Franklin's regional geography course on Europe while he was on sabbatical leave. Europe was a region I had never visited but had been introduced to it in Auckland by Jim Fox's travel-log–like lectures. I remember feverishly preparing lectures until 3.00 am and then dashing to give them to more than 150 sleepy bemused students. At the same time, I was carrying out the fieldwork for my M.A thesis on Indian communities in Wellington City that involved visits to Indian families, their cinemas, their cricket games and the consumption of frequent curries; my first introduction to a cuisine that has become part of my love affair with Asia. This was a very full year and by its end I was encouraged to think of post-graduate studies and I was leaning towards London.

The Victoria Department was intellectually stimulating but very isolated from the other New Zealand ones because of its concern with global issues such as underdevelopment, poverty and social injustice and its focus on Asia and the Pacific. In order to develop these themes the Department began to publish a journal *Pacific Viewpoint* in 1961 that continues in publication today. The early debates about editorial policy, style and focus were vigorous but the journal has succeeded in establishing itself as an important voice of New Zealand geography.

One day in October I was completely floored when Buchanan called me into his office ( his style was to capture you in the corridor), and told me there was the possibility of a job in the Department of Geography in the newly created University of Malaya located in the capital, Kuala Lumpur, and that I should apply. I had my pen out faster than one can say 'geography'. I flew into Kuala Lumpur two months later and began teaching in January. I arrived in Southeast Asia with some preconceived notion that I was going to an under-developed region that was being kept in this condition because of its colonial heritage. In retrospect, I think I was something of a closet Leninist which, had it been known, would not have increased my popularity with the Malayan authorities who were still fighting the tail-end of a communist insurgency. But the move and the notion fitted with my New Zealand nationalist sympathies. So instead of going to London where the tired end of the Empire was being played out, or to the USA where a new empire was being created, I went to Kuala Lumpur where nationalism was in full cry. Thus, the regional focus of my research life was shaped by a fortuitous opportunity at the right time.

I spent five years at the University of Malaya and I now recognize that this period shaped my life more than any other. It gave me the opportunity to start my Ph.D research on Malay migration to Kuala Lumpur City and this required me to immerse myself in Malay culture, language, life and religion over a protracted period. I soon began to realize that in the plural society that British colonialism had created, the Malays had many similarities to the New Zealand Maori people. Certainly both communities had not shared equally in the development that had occurred. I soon realized that the major challenge of the newly independent Malayan government was to correct this situation through policy measures designed to increase Malay opportunities and standards of living. This understanding was heightened further by the rapid movement of Malays to the Chinese dominated cities that was occurring at that time. Here the tensions between the standards of living of the two communities were accentuated. This situation was to come to a head in the riots of 1969, a situation that my thesis predicted. During the period I also took the opportunity to travel widely in Southeast Asia, assimilating the region, its people, tastes, cultures and landscapes.. I was most attracted by the cities of the region— vibrant places in which the street life and the markets were so different from the quiet and emptiness of New Zealand cities. My experiences fueled the writing of *The Southeast Asian City* (McGee 1967).

After five years at the University of Malaya during which time I had learned far more from Malayans than I could impart, I returned to New Zealand driven by a belief that my newly acquired knowledge about Asia would be welcomed. But though my old Department welcomed me, and my new expertise, this was not a time when New Zealand society was willing to embrace the idea of it becoming part of what I believed would be the Asian miracle. New Zealand under a conservative National Government had embraced the Dulles view of the Cold War, most clearly evident in the threat of communist China and the revolutionary war in Vietnam. My experience in Southeast Asia led me to believe that this geopolitical stance completely misunderstood Asian nationalism. I joined protests against New Zealand's military commitments in support of South Vietnam, a puppet state created by the United States. I increasingly realized how alienated I was from New Zealand at that time. Even my love of rugby, an obsession since childhood, could not keep me there. Buchanan, Franklin and Watters were supportive as was Warwick Armstrong, a newly appointed colleague who shared my views on the problems of development in the Third World, and with whom later I was to produce several joint publications. However, the mood of

New Zealand was not for me and thus in 1968 I accepted an appointment in the Department of Geography at the University of Hong Kong.

Hong Kong was my first real experience of living in a colonial society and there were many times over the next five years when my memories of New Zealand nationalism, egalitarianism and sense of the openness of social boundaries made me long to return. The University was impossibly stultifying, administered by a bureaucracy that had developed paper pushing to a fine art. The Geography Department had a strong focus on regional geography and fieldwork which I greatly enjoyed. My colleagues were supportive and professional, and I found ample opportunities to carry out research in Southeast Asia. Surprisingly at this time although I immersed myself in developments in China I did not write about them. Hong Kong was full of 'China watchers' reporting on the country. I was fascinated by the 'cultural revolution,' in full cry at the time, as an experiment designed to reshape socialism. There was also a great deal of collegiality in the Department fostered by the head Dennis Dwyer that centered on departmental sports teams in which I performed with polished mediocrity. All this collegiality was cemented with frequent boozy Chinese dinners.

After five years ( at this point my life had certainly settled into five year cycles), concerns with my wife's health and the education of our son led me to accept an appointment in the Department of Human Geography at the Australian National University in Canberra where a position had been made vacant by the death of Robert Ho, the former head of geography at the University of Malaya who had helped me so much in my early days in Kuala Lumpur. The Department of Human Geography, located in the Research School of Pacific Studies, did not engage in undergraduate teaching, had a small number of Ph.D. students, and ample funding for research. This provided a research environment in which I could flourish, putting together the ideas generated by field experience over the last fifteen years, This 'ideal setting' was shattered by the sudden death of my first wife and the single parent-bonding that occurred with my son. The antipodean sense of mateship was crucial to our survival. Geoff Missen, a geographer from Melbourne University and his wife Jenny, who I had first met in Malaya in the early 1960's, and Gerry Ward and his wife Marion offered immense support. Dave Drakakis-Smith ( recently appointed to the Department) and his wife Angela who were our neighbors in Hong Kong accepted us into their family and became surrogate parents for Tyler. Despite this trauma, I found my involvement with Australian geography and ANU rewarding. There were certain undercurrents of tension created by the contrasts between the over-privileged research environment of ANU and the 'research starved' departments of the 'coastal periphery' but there were ample opportunities for productive interaction including enjoyable joint research seminars between the Monash Department of Geography and ANU held in Beechworth, conveniently located close to excellent vineyards. I would have stayed happily in ANU and Canberra for the rest of my life.

A visit to the Department of Geography of the University of British Columbia in 1976 however, which had been facilitated by Bob Smith ( whose name appears frequently in this volume), resulted in an offer of employment by UBC that was welcomed by my new wife (a Canadian and a Vancouver booster) who was anxious to return home. In the funding climate of the time this offer involved a joint appointment as Director of the Institute of Asian Research in the Graduate Faculty and a post as Professor in the Department of Geography in the Faculty of Arts— theoretically two half-time appointments but as so often happens they soon became more like two full-time appointments. But despite the odd frustration created by wearing two hats, I thrived in the environment where I found excellent research funding opportunities, excellent scholarly standards, a thriving graduate school, and a high degree of professionalism in the university. Canadian geography was well established and the strong collegiality of the profession, most evident at the annual conferences, gave me the opportunity to visit many parts of Canada. I was able to develop an excellent group of graduate students who carried out research in Asia. At the time, the Department had one of the best collection of Asian specialists of any department in North America and this helped attract very good students. I continue an ongoing relationship with many of them. At one point, we even had a web site called the McGlee club in which we shared news of births, appointments, research and so on. As we have grown older the site has disappeared into cyberspace but we still keep in close contact. This ongoing engagement with graduate students has been the most enduring and professionally satisfying aspect of my geographical career.

Despite teaching and research administration ( or perhaps because of it), I have been able to continue a vigorous and productive research life even in my retirement. Once the five year cycle was broken, I have developed a new sense of involvement with one part of a country which I now feel as my own, and at a time when western Canada is becoming more intimately linked to Asia through immigration, trade and educational programs. In some ways what I had hoped for in the New Zealand of the sixties has become true in the western Canada of the present. The cycle has been completed.

## *The research engagement*

Having dealt with the academic framing of my life and the centrality of Southeast Asia to it, I would like now to focus on the issue of my research engagement with this region. For this purpose I have divided my discussion into two parts— first, the research premises that have governed this engagement and second, an illustration of the research through the example of my life-time project on Southeast Asian urbanization.

Six premises have shaped my research. In every sense though, this is a post *ad hoc* rationalization for I did not sit down and write these out like commandments before I began research in the region.

The first is the issue of *vision*. It is important to understand why you are studying Southeast Asia. Although I have occasionally dabbled in the exercise I have never been particularly extended by the need to justify Southeast Asia in its regional context. Certainly, I would not go so far as to agree with the assertion that, 'Southeast Asia is arguably the most insubstantial of world areas, being at once territorially porous, internally diverse and inherently hybrid' (cited in Day 2002, 292). Indeed, I would argue that it is this diversity and hybrid character that creates an intellectual excitement about the region. Nevertheless in my first book, *The Southeast Asian City*, there was really no discussion of this issue. I just got on with the job of describing the growth and features of cities in Southeast Asia at that time. For me Southeast Asia and the part I know best, West Malaysia, was a place to explore issues that related to development and urbanization, and my vision was essentially one of a diverse number of countries negotiating various roads to development. Thus, I was more interested in studying the issue of rural-urban migration as a generic process typical of developing countries in the particular context of a specific Southeast Asian country. I wanted to understand how the local context in which rural-urban migration was occurring influenced the process, and how this effected our views of general theories of rural-urban migration that stemmed largely from Western sources.

The second premise is that I have never been greatly concerned with *disciplinary boundaries*. As a geographer I had always been taught that one way of looking at societal change was to explore spatial change. But this was a particular entry point that on the whole was regarded by other social scientists as a rather minor exercise that did not match the intellectual content of history or economics. Only recently has 'space' begun to be seen as an intellectually challenging concept by these other disciplines. Faced with the perception of geography as an intellectually light-weight subject, geographers have assembled a huge and monstrous collection of theories to justify what is essentially a rather straightforward activity, the art of which is to measure, represent and write about the distribution of activities in space as they reflect societal processes. The geographic contribution has always been to emphasize the manner in which the 'assemblage' of human activities within territorial space aids or hinders development. Thus, in my research on Southeast Asia I have never been concerned about disciplinary boundaries, choosing to use the insights of anthropologists, historians, economists, demographers, sociologists and political scientists whenever they were necessary to elucidate process in order to understand the emerging spatial mysteries of Southeast Asia.

Thirdly, I want to emphasize the importance of *comparison*. Southeast Asia is immensely challenging to the comparative theorist. The diversity of cultures, languages, histories, religions and so on are grist for the mill for those who like specificity. They often say that for every generalization about Southeast Asia there are enough exceptions to invalidate it. On this point I always recall my days at the Australian National University where I used to attend seminars in the Department of Prehistory. There was a vigorous group of scholars working

on the prehistory of the Pacific, and they were totally divided into the generalists and those favoring the specific. At one seminar, a paper given by one of the
generalists on the diffusion of certain styles of pottery through the West Pacific
was used as an argument to justify a theory of the direction of population migration of Pacific peoples, at that time a rather revolutionary idea. The specific
experts were up in arms; each rose, arms flailing and pointed out that in his/her
island this pottery –diffusion theory did not apply. There were more differences
in the pottery than commonalties. These attacks were confronted vigorously by
the generalists and for a time it seemed there would be a physical confrontation. But then someone pointed out the time, 5:00 p.m., a crucial moment in the
Australian day, and all retired to the pub to discuss, in the usual style of drunken
mateship, the performance of the Australian cricket team that was walloping
the English. Thus on the issue of generality and specificity I have always had
an acute ambivalence. While I was intellectually attracted to the excitement of
generalization, operationally I wanted to do specific research involving data collection and fieldwork. To use the analogy of Chinese medicine this represents
the hot and cold side of my academic persona. My compromise is to try and
think about the comparative context of the Southeast Asian specific. For example, it is impossible to explore the development of Singapore in the context
of endogenous development of the city state. You must also understand this
development as part of a particular vision that the leaders have of the state as a
regional node, and its aspirations to be a global city that stems from the broader
ideas of the global city and so on. As another example, can one really attempt to
explain Vietnam's current economic transformation without reference to other
socialist transitions particularly that occurring in China? I would also add that
there is still a paucity of comparative research of this nature apart from that of
historians such as Reid, Lombard and Lieberman that compares process in different Southeast Asian societies. The type of research that dominates presents
a series of examples of different Southeast Asian sites and then tries to draw
some comparative insights. Benedict Anderson (1998) has written eloquently
on this challenge.

The fourth premise is that there is a need to emphasize *openness* in approaches to Southeast Asia. Openness for me has a two-part meaning. First,
that you be 'open' about your research. One of the features of outsiders' research
in Southeast Asia during the flush of nationalism that accompanied the early
days of independence was that we were plagued with concerns about the ability of the 'outsider' to study the 'inside' of Southeast Asia. During my days at
the University of Malaya in the early 1960s this was a particularly touchy issue.
I recall Zainal Abidin, then a historian at University of Malaya, announcing at
a public lecture that no one but Malays could do research on Malays. I understood his position, trying to be open, but it was a bit challenging for someone
embarking as I was on a Ph.D about Malay rural-urban migration. Since that
time, institutional requirements both from the places where research·is being

done, and from where the research is being funded, have forced even greater openness. There is also a growing recognition that being 'open' in research often means working with local researchers and ceasing to be proprietorial about the results. Indeed, increasingly one wonders if the Southeast Asian researchers are becoming new outsiders as their research is increasingly circumscribed by the political control and surveillance of the state. Only a few have the courage to persist, and too often end up producing placid reports that avoid confrontation with the State. A second meaning of 'open' is being open to many interpretations of the research issue you may be exploring. While I am always open about my concern with social justice, I know that this must be tempered by local understandings of the issues that I am exploring. This does not mean that you roll over and capitulate but that you recognize these local realities in your research.

Fifthly, I cannot emphasize too much the importance of *field studies*. Southeast Asia cannot just be studied from the outside, it has to be viewed from within. Language skills are important in this respect. Of course I am very flexible about what constitutes fieldwork, being a bit snooty about political scientists who interview politicians in hotel bars, but more sympathetic to the scholars who immerse themselves in the historical archives. Theirs is a 'dusty' form of field research but none the less a legitimate one. It does not always mean that such historical fieldwork results in correct views on the contemporary. I am reminded of my good friend Jim Jackson ( now engaged in heavenly fieldwork on cloud formations) and his use of history to interpret the present. One Sunday in the early nineteen sixties after a particularly heavy night we were exploring the district of Kuala Selangor outside Kuala Lumpur. Feeling the need of a drink (we were suffering from dehydration in the heat and the consequences of the previous night's excesses), we started to look for a store. Failing in our attempts, Jackson suggested we should drive to the coast where he claimed there was a substantial town. We eventually reached the coast and there was nothing, just a few fishing boats bobbing on a gently undulating sea. ' So', I said to Jackson, 'where is the town?' 'It's not here' he said stating the obvious, 'but it was on the 1872 map'. I conclude this section with a brief reflection on the relationship of fieldwork to theory. I know that the general practice is to do fieldwork to test theory but for me it is a much more fuzzy exercise. For example, as I elaborate on later, the idea of '*desakota*' ( used to apply to the peripheral zones of cities in Asia characterized by intense mixtures of urban and rural activity), was conceived out of series of field studies in Malaysia and Indonesia over a long period of time. This work has attracted considerable interest among academics and planners in India, Southeast Asia and China. The idea of '*desakota*' certainly did not stem from any theory of urban spatial expansion that had been derived from the West.

My sixth and final premise is that it has been important for me to consider the *policy relevance* of the research. This stemmed in part from my concern, developed in my formative years in New Zealand, with issues of class, inequality and social justice. I have generally been fortunate in being able to combine my academic research with policy programs. Policy research funded by the International Development Research Center in Ottawa, the Canadian International Development Agency, the United Nations Development Fund and the United Nations University has enabled me to apply ideas and information gathered in academic research to policy issues such as migration, urban social policy, urban–rural linkages and the role of urban centers in regional development.

## *The Case of Southeast Asian Urbanization*

For most of my academic life my concerns have been with research issues that relate to Southeast Asia urbanization. The knowledge that I have constructed of this urbanization process has been very much a product of the tension between the theoretical views current at that particular time, and the fieldwork in which I was engaged. Looking back on this process, I have come to construct it in my mind as a constant ambivalence in my research between three scales of investigation— the macro level, at which I have sought to explain how the Southeast Asian experience fits into macro-theories of urbanization or development, the meso-scale which is essentially looking through the lens of the nation state, and finally the micro-scale where specific research studies constantly question the relevance of the macro- and meso- generalizations . Much of my research attempts to incorporate all three scales. But my constant goal was to interrogate the macro and meso levels from the local. Thus, when I wanted to deal with macro-issues I resorted to grand-theory. This was and is a very creative tension. For example, the chosen form of representation of my book *The Southeast Asian City* essentially was a normative model drawing on Sjoberg's work (Sjoberg 1961), which was a grand attempt to develop a global model of cities before the industrial revolution that began in the late eighteenth century. At the same time, the interpretation of the urbanization process in my book was based on a theoretical view of the 'development process' that saw the underdeveloped world (often called the Third World) as being de-developed by the forces of global capitalism. This was essentially the 'dependency theory' that had been developed earlier by Raoul Prebisch and Andre Gundar Frank, and applied by them to Latin America. It still has some power and relevance in regions of the world such as Africa.

Thus, as I traveled around Southeast Asia in the early sixties I did not look for the seeds of capitalism so much as for the human distortions of capitalism; hunger, poverty, inequity and social injustice, as well as the growing social and economic inequality that characterized these Southeast Asian societies in their relationship with the developed world. This relationship was further compounded by the demographic fact that most of these countries were experiencing high population growth rates, almost double those of the developed capitalist world. Since the majority of the population was located in rural areas, existing in a low equilibrium state of limited productivity and poverty, this was creating an explosion of rural migrants moving to the city from the countryside. In the cities, because of ongoing neo-colonial relationships, there was little industrialization at this time and they remained primarily service centers. The migrants were forced into squatter encampments, and low productivity service occupations such as vending and transportation provisions such as 'becaks'. This led me to suggest that Southeast Asia was going through a phase of 'pseudo-urbanization' in the sense that the role of the cities seemed to be one of 'providing social safety valves' in situations of low rates of economic growth. This state of affairs also seemed to provide a potential for social, economic and political insecurity that could be revolutionary. However, the persistence of various forms of urban informal activity that involved the activities of the proto-proletariat linked with rural households was an important factor preventing revolutionary change.

At the same time as I developed this macro 'doomsday construction' of the Southeast Asian urbanization process, I was involved in a site specific micro study of the process of Malay rural-urban migration as it was operating in Kuala Lumpur .The results of this study offered a much more optimistic view of the urbanization process than the constructed theory of 'pseudo-urbanization'. Essentially what this study revealed was that in Kuala Lumpur in the early sixties the particular micro-conditions of the Malayan development process were leading to a rather different model. Again my construction of this was influenced by an attempt to suggest that the paradigm of rural-urban differences developed out of Western theory was not applicable to the situation in Kuala Lumpur, for which I make no apologies. The study revealed that the Malays who were moving to Kuala Lumpur from rural areas were not all living in poverty. The squatter areas where they lived had many households that could be described as lower middle class. In some ways this was no great surprise because the national government was investing heavily in rural education for the Malay peasants who were dislocated from the countryside. They were also creating employment opportunities for Malays in the rapidly expanding government sector in the cities. The Malaysian government led by UMNO was determined to correct the socio-economic imbalances that existed between the main ethnic communities in the colonial period. In the later sixties it became clear that these policies were not moving fast enough to alleviate the problems of the growing numbers of urban Malays, particularly the youth. Talking in 1968 to the families that I had interviewed in the early sixties, I sensed a growing frustration with the pace of change that was being channeled into opposition to the urban Chinese who the Malays saw as blocking their access to jobs and opportunities. This led me to predict some kind of urban riots (the US experience) which broke out in May 1969, and led to the strengthening of the Bumiputra policy and an acceleration of Malay urbanization.

My studies of Malay urbanization continued (with fellow Malaysian researchers) with an investigation of the rural-urban connections between Malay female workers in industrial zones of Penang in the nineteen eighties. This research led us to argue that rural-urban migration was just not the relocation of people. Rural and urban areas were in fact better viewed as part of a transactional environment in which people living in rural and urban areas move, convey messages, and shift money and ideas in what must be regarded as a continuous space of interaction. In our selected 'rural villages' we found that most 'household income' came from non-agricultural sources including remittances as a significant proportion. This was greatly facilitated by improvements in communications and transportation that accelerated from the early 1960's. The most recent census of 2000 indicates that Malays of Peninsula Malaysia are now more than 50 per cent urbanized, but only in the sense of their occupation of administrative space defined as urban. They have in effect occupied a transactional space of urbanism for much longer. What did this tell me about the grand theory of pseudo-urbanization? First, that it grew out of constructed knowledge that misread the urbanization process because it was based upon a Western derived theory of rural-urban differences. Second, it was one- dimensional in its assumption of slow economic growth, and wrong about assumptions of the demographic explosion and the inability of local states to mediate the effects of global capitalism.

This of course was hindsight. At the same time as I was working on the Malay study I continued to explore issues relating to pseudo-urbanization. In the mid-1960s, together with Warwick Armstrong, my colleague at Victoria University, we began to grapple with the political implications of pseudo-urbanization. We were heavily influenced by Geertz's remarkably insightful analysis of the urban economy of two small Javanese market towns ( Geertz 1963). Perhaps no other person writing about Southeast Asia has influenced my thinking and research as much as Geertz. In his beautifully written books he has fused macro theory with insightful fieldwork. I only wish I had the space to quote his description of the Balinese landscape in Negara—one paragraph of perfection, a model for us all. The major question we wanted to take up in our study was how long the process of pseudo-urbanization could occur before some kind of breaking point would be reached that would lead to the triumph of either socialism or capitalism. Our hypothesis was that there was considerable capacity for urban societies to involute before they reached a condition of revolutionary change. The processes we observed in Latin America and Southeast Asia suggested that the persistence of rural-urban linkages, and the capacity of the informal sector to absorb population into low productivity occupations, provide evidence of an ongoing set of practices that have not yet disappeared. We also had to recognize that the increase in the surveillance capacities and repressive tendencies of the local state were important in delaying this process. This work culminated in a joint publication, Armstrong and McGee (1985).

For most of the seventies I did research on the survival strategies of the inhabitants of the informal sector, focusing particularly on the street vendors of Southeast Asian cities and Hong Kong. My theoretical thinking about this research was greatly strengthened by the ideas about the ' two-circuit' economy of cities in developing countries proposed by Milton Santos, and the Marxist formulations of Charles Bettelheim and Chris Gerry who showed that the persistence or collapse of the informal sector was primarily a reflection of the dominant capitalist sector and state policies which in times of slow growth engaged in conserving policies, while in times of economic growth they began to dissolve the informal sector. In the seventies and eighties the growth of the new international division of labor that led to the transfer of labor-intensive assembly operations into the developing world ( particularly the urban areas of Korea, Taiwan, Singapore and Hong Kong), affected also the urban areas of the Southeast Asian countries in which I was working ( Penang, Kuala Lumpur, Bangkok, Singapore and Jakarta ). While the informal sector continued as urban income increased, it began to dissolve as more and more people became wage earners in the urban areas. Today, the process is most advanced in Singapore, Penang and Kuala Lumpur but is moving more slowly in Bangkok and Jakarta that felt the full force of the financial meltdown in 1997. In such conditions, the informal sector reasserts itself, as my former students Gisele Yasmeen and Narulman Nira have shown in the case of food vendors in Bangkok. Thus, once again, the micro-scale studies resulted in a recognition that the grand theory of pseudo-urbanization had to be modified or discarded.

During the period of the seventies and eighties, I was also beginning to modify my ideas of the homogeneity of the Southeast Asian urbanization process. In a series of papers (often using the decadal census as a benchmark), I have tried to break down this normative model of Southeast Asia, stressing the idea of different urbanization trajectories that reflected both the variations in economic growth and structural change between Southeast Asian cities, and the pace of integration into the new global system that was a consequence of processes of globalization. In the eighties, these urbanization trajectories varied from the slow growth rates in countries with various forms of state socialism, Burma ( Myanmar), Laos, Cambodia and Vietnam, to countries with accelerating rates, Thailand, the Philippines, Malaysia, the urban involution of Indonesia that still seemed to support the earlier theories, and the city state of Singapore.

In hindsight, I now recognize that from the seventies on this diversification was an incipient reconfiguring of the world economic system that before had seemed rooted in the contrast between socialist and capitalist societies. The oil shock of the 1972, the shift of industrial production to the developing countries, and the surging economic growth of countries such as Thailand, Malaysia and Singapore were only the leading edges of processes that became more universal, if still uneven in their impact, in the region in the 1990s. These developments suggest that my earlier approaches to Southeast Asian urbanization have to be carefully evaluated.

By the 1980s, after a period working as an urban policy advisor in Indonesia, I became more focused on the spatial manifestations of the urbanization process in the Southeast Asian countries of Thailand, the Philippines, Indonesia and

Singapore In these countries, the largest cities that assumed a major role in the colonial period continued to dominate the urban systems. But rapid economic growth, increased industrialization and residential spread had led to the spatial expansion of these core cities into large extended metropolitan regions. This was not a new phenomenon in global urbanization and had been the subject of important research by geographers such as Peter Hall and Jean Gottman. But unlike the European and North American examples, this process of urban expansion was occurring in some of the Southeast Asian countries ( Thailand. Indonesia and the Philippines) in areas of very high rural densities. This was creating zones of intensely mixed urban and rural activities in the peripheries of some Southeast Asian cities. Drawing on my Indonesian experience, in a site specific study of Cilacap on the south coast of Java, I labeled these outer zones of urban expansion as '*desakota*'. I suggested that the existence of such extended zones of dense populations added a new dimension to the process of mega-urbanization that posed particular challenges to urban theory that assumed some convergence of Asian and Western models of urban spatial expansion. Of course, my idea was based upon the transactional model of rural–urban relationships that had grown out of my earliest work on Malay migration.

A group of my students have produced some very fine studies that have modified and criticized the idea of '*desakota*' while not completely discarding it. The idea has had resonance particularly in Thailand and Indonesia where indigenous scholars have seen its usefulness. Its major critics have dismissed its relevance by arguing that a model of convergence with the North American patterns of urban spatial expansion is more suitable to explain the Southeast Asian experience. I liken that kind of thinking to that of George Bush and his advisors who see the American model of democracy as applicable in all societies. Of course, this is only part of a general theory of globalization that assumes we have entered into a period of world history, comparable to the industrial revolution, that is going to deliver global development universally.

There is a large amount of naivety and indeed arrogance in assuming the universal application of systems that ignores the interaction of local forces embedded in different cultural milieus with these supposedly universalizing tendencies. This was an important insight of the work of another student, Phil Kelly, in the urban margins of Manila (Kelly 2000). This is the point where the tension between the scales of global and local becomes most acute. Increasingly, I want to assert the local 'embeddedness' of place as the reality of local groups negotiating their control of the local with various degrees of success. The idea of 'negotiation' enables a major focus to be placed upon the role of local movements engaged in various forms of resistance to globalization. In this approach, the core elements that make up the roots of place— the environment, local culture, local economies, historical layering of 'shared experience' — and the lived experience of place are crucial in explaining global-local relationships. But I would be naive indeed if I did not continue to recognize that 'imperatives' of globalization, masked in neo-liberal espousing of democracy, economic progress and social justice, are not a form of rhetoric embraced by political leaders of Southeast Asian countries: a comforting mask to cover up limited action that enables persistent poverty, income inequality and social injustice to continue. However, we must avoid glorifying the local as some kind of alternative. Only too often negotiation and resistance fail in the face of the overwhelming power of globalization.

## Conclusion

I would like to conclude this essay with the following points. First, I want to return to the quotations that I placed after my title. One of the consequences of spending a lifetime in research and writing is that (assuming you do not forget it, which is a strong possibility) you do acquire a lot of detail ( Robert Plant) and your sense of running out of time creates a certain imperative to try and give meaning to that detail (Cohen) So in every sense this essay has been driven by reflection upon a life of enquiry carried out in a variety of universities, and I have attempted to show how my search for geographical knowledge was intimately related to the places in which I have carried out this research. My second point relates to the collegial experience of academic life. None of this work I have carried out could have been done without constant interaction with students and colleagues. As I often say, they have taught me far more than I could offer them. Third, I must emphasize that my efforts to interpret social, economic and political change in Southeast Asia over the last fifty years have relied upon the contributions of Southeast Asians from all walks of life who have enabled me to sharpen the lens of the outside researcher struggling with ambivalence in attempting to understand the 'inside'. Finally, it is important to emphasize that the antipodean diaspora's experiences involve different life trajectories that are always intertwined but ultimately embedded in those formative years of nationalistic pride that now seem muted in an era of increasing internationalism.

### ACKNOWLEDGMENTS

Parts of this essay were originally given as a keynote address to the Canadian Council of Southeast Asian Studies Biannual Conference held at York University, Toronto, October, 2005, which was published as McGee, T. G. 2007 ' Many knowledges of Southeast Asia: Rethinking Southeast Asia in real time' *Asia Pacific Viewpoint*, 48(2), 270-280. I am grateful to the Editor-in-Chief of *Asia Pacific Viewpoint* for permission to include some portions of my earlier article in this essay.

### REFERENCES

Anderson, B. 1998 *The spectre of comparisons: Nationalisms, Southeast Asia and the world* (London and New York: Verso)

Armstrong, W. and T. G. McGee 1985 *Theatres of accumulation: Studies of urbanization in Latin America and Asia* (London: Methuen)

Daly, T. 2002 *Fluid iron: State formation in Southeast Asia* (Honolulu: University of Hawaii Press)

Geertz, C. 1963 *Peddlers and princes: Social change and economic modernization in two Indonesian towns* (Chicago: University of Chicago Press)

Kelly, P. 2000 *Landscapes of globalization: Human geographies of economic change in the Philippines* (London: Routledge)

McGee, T. G. 1967 *The Southeast Asian City: A social geography of the primate cities of Southeast Asia* ( New York: Praeger)

Sjoberg, G. 1961 *The preindustrial city* (New York: Free Press)

# NAVIGATING UNCHARTED WATERS

## Janice Monk

IN THE 1950S and early 1960s, ships leaving Australia were laden with young Australian women. We used to speculate that there were ten of us for each young man aboard. As Ros Pesman argues in *Duty Free: Australian Women Abroad* (1996), these were middle class women whose journeys reflected the circumstances of their times: their participation in the expanding system of higher education, the relative affluence of the period, and cheap fares on ships that had brought migrants to Australia. They were attracted by visions of Europe as the center of culture and 'freedom', as a place to escape, if temporarily, the confines of family, neighborhood, and the seemingly inevitable future of settling down as a suburban housewife. Using this era as a starting point, Pesman traces a passion for travel by Australian women that dates back to the late 19th century. Some went with families, some alone. Many returned, but some stayed abroad. Their motives varied: some went to seek status and 'finishing', others to pursue education or careers in the arts, literature, theater, the sciences, or to learn foreign languages. Often (and possibly combined with these other motives) they sought to establish their independence, to form new understandings of self, or to test themselves by venturing out. I can identify with the travelers she chronicles and shared several of their motives. I graduated from the University of Sydney in 1958 and held a junior position in its Department of Geography until my departure in 1961 to enter a Master's degree program. Yet my journey was also different from those that Pesman describes. Generally young Australian women were heading to Europe, whereas I went directly to the United States. Further, though my education had opened the way into middle-class culture, I grew up in a working-class suburb. The family finances always had to be watched very carefully.

Although outside the norm in choosing the United States, I was not, however, the first Australian woman geographer to make that voyage to North America. In 1936, the year before I was born, Melbourne graduate Ann Nicholls (subsequently) Marshall (BSc 1929, MSc 1930) went to Toronto as a lecturer, invited by Griffith Taylor. He later encouraged her to study at the University of California, Berkeley where she earned an MA in 1938. She returned to work in Melbourne, then, on her marriage, moved to Adelaide where she sustained her career at the University of Adelaide until her retirement in 1974. In 1989,

Ann Marshall was the first recipient of the Institute of Australian Geographers' Griffith Taylor Medal for distinguished contributions to geography in Australia ( Gale 2001). A decade after Marshall, Patricia McBride (subsequently Bartz), who also earned her BA and MA (1940, 1945) at the University of Melbourne, became the first woman to be granted a PhD in geography at the University of California, Berkeley. She did not pursue an academic career however, living outside the United States as the wife of an American diplomat for more than twenty years. That experience led to her book, *South Korea* (Bartz 1972). My experiences differ from those of these predecessors. I have spent over forty years practicing geography as an Australian in the United States, beginning my career at a time when few women of any national origin were studying geography in American graduate schools or holding faculty positions in graduate programs in geography. I was venturing into largely unchartered waters.[9]

In reflecting on my voyage, I have turned to perspectives offered by scholarship on the life course. This work points to integrating five considerations. It advocates recognition: first, that individual development continues throughout life and is not confined to childhood and adolescence; second, that individuals have agency as they exercise choice within the constraints and opportunities of history and social circumstances; third, that place and time (both period and cohort) are important considerations; fourth, that the timing of life transitions has an impact on how they are experienced; and finally, that individual lives are linked with others through a network of shared relationships (Elder et al. 2003). I also find useful Mary Catherine Bateson's essays on women's lives (Bateson 1989) in which she meditates on improvisation rather than of following a predetermined path, on continuities and discontinuities. These ideas will emerge throughout the story I tell. I also recognize that it is a partial story – both in the sense that it represents my views looking back at a particular point in life, and that some experiences belong only to those involved, not to the wider world. As is evident from the chapter's introduction, I will be integrating attention to themes of class and especially gender.

## *Home Port*

What was it about time, place, personal inclinations, aspirations and connections that led me eventually to an academic life in American geography? Those seeking to answer such a question often begin by reflecting on child-

---

9   I am not aware of Australian men completing graduate education or being employed in North American geography before the mid 1950s, with the exception of British-born Griffith Taylor who earned degrees at the University of Sydney and had his first academic employment there. He was Professor of Geography at the University of Chicago (1929-1935) and at the University of Toronto (1935-1951), and had the unique distinction of being President of the Canadian Association of Geographers, the Association of American Geographers, and the Institute of Australian Geographers. Taylor appears to have been supportive of women as geographers. He long resented that his sister was not retained on the Geography staff by his successor at the University of Sydney. He prompted Ann Marshall's work in North America. I have a clear recollection that he welcomed me personally in 1961 at the Institute of Australian Geographers conference in Brisbane, saying 'Good to see you here. Ellen Churchill Semple was one of our greatest'.

hood and family experiences. For me, they certainly did play a part. My parents' education had ended in their early teens, neither having completed high school. Prior to marriage in his late twenties, my father was employed as a clerical worker, but his real love was travel. With friends he visited Victoria, South Australia, Queensland and Tasmania. As a child, I looked often at the photo albums recording his journeys, and clearly recall an image proudly labeled 'this is the fella wot did all that'. Journeying, especially railroading, was clearly in his heritage. His father had been a locomotive driver, his paternal grandfather an inspector of railroads for western New South Wales. By contrast, my mother had stayed close to home, not traveling beyond New South Wales until well into her 50s. Her family had few resources, and she went to work at age 15, learning to operate a 'comptometer' (adding machine) to work with accountants and auditors. They married in 1930, and soon faced severe economic problems when the firm for which my father worked folded in the Great Depression. My brother was born in 1931, but the times inhibited my parents from having other children, as did the need to take in and care for my maternal grandparents who had few resources. I was born in 1937, just as my father found long-term employment, this time as an office cleaner, then as a storeman in a pharmaceutical company. Money was limited, though my mother's experience with its management became key as the years went on. Nevertheless, the constraints of finances, responsibilities for elder care and the limits of life during World War II meant that family travel was not on the agenda during my childhood.

My father, however, found surrogates. He avidly collected the timetables and magazines of railroad companies from around the world, but especially from US ones. He corresponded periodically with a railroader in Southern Rhodesia and a magazine editor for the Illinois Central Road. From time to time, possibly when I was about seven years of age, he and I would rise early on a Saturday morning and take a train or bus to the end of the line. For me this travel was a treat. With my brother his activities focused more on sports, as he took leadership in organizing youth cricket and baseball teams. This was just one of the activities he promoted at the local Church of England to engage youth. He was expressing a value that social service was more central in his life than paid employment. 'We work to live', he often said, 'not live to work'.

My mother's role was to make ends meet, see that we were well-cared for, and that we kept up with our school work. I learned to love reading early, was given books at birthday and Christmas, and became an active user of the children's sections of local libraries. Among my favorites were Lucy Fitch Perkins's 'twin' books on the lives of boys and girls in other countries and Joyce Lancaster Brisley's stories of the mild adventures of Milly-Molly-Mandy, a little girl in a small English village (who became an alter ego for me). I still have Brisley's books which were illustrated with detailed maps. So too were Arthur Ransome's English children's stories which I encountered a little later.

Fortunately for me, the education system in New South Wales at the time offered 'opportunity schools' for children who scored well on intelligence tests. I qualified, and after considering whether it was desirable for their nine-years old daughter to venture beyond the local neighborhood and travel by public bus to another suburb, my parents decided I should go. Thus my educational advancement began. We had a special curriculum, periodic field trips, and were coached for highly competitive state exams that would give us modest scholarships in our high school years. The daily travel also gave me some freedom and confidence to explore different routes. Additionally, my classmates, though from working and lower middle class families, represented a broader social mix than did my neighborhood.

My high school years, beginning in 1949, further widened my horizons, though still within gendered and, to some extent, class constraints. The public school system was highly stratified. Co-education was only for the first years of schooling; from the age of eight I was in classes for girls. Secondary education divided students not only by sex but by performance and curricula. Qualifying, as did my classmates from the opportunity program, for a highly selective academically-focused high school, I began at Fort St. Girls High. One of the oldest schools in Australia and located on the city approaches to Sydney Harbour Bridge, Fort St. was celebrating its centennial. Distinguished women alumnae (academics, musicians, actresses) were brought to our attention. Our teachers were women graduates, some of them leaders in the state's educational establishment, notably the headmistress, Fanny Cohen, who had earned an overseas scholarship to study mathematics at Cambridge as a young woman. Sewing classes were for first-year students only and cooking was not offered, though these were standard offerings, along with typing, in the local 3-year junior secondary schools. We were expected to work hard, identify proudly with the school, and excel academically. Nevertheless, the curriculum did reflect gendered visions. We studied literature, history, foreign languages and only modest amounts of mathematics and science. At the counterpart boys high school, the latter were emphasized. Geography was mandated in the first year, thereafter being for students who took only one foreign language, two languages being the preferred curriculum for girls who had demonstrated higher achievement than their peers. I took five years of French and four of German.

In class terms, the student body was somewhat wider than it had been in my primary school, yet it is clear from Jill Ker Conway's reflections on her education at that time at one of Sydney's most exclusive private schools for girls (Conway 1989), that we experienced different worlds from Sydney's wealthier classes. In general, our expectations were that most of us would go on to a teacher training college, some to university, some to clerical work. It was a period when job advertisements in newspapers were categorized separately for men or women, and the governmentally-established basic wage levels were higher for men than for women. Though marriage, 1950s style, was in our anticipated futures, I nevertheless do not recall the culture Conway identifies at her school of aspiring to and preparing for the 'right' marriage and social milieu. Nor did we forge networks, as might students in the boys high schools, that would advance us later professionally. Nevertheless, beyond the academic or professional, Fort St. offered me friendships with a wider array of girls than I would have encountered in my local setting, some of which I have maintained for over fifty years from across the globe.

## Voyaging Out

My voyage out and engagement with geography began at the University of Sydney in 1954. At that time, higher education was expanding as was government financial assistance. Given my background, I anticipated pursuing the two-year teacher training program. I applied for a scholarship from the New South Wales Department of Education and also for a Commonwealth Government scholarship for university studies. I was offered only the former which would have paid a living allowance and fees though it required I sign a bond to commit to teach for the state or pay a penalty. The Commonwealth scholarship did not offer comparable resources, but neither did it have an obligation for later employment.. Before the academic year began, as the Commonwealth program proceeded down the merit list, I was offered a scholarship. Simultaneously, the Department of Education changed its offer from the two-year to the four-year program that covered the three-year B.A. followed by a one-year Diploma of Education which would lead to teaching in a high school rather than a primary or junior secondary school. Holding both awards meant that my fees were paid, I received the Education Department's living allowance, and the Commonwealth paid for some ancillary expenses. At this point, I began down a path which I subsequently see as one on which I have often trod – when doors open, I tend to think 'why not?' rather than 'why?' Though my mother questioned the economic advantages of my spending more years in training, it was possible with the combined awards to more or less support myself, living at home but contributing a modest weekly room and board payment. At this age, I see that I was also beginning to make my own decisions. I opted for university.

The Department of Education scholarship required that I enroll for four courses, one of which had to be psychology or philosophy, and two a recognized teaching combination. I chose English and history for the latter. That left a fourth choice. An advisor suggested economics, but it did not attract me. So I tried geography, reflecting, I suspect, my childhood background and an emerging sense that I could make my own decisions. Not only the content, but also the pedagogy of undergraduate education set my eventual course. English and history had large lecture classes. In three years of English (which qualified as a major, to use the US term) and two years of history, I diligently took notes, but do not recall ever speaking to a faculty member. There were one or two required long essays each year and a final exam. Essay topics were to be chosen from a prescribed list with readings being identified for each. While this system meant we took on some challenging topics and reading, more sophisticated than work I often subsequently saw in the student-designed term papers of American undergraduates, we were not prompted to identify problems for ourselves and we received little feedback on our work, other than a grade on the essay and our end-of-year examinations results that were published in the *Sydney Morning Herald* early in the following year. British literature dominated our literary studies. In three years, we studied only one Australian writer who happened to be the lecturer's research interest. No other English-language literature was included. In first-year history, we studied Tudor and Stuart constitutional history and the European renaissance and reformation. There was an ambiance of 'sink-or-swim', with instructions given in our first year to look to the students on either side of us in lectures, since only one in three would be back next year.

Geography, by contrast, was a fairly small department with about fifty students in the first year. In addition to lectures, there were weekly practical classes given to two sub-groups of the students, and several required Saturday field trips. The lecture component, much of it delivered by Professor Macdonald Holmes, was not especially stimulating as he frequently relied on old (1930s?) slides along with assurances that the trend was the same. The practicals and field trips were another matter. Students worked in small groups, got to know each other and the faculty, including the informal and friendly Jack Devery and the New Zealander Ken Robinson. The small group of us on Department of Education scholarships also had weekly tutorials at the Sydney Teachers College, located in the university grounds, led by George Muir. We learned how to tackle the assignments.

At the end of the year, I earned a 'credit' in geography, a 'pass' in English and psychology, but failed in history. Fortunately, keeping my scholarships required passing three of four subjects, so I was not one of the students who disappeared. My results in geography meant I was eligible to enter the honors group, which I did, continuing with English II and successfully repeating history as a night class. For some reason unknown to me, in second year geography, which dealt with systematic subfields, we had an array of visiting faculty, among them the Australian David Simonett, Sydney's first PhD in geography (1954) who was then teaching at the University of Kansas, the genial Yorkshireman, Joe Jennings, and others. I gained some sense of the wider horizons of geography as a profession. In third year we did regional geography, including studies of development issues in Asia and the geography of North America. Teachers included Ray Mathieson, an Englishman who had worked in India and studied at the University of Washington, John Andrews, always eloquent, who had worked for a period in New York (with the United Nations if I recall correctly), and Trevor Langford-Smith, a recent PhD from the Australian National University. I continued to do relatively well, earning 'distinctions' for the extra work in the small honors group. We also were able to choose some topics for our own papers. One I wrote for the North American unit addressed the theme of black Americans. At the time, US-authored geography texts were race-blind, but I found material by a Canadian author, J. Wreford Watson as I recall. My choice possibly reflected a growing interest in race and ethnicity, prompted by the increasing diversity of the Australian population, especially the presence of southern Europeans in my residential neighborhoods, and by ongoing discussions at the time about the 'White Australia' policy.

At the completion of my third year, I had enough courses to graduate and take the Diploma of Education course at Sydney Teachers College. The other option was to continue to the fourth year for an honors degree. This required extending my legal obligation to the Department of Education: to increase the amount that would have to be paid as well as the number of years of required teaching. Again my family discussed the financial implications, especially in terms of foregone salary, with my mother being particularly cautious. I nevertheless decided to go on. The honors year was largely devoted to independent research for a thesis. Even though we had done occasional small library-based projects or field trip reports, we had no training for framing or carrying out larger independent research projects. I was at something of a loss for a theme when the University Archivist came to the department looking for someone who might work with a recent donation to the university of the papers of the Scottish Australian Investment Company. Since I was looking for a topic and had two years of history (despite my first year performance, I did better in the second), I took up the task and settled down to reading decades of handwritten correspondence from the late nineteenth century about the company's changing challenges and policies in north Queensland.[10] It never occurred to me that this task would lead beyond a degree. Surprisingly, however, the following year, Macdonald Holmes had funding for a research assistant to help him complete a languishing book project on northern Australia. The task required synthesizing materials from theses written by earlier students whose research had been (at least partially) funded by his larger project. He offered me the position for a year if I would take leave from my scholarship commitments. Once again, I walked through the door. I was beginning to prefer being at the university than to taking up high school teaching.

Macdonald Holmes did not finish the book that year. He offered me another appointment, this time to combine the research with work as a 'demonstrator', mainly teaching practical classes to evening students, many of whom were two-year trained teachers returning to earn their B.A. I made the jump and resigned from the Department of Education, using my salary to pay off my bond. At that point, I think, on a salary of 1,000 Australian pounds, I was earning more than

---

10   I did not think of publishing this research and no-one suggested that I do so. Just before leaving Australia, I learned inadvertently that the University archivist, to whom the Department had shown a copy of my thesis, published an article under his own name which took whole paragraphs from my work, writing himself only a short introduction and conclusion and indicating in an endnote that the paper 'draws freely' on my thesis.

my father. Interestingly, the bond would have been reduced in terms of time and money if I had resigned to marry, and waived if I had born a child. I was also well aware that, had I taught high school, despite having the same credentials as the men with whom I had been a student, I would also have received a lower salary. The inequities and ironies did not escape me. But this was the 1950s. Women's roles were more closely identified with marriage and motherhood than careers.

I was not really thinking long-term. I just liked what I was doing. There was little indication around me of women advancing in academic careers. The other women with degrees who worked in the Department during my years there were librarians (though not trained in that field), a cartographer, a secretary, and another tutor-demonstrator. I began to think of doing an M.A., possibly about journey-to-work in Sydney, but had little idea of how to go about it. I was saving money, however, despite paying off the bond and increasing the room and board I paid to my parents. The notion of the standard Australian girl trip 'overseas' was on the horizon, but the school friend with whom I would have traveled to Europe was still working out her bond, teaching foreign languages in rural New South Wales. I was also in no hurry to marry and settle down in suburbia. Since my parents had not married until each was 28 years of age, they were not pushing me to hurry in that direction. Neither, however, did they promote a long term career. My father used to say ' a woman's place is in the home' and my mother had not sought employment outside the home after marriage, despite our limited finances, engaged as she was for almost twenty years with both parent and child care.

Meanwhile, I saw advertisements for American graduate programs along with their mentions of assistantships to support graduate education appearing in the department. I also had become friendly with an American student who was on a Fulbright fellowship in Australia. I liked the idea of going on, especially since it would involve advanced class work, not only solo research. I decided to apply, selecting about eight departments recommended by an American contact of Macdonald Holmes. An early offer came from the University of California, Los Angeles, but I turned it down. California seemed too much like Australia, and they wanted an answer before the date other institutions were announcing. Some departments offered me admission but not funding, others did not make offers. It looked as if I would not go, but then I received a cabled offer from the University of Georgia (a new Ph.D program to which I had not applied) and shortly thereafter one from the University of Illinois which had previously rejected me. Since my mother's niece (whom I had seen frequently as a young child) had married a World War II American soldier in Australia and moved to Chicago, going to Illinois at least meant I would have a nearby family contact. It set my mother's mind somewhat at rest about this odd venture. My father was enthusiastic – after all, the Illinois Central Railroad line went through Champaign-Urbana. As fate had it, my father died just a few months before I was due to leave. My brother's reaction was that I should now remain at home with my mother, though he was still single and living at home. As a new widow, committed to her husband's memory, my mother became a stronger supporter of my going than she had been earlier. Of course, we all assumed it was a temporary departure. I booked passage in a four-berth cabin on a P.&O. liner that was on a round-the-world cruise. It called at Manila, Hong Kong, Kobe, Yokahama (I traveled on land to Kyoto and Tokyo with shipmates between those ports), Honolulu, then Vancouver. The ship was returning to England via Los Angeles and the Panama Canal. I disembarked at Vancouver, took the Canadian Pacific train, stopping off in Banff, then on to Winnipeg, Minneapolis and Chicago, where I was met and driven to Champaign-Urbana by my cousin and family. It was a five week adventure, and my first alone.

## Cross currents

I remained at the University of Illinois from 1961 to1980, first as a graduate student and teaching assistant, then as an instructor, and finally as an assistant professor. During those two decades, much changed in American society, in higher education, in the discipline of geography, in the department, and in my own developing orientations and connections. When I arrived, people asked me what I was doing there. I was the only woman graduate student in the Department of Geography, and there was no recognition of the earlier generations of women geographers who had earned graduate degrees and made careers, mostly in teachers colleges, government, or other arenas. Some had even studied and taught at Illinois. Several years later, I learned that my initial rejection had been the unilateral decision of the department Head. Though the faculty had placed me on the list to receive an offer, he had removed my name because, as he reported, he did not take women: they had been 'trouble' at Michigan. The younger faculty members persuaded him to reverse his decision. I was, however, given a desk in a map storage room, along with one older married, male doctoral student; all the other graduate students were quartered in a single large basement office. I have written elsewhere about the gendered culture of the times (Monk 2004, 2006), and of the experiences of women in graduate geography a decade later, and so I will not go into depth here except to note how the larger cultural and social climate had implications for who studied geography, and later had effects on what and how.

My entering graduate class was unusual for Illinois. The department had taken the step of bringing in several Commonwealth students— Bill Clark from New Zealand, Kevin Cox from England, Lorne Russwurm and Alex Blair from Canada. This countered its more usual midwestern American orientation and was not repeated over the next decade. It may well have been influenced at the time by the outstanding work and diplomatic presence of Warwick Armstrong who had come from Auckland a couple of years earlier. I thoroughly enjoyed those early graduate years. My fellow students and others that I met on campus offered friendships and a lively social life; it was great to be independent rather than a daughter in the parental home. In a large state university in a nation where social elites often attend prestigious private institutions, there also seemed to be less class awareness in the social life than there had been in my undergraduate days at Sydney. Perhaps it was just that I was identified at the national or city scale, an Australian from Sydney, and people did not ask or know the specific suburbs. Perhaps it was being in a group of graduate students who were supporting themselves on teaching assistantships. Or perhaps it was also that geography as a profession was not represented in most of the elite private institutions and had a different culture. Whatever the reasons, my memories of graduate school bear little resemblance to those reported by Jill Conway of her days at Harvard in the same period (Conway 1994).

The curriculum was in transition. We had to take quantitative methods, but still do cartography, a summer field course, and a detailed field project analyzing anything we could about a couple of square miles of the local farmlands. In some ways, I thought the geography was not much more advanced in complexity over my undergraduate classes, but I did find the methods courses new. Possibly more important were those that I took outside the department which widened my intellectual range. At Sydney there had been no sociology department, anthropology had been an option only in second and third years and was heavily influenced by British interests in kinship systems, and as I have noted, history was British and European, with a considerable emphasis on political and high cultures. At Illinois I took two classes in American social and economic history, and sociology courses in theory, survey methods, and race relations. In anthropology, I took a two semester seminar with the distinguished scholar Julian Steward who was exploring culture change and development issues within a broadly ecological framework. These choices reflected not only my interest in gaining access to ideas that had not been on the agenda at Sydney, but supported my developing interest in ethnic and racial issues, including their expression in Australia. As I prepared to craft my dissertation project, I drew substantially on this work outside of geography.

My dissertation was a contextually-oriented comparative social ecology of six part-aboriginal communities in New South Wales. As with much of my work during the time at Illinois, this was stimulated by personal experiences and situations that I observed in the field, rather than by what was then 'hot' in the discipline, such as quantitative model building. Neither Australian nor American geographers were engaging with indigenous studies at the time, Fay Gale being the exception in Australia. Further, American geographers did not turn significantly to 'race' questions until prompted by the Civil Rights movement later in the decade. My engagement grew out of a summer work camp in which I had been a volunteer not long before leaving Australia. A group of recent graduates, with funding support from the New South Wales government pursuing its assimilation policy, built a house for an aboriginal family within the white community of Kempsey, a small town which had an aboriginal reserve on its outskirts. That experience had raised questions for me about the intersections of who lives where, who decides, of race relations and economic conditions. Wider social and political currents around civil rights were also rising in Australia, and I was able to link my dissertation research with a large project directed by Charles Rowley that subsequently was associated with significant changes in Federal policies on aboriginal affairs.

My later socially-oriented research projects while at Illinois were stimulated first by experiences and interests in Australia's changing ethnic make up. I completed a study of Asian professionals as immigrants in Sydney. Additionally, I did several projects in rural Puerto Rico taking up aspects of population and economic changes, including my first project that addressed gender issues, just then emerging in academic research as an outgrowth of the women's movement of the late 1960s and early 1970s. These studies were prompted by observations I had made in the field when assigned to co-teach the department's summer field course. All were based on field observations, mapping, archival work and interviews with relatively small samples. With the exception of the work in Sydney, they were in rural communities. I was thus outside the mainstream orientation of the period towards larger scale, quantitative model building and urban research.

The late sixties and early seventies saw an expansion of US federal government funding for research and higher education which had long term implications for my career. One of those came via grants to the University of Illinois and its Office of Instructional Resources (OIR). OIR was seeking departments with which it could collaborate in research to evaluate teaching and learning. The Geography Department was interested. Though I was still a graduate student at the dissertation writing stage, I was asked to serve part-time as a research associate supported by a federal grant to the OIR, with the rest of my salary earned in teaching an honors section of the introductory physical geography course, then taught by Charles Alexander. In the process, I learned a lot about approaches to teaching and learning in higher education, published several co-authored articles related to the project, and a book of teaching activities with Alexander to complement a recent introductory college text he had co-authored. I thus began to develop work on geography in higher education, an area which I have sustained to the present.

Based on my research with OIR and on interests in the department in strengthening geography education by supporting the preparation of its teaching assistants, I was well positioned when the Association of American Geographers (AAG) sought partnerships with doctoral programs for a multi-university project funded by the National Science Foundation, 'Teaching and Learning in Graduate Geography'(TLGG). Illinois applied to become one of the participating campuses and I directed its program under a sub-contract. About this time, the department was able to secure university funding to place me on a tenure-track line as an Assistant Professor, with dual responsibilities for education and social geography, but with the former as a key component of my work.

As an AAG project, TLGG substantially expanded my national and even international network. One key event was an invitation in 1976 to offer, along with the TLGG's Associate Director, workshops at an International Geographical Union symposium in Leningrad. The various educational projects also offered new opportunities for publication, given the obligations to disseminate the findings of the funded research. It did mean that my time and publications were divided between two arenas, however. Also, I was beginning to realize that continuing my research in Australia would be hard to fund from a U.S. base, that I was now in a much larger job market, and that I was undertaking work of a kind then not widely included in Australian institutions. I liked what I was doing, the people I was meeting, and the continuing appointment. I did not look seriously for any opportunities to return to Australia.

Other contextual changes meant both new constraints and new opportunities. By the early 1970s, the expansion of the academic labor market that had been supported by enrollments of the baby boom generation was passing. Simultaneously, the investments in graduate education that had stemmed from cold-war politics, such as the National Defense Education Act fellowships were being curtailed. In the post-Vietnam war era, male students who had sought draft deferments to stay in graduate school also moved on. Higher education, including geography programs, felt the pinch. With these conjunctions, male student membership of the Association of American Geographers dropped from 1,897 to 879 between 1973 and the end of the decade. Countering this in a modest way was the increasing entry of women into graduate programs in geography, their student membership in the AAG rising in the same period from 346 to 459 (see, Monk 2006). The women's entry reflected motivations prompted by the women's movement with consequences not only for the labor market but for scholarship, program development, and for me personally.

At the University of Illinois, and in the Geography Department, structural and personnel changes were underway that would affect my career, The College of Liberal Arts and Sciences was reorganized to have Schools as sub-units made up of several departments. Geography was located within a School of Social Sciences under a Director who was a specialist in Asian history. In several ways it became evident that his vision was not going to support the kind of work I was doing, neither in education nor in the feminist work that was becoming increasingly of interest to me and other women. When a group of women faculty, including some senior women in other departments, met with him to discuss developing courses in women's studies, he was dismissive, arguing that women's studies was not like interdisciplinary area studies, since women 'had no culture'. The interim Dean by the end of the decade was also conservative on matters of gender and 'racial' equity and advancement. It was not the fault of the university, he argued in a letter to the Faculty Senate, that blacks were not in higher education, it was because they were developmentally limited. With women, the problem was that socialization meant they lacked mathematical skills. By the end of the decade, the headship of the Geography Department also changed; a new Head recruited from the outside did not share the visions of his predecessor who had supported my hiring and work.

Nevertheless, in several ways the feminist developments of the decade had multiple positive implications for my work and status. I found the new scholarship in the social sciences and humanities attractive and began to publish and teach in the area; simultaneously, it offered opportunities to extend my networks nationally in geography and on campus. In the AAG's Committee on the Status of Women in Geography, political activity rose with efforts to advance women in the discipline and in AAG leadership. One outcome of this was my nomination and election as a national councilor of the Association (1978-1981); I was one of the few potential candidates who was a faculty member in a doctoral granting department. I was also co-principal on a federal grant administered through the AAG, *'Women and Spatial Change'*, to develop curriculum modules that could be integrated into introductory human geography courses. At the local level, federal Affirmative Action policies, which had taken effect in higher education in the early 1970s, mostly meant more service work for the few women faculty on campus with our appointments as 'the woman' member of various committees. At one point, I was serving simultaneously on about ten committees, as well as being the undergraduate advisor for the department, on the AAG Council, and on some of its committees such as the one that developed the system of Specialty Groups. 'Just saying no' did not seem an option when the appointments were made by supervisors or national leaders.

The negative side of this work was the heavy amount of time it took and the lack of value generally assigned to it. The positive side was that between it, my grant-funded projects and related publications, I learned new skills in proposal writing, administration and publishing. These skills stood me in good stead when I was denied tenure in 1979. Although departmental colleagues had voted positively, the new Head did not accept the recommendation, indicating I lacked 'potential' for the Department's programs. I have discussed the case in more detail elsewhere (Holcomb et al. 1987, Monk 2007), and will not elaborate here, except to indicate that I appealed at several levels, motivated politically more than by a desire to remain. The appeals committees at several levels found evidence of procedural problems and sex discrimination, but the eventual University judgement was that there had been 'irregularities but not errors'. The decision meant that I had to find a new position in a tight labor market.

## *On the bridge*

In the fall of 1980 I arrived at the University of Arizona to take up a grant-funded position as Associate Director of the Southwest Institute for Research on Women (SIROW). I have remained at the University since then. I learned of the position after having declined an offer to chair a small midwestern department where I would have had to lead a divided unit as a non-tenured associate professor with, I thought, low prospects for success. I was also a finalist for a two-year position as a program officer at the National Science Foundation, but for this I was disadvantaged in having no academic position to which I would have the guarantee of return after the short-term appointment. Those considering me for both these prospects saw the administrative experience I had gained through professional service and grant activity as useful credentials. There were however, no significant geography faculty positions open.

The SIROW appointment had no commitment to continuity, but it drew on the range of experiences I had built, though I had not been thinking of where they might lead. Women's studies was a new interdisciplinary field, without an established pool of applicants. The Ford Foundation had recently initiated funding of an array of research centers on women. At Arizona, Myra Dinnerstein, an Africanist historian, had been appointed on one-year contracts since 1975 to chair a Women's Studies program. An astute and imaginative administrator and politician, she and colleagues identified the concept of a regional research center as one that would appeal to the University's goals of enhancing its research and bringing in external funds. She made national connections with leaders in Women's Studies who introduced her to the Ford Foundation and proposed the regional model as a way to compete with, and stand out from other universities, especially those that were more visible to the eastern establishment. The application was successful. It proposed a model that would draw on the talents of scholars in over twenty regional colleges and universities, engage in research, curriculum development, and community outreach, and attend to the ethnically and culturally diversified nature of the southwestern United States. There was the hope that the initial three-year award, under her Directorship, would lead to additional grants and sustained funding. In the first year, a junior temporary assistant director was hired with the intent to search for a more established Associate Director.

My experience meshed with the Institute's needs. As a geographer, I had the background to identify themes that had a regional focus. I had also sustained study in several fields (literature, history, sociology, and anthropology), as a geographer had worked with natural scientists, had done curriculum and faculty development work, written and managed grants, and networked nationally in my own discipline. Once hired, I quickly found my colleagues and the institution stimulating and open. We successfully developed a range of funded projects and gained an additional three-year grant from the Ford Foundation for core operations. In the second year of that cycle, with the support of a canny Dean, we obtained state-funding that included a research appointment for me on a continuing status track, the equivalent of tenure track for a non-teaching appointee. My title was advanced to Executive Director.

Over the next two decades I was on the bridge in multiple senses of that metaphor. On the one hand, I was bridging fields and types of projects. I was also striving to maintain my work in and ties to geography, though the type of field research I had undertaken previously needed to be modified to fit with the administrative responsibilities. Additionally, I had opportunities to take leadership in fostering work and perspectives that I valued.

In reflecting on my work at SIROW, I will address aspects of it that most closely connect with geographic perspectives. One highlight of my career was to initiate an interdisciplinary project on the ways in which southwestern women writers and artists responded to and represented the landscapes of the region. Vera Norwood, an American Studies scholar at the University of New Mexico, and I brought together an interdisciplinary team, secured a grant from the Rockefeller Foundation, and co-edited the book, *The Desert Is No Lady*. It interpreted the writing and art of American Indian, Hispanic/Chicana, and Anglo-American women over the period 1880-1980. Its comparative focus reflected the character of the region and my long-standing interests in exploring ethnic diversity. We showed cultural connections and differences, changes over time in relation to shifting contexts, and in particular how the women's visions and creativity drew strength from the landscape. Unlike the perspectives in much of the canonical regional literature about the American West written by Anglo-American men, these women did not see the land as a virgin to be conquered, a garden to exploit or conversely as a wilderness to protect from human exploitation. Published initially by Yale University Press (Norwood and Monk 1987), and later by the University of Arizona Press, it circulated widely and won a regional book award. In the 1990s, an accomplished British film maker approached me to discuss creating a documentary inspired by the book. Completed in 1995, after intensive grant-writing to secure funding, it won a national award and is still being sold, mostly to educational libraries.

A second sustained initiative that I advanced at SIROW was faculty and curriculum development to bring international perspectives into the Women's Studies curricula in the region, and to bring Women's Studies scholarship into international studies. Funded by an array of granting agencies, for over a decade we led summer institutes for faculty from regional institutions, edited related publications, and joined with colleagues across the country in fostering such work. In participating in these projects I had the opportunities to consult on other campuses in the US, and also on behalf of the Ford Foundation with universities in Israel.

A third extended effort involved collaboration with colleagues in northern Mexico in joint leadership of the 'Transborder Consortium for Gender and Health at the Mexico-US Border'. This work, beginning in the 1990s, continues into the present. Conducted with colleagues in anthropology, public health, political science and other fields, it has incorporated research, faculty development, and substantial community outreach. An important aspect of my participation has been to reflect and write on the processes of collaborating across multiple boundaries – national, disciplinary, and university-community (see, for example, Monk et al. 2002, Denman et al. 2004)

Within geography, much of what I was able to sustain was at national and international levels, by way of co-authoring, co-editing, and service. Especially important have been the ties with feminist geographers through the International

Geographical Union. We first gained approval of a 'Study Group on Gender' at the Sydney Congress in 1988, and subsequently built an active Commission on 'Gender and Geography' that has sustained an international program. It was especially rewarding for me to be invited by Australian geographers to give one of the plenary addresses at that Congress, speaking on international developments in gender research in the discipline. Through the IGU work, and as editor of the Commission's newsletter, I have made friendships in numerous countries, and especially close ties at the Autonomous University of Barcelona which I have visited many times and where I have held short-term appointments. It has been a pleasure to host international geographers, a number from Barcelona, in Arizona,. Also gratifying has been the opportunity to bring the work of scholars from an array of countries into wider circulation through a book series, *International Studies of Women and Place* (published by Routledge) that I co-edit with Janet Momsen, the founding chair of the Gender Commission. The introduction to one of the books in this series (Garcia Ramon and Monk 1996), makes the observation that it gives more emphasis to southern Europe than is common in studies of western Europe. We saw this as a reflection that we were both 'women of the South', in my case doubly so coming from Australia and from the southern border region of the US.

I have also sustained my work in geographic education, focusing on faculty and curriculum efforts in higher education. This has involved much collaboration. Officially now retired from the University of Arizona, I am engaged with colleagues in a large multi-year project, 'Enhancing Departments and Graduate Education in Geography,' funded by a National Science Foundation grant to the AAG. We are researching the cultures and climates of graduate programs in the discipline with the aim of developing strategies and resources that will help to widen the career opportunities and preparation of the next generations of geographers within the academy and beyond.

In 2001-2002, I had the great privilege of serving as President of the Association of American Geographers, a role I could never have imagined as an undergraduate finding my way into geography and academia in Sydney in the 1950s. In my first column for the AAG Newsletter, I wrote on the theme of valuing service, an activity that young scholars are often cautioned to avoid. Certainly, my career might have taken different directions if I had not been charged with so many service tasks in my years at Illinois, partly because of my role in educational projects, and partly because of gender and feminist politics. It is also not surprising that among my Presidential initiatives was one to strengthen international collaboration by, for example, initiating a reception to welcome geographers from abroad who attend the AAG's annual meeting, and prompting the Association's 'Committee on International Research and Scholarly Exchange' to secure funding for a joint research workshop with South African geographers on 'race' and space issues. With the privilege of arranging the Presidential Plenary, I invited the then women presidents of the Institute of Australian Geographers (Ruth Fincher), the Canadian Association of Geographers (Audrey Kobayashi), the Catalan Geographical Society (Maria Dolors Garcia Ramon) and the Californian Geographical Society (Jenny Zorn) to offer their perspectives on 'Points of View, Sites For Action'. Also at that meeting, I was able to invite as speaker for the Opening Session the distinguished Mexican American poet, Pat Mora, who gave an inspiring presentation, 'Spirit and Space'. It was the first occasion on which I can recall a woman speaker being invited to give the opening presentation, and only the third on which the speaker represented an American ethnic minority group. When time came for my Past-Presidential address, I used that platform to present research on issues of women and gender in American geography (Monk 2004).

Throughout my career, and especially in the service and administrative roles, I have enjoyed many gratifying rewards: friendships, opportunities for learning, contributing in support of collective endeavors. I have also learned that taking chances, and venturing into waters that were unchartered and unknown to me when I grew up in Australia, continues to offer exciting prospects.

**REFERENCES**

Bartz, P. M. 1972 *South Korea* ( Oxford: The Clarendon Press)

Bateson, M. C. 1989 *Composing a life* ( New York: The Atlantic Monthly Press)

Conway, J.K. 1989 *The road from Coorain* ( New York: Alfred A. Knopf/Random House)

Conway, J. K.1994 *True north* ( New York: Alfred A. Knopf)

Denman, C., Monk, J. and Ojeda de la Peña, N. eds. 2004 *Compartiendo historias de ronteras: cuerpos, géneros, generaciones, y salud* ( Hermosillo, SON: El Colegio de Sonora)

Elder, G. H., Johnson, M. K. and Crosnoe, R. 2003 'The emergence and development of life course theory' in Mortimer, J. T. and Shanahan, M. J. eds. *Handbook of the Life Course* ( New York: Kluwer Academic/Plenum) 3-10

Gale, F. 2001 'Obituary: Ann Marshall 1909-2001' *Australian Geographical Studies* 39(3) 365-367

Garcia Ramon, M. D. and Monk, J. eds. 1996 *Women of the European Union: The Politics of Work and Daily Life* ( London and New York: Routledge)

Holcomb, B., Kay, J., Kay, P. and Monk, J. 1987 'The tenure review process' *Journal of Geography in Higher Education* 11(2), 85-98

Monk, J. 2004 'Women, gender, and the histories of American geography' *Annals of the Association of American Geographers* 94 (1), 1-22

Monk, J. 2006 'Changing expectations and institutions: American women geographers in the 1970s' *The Geographical Review* 96 (2), 259-277

Monk, J. 2007 'Outsider/insider: Traveling across divides' in Wheeler, J.O. and Parker, K. C. eds. *Inside Geographers' Lives and Minds: Autobiographical Insights* forthcoming

Monk, J., Manning, P. and Denman, C. 2002 'Working together: Feminist perspectives on collaborative research and action' *ACME: An International E-Journal for Critical Geographies* 2(1), 91-106

Norwood, V. and Monk, J. eds. 1987 *The desert is no lady; Southwestern landscapes in women's writing and art* (New Haven: Yale University Press)

Pesman, R. 1996 *Duty free: Australian women abroad* ( Melbourne: Oxford University Press)

# GEOGRAPHERS BY INSTINCT?

## Warren Moran

I AM NOT sure when I first read these words but it was certainly while I was a student studying at Auckland University College in the 1950s. They were written by P. Marshall the author of *The Geography of New Zealand* first published in 1905. The full quotation reads, 'The fortunate inhabitants of New Zealand should be geographers by instinct.' Marshall, a geologist, was primarily referring to the rich diversity of New Zealand's natural landscapes especially its geomorphology and its endemic plant and animal life. His words could equally well evoke references to the cultural diversity of the nation, its original settlement by Maori, its colonial history, its ambivalent and evolving relationship with the rest of the world and the diverse economic and settlement landscapes that clothe and scar its natural landscape. Seen through the eyes of its 'fortunate inhabitants', from the first Polynesian migrants through its second colonization by primarily Anglo-Celtic peoples to the late twentieth century accelerated settlement of people from China, Korea, and the nations of Southeast Asia, and many other parts of the world, the country has many geographies.

While the New Zealand cultural and natural landscape may well have been an underlying instinctive inspiration for many of us, it was the philosophies and perspectives of our formal training that provided the equipment to interpret this landscape, and to understand other places through asking different questions as a result of understanding our own place. Our generation, both Maori and Pakeha, were the first of the professionally trained indigenous geographers, albeit from a European cultural perspective, on these islands. In this chapter, I use my personal experience and that of my contemporaries to reflect on the interaction among what Marshall called 'instinct' and education, research, teaching and administration in shaping the understanding of our generation of geographers.

### Growing up on the public service circuit

I was born in Auckland, the second of three children, but spent very little of my childhood education there. My father was employed by the New Zealand Post Office in its main Auckland office. The year I was born he was appointed as a supervisor in the Hastings Post Office in Hawke's Bay, This was the beginning of the family's public service circuit. Employees in the public service were encouraged, even required in the case of teachers, to spend part of their career in the rural parts of New Zealand. By the time I started primary school we had moved to the nearby city of Napier where my father was Postmaster of its Port Ahuriri office. Strong memories from the time are of learning to swim from the stony beach on the open coast less than one hundred meters from the school, and of the canoe that I was given when I was six. My parents let me use this to explore the estuary adjoining our house, and summer days were spent paddling, beaching the canoe on shell banks, reading and lying in the sun.

From there we moved to Kaikohe in Northland where I completed most of my primary school education. In 1948 we moved to Helensville, a rural service town about 60 kms from Auckland, and there I attended the local District High School, now Kaipara College, but at the time a school of about two hundred students. It was a well-organized school with some very good teachers but with a small choice of subjects. Nevertheless, the school and clubs in the small town offered a full range of sporting and other activities, tennis, track and field, cricket and swimming in summer and rugby in winter, and I took full advantage of those opportunities. Towards the end of 1953, my final year at school, my father was appointed Postmaster at Henderson, a growing town, and now a suburb on the western edge of Auckland. This move was not coincidental. My parents wanted to give my elder sister and me the opportunity to attend university, a step encouraged by our teachers, and for which we had completed the necessary examinations. It was from there that I attended what was then Auckland University College.

I have occasionally considered whether these experiences of different places enlivened my interest in geography. They certainly provided an historical perspective, and an understanding to be built on that later proved invaluable. The phrases 'the road-less North' and 'winter-less North' still stick in my mind. I have clear impressions of the Northland of that time with manuka and other low scrub dominating the landscape, although the area immediately around Kaikohe where we lived was mainly in pasture. I recall too the rolling, volcanic landscape of Waimate north, one of the earliest agricultural settlements in New Zealand, as being almost idyllic. In summer though, everything near any road was dusty.

## University life as a student

At Auckland University College, English and geography were my first choice of subjects for the BA degree. My high school geography had been well taught and mainly from interesting materials. We were among the first of the students to have a comprehensive course in the regional geography of New Zealand using the set of post-primary school bulletins that had recently been written by university geographers and edited by Kenneth Cumberland. I recall clearly the contrast between these and what I later recognized as the dull world geography of Dudley Stamp, the text in our final year of high school.

A foreign language was compulsory in the Bachelor of Arts degree. I took French, although it had been taught only to third year of our high school. The only science available at my high school as a specialist subject beyond third year was biology and I took that and rounded out my undergraduate degree with two courses in each of history and education. By the final year of the BA, I had two choices as a major — English or geography. I had received much better grades in English but chose geography and have never regretted it.

Ken Cumberland, the sole Professor and Head of the Department of Geography until he retired in 1978, was clearly its most influential figure (Anderson 1980). At the time he taught the first year course with other staff invited to give a few lectures. His lectures were models of clarity and always interesting, features that were later displayed publicly in his presentation of the highly successful Television New Zealand program *Landmarks* on the historical geography of New Zealand. He also had a definite philosophy of the discipline that became clear as we advanced through the geography courses at Auckland (Cumberland 1946). He insisted that the practising of geography be stressed in the curriculum. Laboratory classes and exercises began in the first year and continued throughout the undergraduate degree. In second and third years they were linked to residential field courses of a week to ten days with research projects and practice as the main outcomes.

An aspect of Cumberland's reputation was revealed, as many events are in universities, by students, in this case through an incident on the first Stage 3 field-trip that I organized. It was based in Lytton High School, Gisborne, with the students camped in sleeping bags on the classroom floors. When the students were out on survey work one day I walked into one of those rooms and written in bold letters a meter high on one of the blackboards was 'GOD ROLLS HIS OWN'. At the time, Cumberland smoked the brand of loose tobacco called 'Park Drive'.

Cumberland was already an active voice in the community. Along with his colleague Jim Fox he served as a commentator on a weekly national radio program on international events. He was also a member of the Auckland Regional Authority, as it was then called, and for a period chaired its planning committee. In this capacity he was especially influential in the planning for Auckland's first motorway system. As foundation editor of the *New Zealand Geographer*, Cumberland contributed both papers and commentary, as did many of the staff.

Cumberland's philosophical position was always a strongly argued one although even at the time it was tempered by others in the Department such as Les Curry and Gordon Lewthwaite. Curry who had a deep and lasting influence on me was then completing his PhD on the climatic resources of New Zealand pastoral farming, a sophisticated work that in many ways demonstrates the best qualities of quantitative geography (Curry 1963). He rejected the oversimplification of areal differentiation as a primary objective, preferring to argue from theoretically based ideas, though not always to his advantage. I remember vividly a first year climatology lecture from him. He began his interpretation of planetary pressure and wind systems with theory but unfortunately, by the end of the lecture the northeast and southeast trade winds ended up as westerlies on his blackboard map. His response was to gaze at the map quizzically, throw the chalk in the air, and exclaim, 'oh, what the hell, anyway'. Lewthwaite introduced us to the research of United States agricultural economists on the theorizing of inter-regional land use competition, and he also made Carl Sauer's work compulsory reading. These were more sophisticated ideas than we had confronted in our regional geography courses.

What were the strengths of the program in geography at Auckland in the 1950s and 1960s that enabled its graduates to succeed internationally as well as locally? Four inter-related elements stand out. First, a staff who were practically and philosophically knowledgeable in the discipline. Second, a syllabus that covered in reasonable detail physical, human, and regional geography. Third, an emphasis on fieldwork and student research projects in the undergraduate and graduate degrees and fourth an expectation, even requirement, that students be encouraged to teach themselves and others in the course in a demanding seminar program. In the third (and final) year of the undergraduate degree, the students themselves did much of the teaching. After a few introductory lectures by the staff member in charge of the course each student was assigned two seminars that they presented as part of the structured program. Two seminars made up the weekly two-hour session for each course. Oral presentations were about forty minutes long followed by discussion, with another member of the class presenting the first assessment of the presentation. We students saw this arrangement as an easy ride for the staff and a rough one for us. Few if any of us recognized how much we were learning.

The MA/MSc degree of the time was a two-year program with all assessment at the end of the second year. Again, we students complained about this and only retrospectively recognized some of the advantages that it provided. At the end of the second year we were required to sit the four papers that we had chosen, and hand in the substantial thesis that had been completed over a fifteen-month period. This, of course, required that we be well organized and able to use one's own work and that of others to prepare for the examinations. The course mirrored the same pressures that we were to encounter in most jobs. A single paper on the history and philosophy of geography was compulsory. By the end of these two years we all had a good understanding of our own strengths and weaknesses as well as those of the other students in the class. I was surprised when Gerry Ward, then a junior Lecturer in the Department, approached me after a seminar presentation on regional variability in the agriculture of the Pacific Islands and its relationships to demographic change, with a suggestion to use it as the basis for a joint paper. That was my first publication.

We were also lucky to have regular visitors from the northern hemisphere. Cumberland had persuaded the University to allow him to keep one academic post open and use the funds to invite visitors. In 1957, the first year of my Master's course, H.C Darby from University College, London, visited. His warmth and affability surprised us all. Late in the afternoon he would wander into the graduate workroom and say, 'I'm off to the Station for an ale. Would any of you like to join me?' Invariably, some of us would and the discussion was always rewarding. Darby inquired about my thesis topic, discussed it with me, and suggested that I write to Roger Dion who had recently published prolifically on the French wine industry. Dion replied by postcard followed by a package of his papers. I struggled through the French. His powerful cultural, economic, and socio-political arguments helped provide me with a central theme for my thesis on the New Zealand wine industry – the influence of culture on its location and regional organization. Little did I know then how immersion in Dion's ideas would influence my research. At the time the wine industry, especially near Auckland, was dominated by Croatian migrants from the Dalmatian coast. Darby also suggested a contact at Zagreb who directed me to sources that helped tease out the conditions that saw these Croats migrate to New Zealand from the end of the 19th century.

The final year of the Masters degree was intense but surprisingly enjoyable. It was complicated because it coincided with my year of teacher training. Averilda Gorrie, later a colleague at the University of Auckland, gave the history and geography thesis students in her class great flexibility, especially when they were completing their degrees. In the same teacher training class was Pauline Dickson who was completing the last two units of her BA in history. We started going out together at the end of 1958. By then Pauline had already accepted a job teaching at Hutt Valley High School in Wellington and I had accepted a position at Henderson High School in Auckland.

When the Masters results were announced I was asked to meet with Cumberland who suggested that I should begin a PhD program at either Nottingham or Wisconsin. But after five years at university and the intensive two years of the Masters degree, I was looking forward to spending time with Pauline, enjoying club rugby with Waitemata, and with luck continuing to play for Auckland while beginning a teaching career. We both knew about the excellent teaching conditions and salaries in Canada at the time and were keen to travel. We were married in January 1961 in Hawera, Taranaki and two months later left for Canada on the P.& O. Line vessel, the Orsova, traveling via Suva and Honolulu to Vancouver. It was a lively voyage. The numerous recent graduates on the ship were heading to the United States or Canada for further education or to take up jobs, and even though we were traveling in cabins on the lower decks on the lowest possible fares, this New Zealand contingent somehow often ended up at parties in first class. Groups of us made full use of our one-day stopovers in Fiji and Hawaii, getting out to remote villages and seeing as much as we could.

## Teaching in Toronto, Canada

Teaching in Canadian high schools made me realize how well trained we were at Auckland both in geography, and in our teacher training. Pauline and I had purposely arrived in Toronto for Easter 1961, the week when most hiring took place for the beginning of the school year in September. Most Ontario boards of education interviewed in Toronto hotels, and each of us attended a number of these and were both offered several positions. We spent until June 1961 'supply teaching' at different schools in Toronto and North York. Without our own transport we soon got to know the city well.

I still harbored thoughts of doing a PhD. Pauline offered to teach and support us both. I made an appointment at the University of Toronto Department of Geography with Jacob Spelt, chairman at the time. He assessed my record and references, read my thesis, and offered me a position in their PhD program. But within two weeks of this we found out that Pauline was pregnant, and the principal of her school immediately asked her to sign a letter of resignation. Those were the 1960s. At about the same time the principal of Bathurst Heights Collegiate school contacted me because the head of their geography department had resigned. He offered me the job and I accepted. The PhD would have to wait.

Those were the halcyon days of high school teaching in Ontario. Salaries were high, sufficient to attract qualified people from other professions. Schools had substantial budgets and we were encouraged to be innovative in our teaching. Interest in geography was high and enrollments strong. No sooner had I taken up the headship than I had three posts to fill in the department. A strong group of applicants came forward and we were able to fill the vacancies with honors graduates, two from Toronto and one from Western Ontario. With six well-qualified geographers in the department we set about attracting good students. We established a good library including subscriptions to journals such as *Economic Geography*, the *Annals of the Association of American Geographers* and the *Canadian Geographer*. Quentin Stanford (the deputy head) and I introduced an advanced placement course in geography which enabled a selected group of grade 10 students to take the grade 11 course in geography, and to continue this advancement in the following two years thereby completing final grade 13 geography in their second to last year. In this way, we attracted a group of talented students, many of whom were primarily science students who would not otherwise have taken geography in their senior years. From the first of these classes twelve students went on to complete honors degrees in geography at the University of Toronto.

Bathurst Heights Collegiate was a large school of over 2000 students with a catchment that at that time was dominated by students of Jewish and Italian descent. A stimulating place at which to work, it was very strong in the academic subjects and in music and sport, and also offered a substantial vocational training program. The history department rightly took pride in being among the best in the Province. We set about to become as well respected. In the1960s the High School Geography project of the Association of American Geographers was seeking to strengthen high school teaching of the subject, and I attended the mid-western regional conferences held in connection with it as one of two Ontario delegates. We began using materials produced from the project in our senior classes.

A consulting engagement which I had in the early 1960s with the Toronto office of the Oxford University Press led to discussions about the writing of a senior high school geography text. Quentin Stanford was keen to participate. His degrees in geography and planning and expertise in urban geography and geomorphology complemented my interests in economic geography and climatology. We signed a contract and wrote the book over the next three years. It was well received in the western provinces as well as in Ontario and went through several editions. I think it did help change Canadian high school geography which at the time was relatively traditional with physical geography dominating the syllabus and with a strong emphasis on geomorphology. That emphasis had certainly improved my knowledge of the glacial geomorphology of the continent and served me well when I took the examination for the Type A teaching certificate. Two years later, in 1964, I taught the summer school for this certificate at the Ontario College of Education.

Our five years in Toronto were packed with activity. As well as the classroom teaching, I coached the track team and entered fully into the life of the school. Bathurst Heights also had an active night school program where for two years I taught English to 'New Canadians'. It was some of the most enjoyable 'work' I have ever done. The teaching resources and materials were excellent and the people full of ideas and receptive, though they probably ended up with a New Zealand accent. Rugby offered me another way of meeting different people. I played for the Toronto Irish, for the Nomads which was mainly a mixture of Australians, New Zealanders and South Africans, and for Ontario. An opportunity in the following year to tour England and Ireland as a member of the Canadian team had to be turned down when the Board of Education refused me leave. Toronto offered an almost overwhelming choice of music, both classical and popular. During the 1960s it was in the top four or five North American cities for the quality and number of jazz groups that visited regularly. The Ellington and Basie big bands visited annually while small groups from across the jazz spectrum were always in town. They played mainly in downtown taverns such as the Town and Colonial and we were regular patrons.

To see something of the United States and Canada when we first arrived we had taken ten days by Greyhound bus to get from Seattle to Toronto, via Chicago, with some short stopovers. For the next two summers we traveled by car extensively, as well as taking numerous weekend trips in southern Ontario. The first summer we took six weeks traveling and camping through Quebec, Maine and the Maritime provinces, and the following year completed a 15,000 mile trip north of Lake Superior across the Trans Canada Highway, south through Washington and Oregon into California and then zigzagging back to Toronto through the west and Midwest. We organized this trip around the National, Provincial, and State Parks of Canada and the United States. Our son Michael who was five months old came with us and we again camped all the way.

On this trip we made a point of stopping for picnic lunches not far from farmhouses, and I would chat to the farmers about their farms before we had lunch. In the Napa valley and other vineyard areas of California I made a point of doing this and was able to gain a good understanding of their organization in the early 1960s prior to their rapid growth. By the time the two-month trip was finished, I had put together my own interpretations of the North American rural systems that were invaluable in my teaching.

With five years of teaching behind me in Toronto, it was suggested that I begin to apply for Vice-Principal positions. Then I knew that it was time to consider going home. I was enjoying teaching and still thinking of doing it at higher levels but I was not ready to become an administrator. Pauline was even more enthusiastic to get back to New Zealand, and for our two children to get to know their grandparents. A week after arriving home however, the reality of being back in Auckland had Pauline, in particular, but me as well pining for Toronto.

## My return to the Auckland Geography Department

When we decided to return to New Zealand I had let some of my contemporaries know that I would be looking for a position in geography and I received an offer from a new west Auckland school. My ambition to do research was still strong however, and when a position for a lectureship in geography at the University of Auckland was advertised in 1967 I applied for it and was appointed. The timing was fortunate because I was one of the last of the people to be appointed without already having a PhD.

When I took up the position at the beginning of 1968 only Ken Cumberland remained of the staff who had taught me a decade earlier. Peter Hosking, a Canterbury graduate who had completed his PhD at Southern Illinois and had been teaching at Wisconsin, joined the staff at the same time as me. The Geography Department then adjoined the Geology Department with the two groups sharing a common room. My office was next to Peter's and for two weeks he thought that I was a member of the Geology Department. Over the next decade, the two of us were to be active in promoting curricula and administrative changes in the Department. On most issues we were of a like mind. In addition, Peter who was both well trained in and a superb teacher of quantitative methods, was a source of inspiration and help to me in my research and teaching.

Grant Anderson and Rilda Gorrie, both Auckland graduates, had been appointed while I was away and remained on the staff until they retired. Within two years, four of the existing faculty members had accepted positions else-where while Bruce Rains, another Canterbury graduate who had completed a PhD in Edmonton, Mike Taylor, a University College, London graduate and Dave Rankin from Nottingham joined the staff. This total of five appointments in two years reduced the average age of the department's staff by ten years.

During my first year, Clarence Olmstead from Wisconsin, spent six months in the department. He had been invited as a result of Cumberland's and later Gordon Lewthwaite's time at Wisconsin. He participated in a graduate course in agricultural geography that Grant Anderson and I were teaching. I knew Olmstead's work from his paper on American orchard and vineyard regions that had influenced my approach in my M.A. thesis. At the time he was writing what was to become an influential paper in rural studies (Olmstead 1971), especially for geographers of the next generation and he presented this in our course. His deep conceptual thinking in this work, and his sophisticated approach to spatial scale were underpinned by an extensive empirical knowledge of American and world agricultural systems.

I was quickly thrown in at the deep end of university teaching. In my first year I jointly taught the third year New Zealand course with Cumberland, organized an associated ten-day field course, taught a third year regional course on North America, and jointly taught the graduate course in agricultural geography with Grant Anderson. In my second year, I added the economic geography section of the main undergraduate human geography course. In these first two years we were fortunate to have a particularly strong and active group of MA/MSc students, four of whom continued on to PhD programs in Canada and the United States. Their presence made the department a lively place.

Peter Hosking and I led a curriculum reform project that introduced more courses in systematic geography, as they were called then, at third year, and limited the number of regional courses. A compulsory statistical methods course had been introduced earlier in second year and a more advanced third-year course as well. My enthusiasm for these developments was heavily influenced by some of the limitations I perceived in my own undergraduate and graduate training.

With Michael Taylor (now at Birmingham), I was involved more personally in the development of teaching material focusing on the firm and its relationships with regions, industries, and policy in urban and rural contexts. This was the basis for a new course entitled *Regional processes and development* introduced in 1985 and taught by the late Steve Britton and me. Under Steve's influence it became more heavily political-economic in approach with a stronger emphasis on economic development under capitalism, and comparing New Zealand developments with international ones. It reflected also my research interests at that time with the neo-liberalization of the New Zealand economy and the role that the rural sector played in it.

My most rewarding undergraduate teaching assignment, although also sometimes the most frustrating, was the third-year undergraduate course that became *Research Design and Methods in Human Geography*. It included a field course of about a week where students completed their own research projects. A series of methodological and philosophical lectures, seminars and practical examples of the research process preceded and followed the week. Students presented their results to their peers. It was rewarding because some excellent work always emerged, and frustrating because some students always struggled.

Even more enjoyable was the Masters paper, initially called agricultural geography and later land use studies, that I taught for the whole of my time at Auckland. The demanding masters program, with a compulsory thesis remained a strength of the Auckland Department throughout the 1970s, 80s and 90s. The quality of the best students who were attracted to the graduate program at Auckland, and other New Zealand geography departments has always impressed me. I count myself privileged to have supervised the theses of over ninety of them. The best of these students were welcomed into the PhD programs of prestigious geography departments.

In 1974 when the IGU regional Conference was held in Palmerston North, Bruce Rains and I organized a field trip on the settlement, land use, and natural environments of the central North Island. Bruce was working on the river terracing sequences of parts of the North Island, and was studying the tephra layers that play such an important role in the geomorphology, soils and land use of the region. His lucid explanations in the field combined with Graham Campbell's insights into the economic evolution of the Central Plateau were invaluable. Most of the staff in the Auckland Geography Department wrote chapters for the field guide that was later published. For a decade it became the tour guides' bible for the central North Island. This and the lively conference held at Palmerston North with many of the down under diaspora was my introduction to the International Geographical Union (IGU). Jean Dresche, its President at the time, was on the North Island field trip but I met him personally only later in France when he insisted on my talking to Roger Dion.

In 1976, Reg Golledge visiting from Santa Barbara, organized a group of us to respond to a request from the Auckland Regional Authority for comments on their urban growth strategy. We each wrote chapters for the comprehensive document we presented to the executive and politicians. This initiative prompted us to organize a more permanent research cluster of staff and graduate students that was later formalized as the Regional Research Unit in 1985. Over a 15 year period various combinations of staff and graduate students conducted a series of studies for local, regional and central government agencies and private sector firms, and many of these studies were published as technical reports either by the Department of Geography or the agencies themselves

## The importance of research and sabbatical leaves

The Colleges of the old University of New Zealand established a generous leave system that continues today. These leaves are invaluable for without them it would be much more difficult to keep an active research program moving, and to have much contact with international colleagues. For me over a period of thirty or so years they have served to shape and strengthen my research and teaching interests.

From September 1971 to May 1972 while at the Universities of Toronto and Guelph I refined the approach that I was planning for my PhD at Auckland. I was primarily interested in land use competition on the urban periphery, rent theory, and the localization of agricultural production. I knew Toronto and its urban edge well from the field trips my colleague Quentin Stanford and I had run from Bathhurst Heights. The local authority of Peel County, Ontario, had some excellent data on land ownership and sales as well as property tax and its relief. This provided an opportunity to test my ideas on the impact of reductions in property taxes on the land market, land values, and land development on the urban periphery. There was at the time a lively interest among Canadian and international geographers in the urban periphery and the book, *The City's Countryside,* published a few years later reflected that interest (Bryant et al. 1982).

Stimulated by the Canadian experience I finished collecting my Auckland data, spent the necessary nights running the models on the University's 1130 computer, and was awarded the PhD in 1976. Peter Hosking was a constant source of statistical and computing expertise and help. I learned much. Although the quantitative work was invaluable in identifying the evolution of interaction between accessibility and land quality through time, it was the political and institutional processes of manipulating property tax and property rights, and their influence on land use change, conversion, and urban and peripheral-urban form that really intrigued me.

My leave spent in Languedoc and University College, London in 1976-77 was primarily to continue with work on urban peripheral land use change in different contexts. I had long admired Richard Munton's (University College) work on the urban green belt of London and other British rural themes, and the theme was also current in France.

In the Languedoc while at the University of Paul Valéry, Montpellier, we lived in the small village of Montpeyroux, Hérault, where the cave coopérative was the axis of village life. No geographer interested in the vine and wine could avoid absorbing huge amounts, and raising more questions than one could answer. The left-wing daily paper, the *Midi Libre,* was essential reading because the vignerons of the Midi were actively protesting the competition from Italy and Spain as the formation of the European Union was beginning to bite. I remember vividly this unrest spilling over in their disgust at Chablis being allowed a large increase in their appellation whereas much of the south had been refused. The paper headline read – *Si la viticulture marche sur la tête, ou donc les crus mettent-ils les pieds? (If viticulture is in disarray where are the crus trampling?)* I considered myself very lucky to have had a taste of this Midi perspective when I later began my research on the French wine industry in the prestigious appellation of Burgundy.

Although the wine industry was the subject of my MA thesis and continued to inform my thinking, I did not again actively research and publish on it until I became intent on unraveling the appellation system as a system of intellectual property yielding economic rent to those eligible. Leave at the Université de Bourgogne in 1986/87 with Robert Chapuis provided the opportunity for fieldwork, access to primary data and interviews, and a widening of academic contacts in Dijon and other French universities and research groups, notably in the Institut National de la Recherche Agronomique (INRA), Dijon, through my colleague Philippe Perrier-Cornet. On this leave I gathered material in the Regional Office of the Institut National des Appellations d'Origine, Dijon, on the historical origins of the Burgundian Appellation system and its contemporary structure. Although based in the Geography Department at Dijon we lived in wine villages of the Côte, successively Baubigny, Ladois, and Chaux on different leaves. This participant observation and especially the insights provided by the Cornu family of Ladois and Martha Veau of Aussey-Duresses were invaluable.

In North America and internationally, during the late 1970s and 1980s, geographers interested in these themes coalesced around two groups – the specialty group CARLU (Contemporary Agriculture and Rural Land Use) of the AAG and the IGU Commission on Rural Systems. During the 1980s, regular attendance at their meetings stimulated me to relate the New Zealand circumstances to international studies of trade and rural change. The neoliberal reforms of the New Zealand's Fourth Labour Government of 1984, under the superficial mantra of the 'level playing field,' were being held up as one international model for agricultural reform. When the Thatcher government began to apply similar principles to agricultural policy in the United Kingdom, the New Zealand case began to receive increased attention in many countries as well as in the sequence of GATT rounds, and later in the World Trade Organization (WTO). Ironically, the origin of New Zealand's reforms rested directly on the United Kingdom's entry into the European Union, and the transitional arrangements that were made to give New Zealand and other former colonies the opportunity to diversify their markets before all reciprocal trade arrangements disappeared. At the time of writing, twenty-five years later, the remnants of the transitional arrangements are still being debated. In these international negotiations on trade, the Cairns group of agricultural nations organized by Australia and New Zealand became a lead lobbying group.

Many of us responded by both writing papers for the international journals and by contributing to the books edited by colleagues (Britton et al. 1992, Le Heron and Pawson 1996). These two editions were essentially assessments of the impact of the neo-liberal reforms on the geography of New Zealand with emphasis on the privatization or transformation into state owned enterprises of both services (electricity generation and supply, post office, railways, advice to farmers) and production (state forests, state farming operations, and the producer boards).

My renewed interest in the New Zealand and international wine industry had a direct connection. One response to the rhetoric of free or fair trade has been the French and European Union's efforts to protect origin-labeled products, notably wine, but then widened to a range of other products. When in 1991 I was on leave at the Université de Bourgogne in Dijon, I was asked by the Wine Institute of New Zealand to attend the annual meeting of the OIV *(Office International de la Vigne et du Vin)* in Paris. Robert Tinlot was director at the time. I was co-opted to the economic and legal working group dealing with issues of geographical indications and their relationship to European and international wine law and practice, and attended regular meetings for the next four months. These discussions, mainly with French scholars, and access to a wider range of literature gave me a much deeper understanding of the French appellation system, and that led me to challenge some of its environmental assumptions (Moran 1993a & 1993b).

## *The International Geographical Union*

In 1991 when I was asked by the New Zealand Geographical Society if I would be prepared to stand for one of the Vice-President positions I agreed without really knowing what I was getting myself into. I was elected in 1992 at the Washington DC four-yearly Congress of the IGU. It was only later when I knew more about the IGU that I realized how vigorously these positions are contested, especially in Europe. Embassies hold cocktail parties for their candidates and lobbying is vigorous. Being from a small and remote country probably gave me an advantage although it turned out that I did have the support of the Francophone community. IGU is affiliated to the International Council of Scientific Unions (ICSU) the headquarters of which are in Paris. Among European scholars positions on the Executive of any of the scientific unions are highly sought after, both in their own right, and because they offer access to knowledge and research funds for scholars of their country.

Although dominated by Europeans the IGU Executive that I joined had a good smattering of people from New World countries who were prepared to express their distinctive points of view forcibly. In particular, Bertha Becker from Brazil was fearless in her pursuit of encouraging younger people to participate, and to widen the research agendas of the organization beyond the conventional. Eckart Ehlers from Bonn, was Secretary General for the eight years that I was a member. He was both efficient and always prepared to accept new ideas. The two Presidents I served under, Herman Verstappen, a geomorphologist from the Netherlands and Bruno Messerli, a physical geographer from Switzerland had a more conservative and Euro-centric view of the organization. The Europeans gave the impression of treating the IGU as their fiefdom. I recall vividly when one of our meetings was held in Seoul and the Korean Geographical Society presented each of us with a package of materials that introduced their country. Only three of us had seen a map of the world centered on the Pacific. The Europeans viewed it with suppressed amusement, almost disdain.

After finding my feet in the organization, I suggested that we make more of an effort to monitor our own performance just as we did with the research Commissions that reported to us. During my first term the committee asked me to develop a set of criteria for this assessment that were put more firmly in place when Bruno Messerli became President in 1996. Despite the willingness of the Europeans to be open to new ideas the Executive almost inevitably continued to have a European focus partly because the President and Secretary were based in Europe, as are the headquarters of the main international agencies that fund research. Nevertheless, we did manage to make progress in opening the organization to the wider world. Eckart Ehlers in particular, but supported by the two Presidents and the rest of the Committee, including Bertha Becker, managed to support a regional conference in Cuba in 1995. Its primary intention was to bring the Latin American geographers into closer contact with their colleagues elsewhere. This was at least partly successful largely because of the Secretary General's open and inclusive manner, and buoyant, 'almost Latin style' as the locals said.

In my second term, the Executive Committee appointed me First Vice-President. Should the elected President be unable to perform their duties the First Vice-president takes over the Presidency. Although no guarantee of election by the General Assembly, this confidence shown in me by the Committee encouraged me to accept being nominated for the Presidency. The Executive Committee, with the election to be held at Seoul in 2000, endorsed me as the preferred candidate. Unfortunately, the same year I was diagnosed with prostate cancer and at short notice underwent surgery. This left me not knowing what the state of my health would be after the operation. I decided reluctantly that the best decision was to withdraw my nomination. One of the other Vice-Presidents, Ann Buttimer from Ireland, was asked by the committee to stand as President and was duly elected. I was disappointed with not having the opportunity to take the IGU in new directions. As it turned out not being President enabled me to make progress with some of the research that I was keen to finish.

## As Dean of Arts

Three main circumstances influenced me to stand for the position. I had the experience at the departmental, university and wider community level to understand the dimensions of the job. I was satisfied that I would have the support of the Faculty, and was confident about chairing its committees and representing it in the university and wider community. My experience of being head of a department that was a full member of both the Arts and Science Faculties provided an understanding of the range of different university disciplines and cultures that is difficult to achieve in other ways. That the position was full- time was also important. The prospect of having the opportunity to be in on the ground floor of the organization of a new university and faculty structure and able to influence both was appealing. The Arts Faculty at the University of Auckland includes the humanities, the languages and the social sciences, with geography, psychology and mathematics also being members but line-managed by the Science Faculty.

I also found my experience as Senate representative on the University Council and chairing reviews of several departments extremely valuable. In 1981, after being appointed as Professor of Geography, several members of our Senate (Professorial Board) had asked me to stand as one of its representatives on the University Council. I was elected and served a five-year term. As a Council member I was appointed to two of its most important committees, Education and Finance, and I also chaired some committees that at times were highly contentious. One of these was the Student Appeals committee and that was at a time when the Student's Association was very aggressively bringing complaints to the Council. I was fortunate in having a strong committee that included the former Attorney General, Martin Findlay, as a member. With his advice and the support of the committee, we managed to deal with the appeals equably even though many of them were highly contentious.

In my response to the University Council's offer of the position as the first Executive Dean of Arts I negotiated two conditions that related to the Geography Department. First, that although I retained my position as Professor of Geography my chair should be advertised immediately, and second that I be provided with some support and space for research. These were agreed to and the Vice-Chancellor went further by offering me teaching relief for the remainder of 1992. I had recently received a letter from Willie Smith who had finished his term with the Science Council of Canada and was seeking an academic position. He accepted the offer of a temporary position to teach my courses, a position that was later made permanent.

The decision to appoint executive deans at the University of Auckland reflected the political philosophy that had been the foundation of the 1984 Labour Government's policy and continued by the National Government that succeeded it. At that time, all Heads of Departments of the University reported directly to the Vice-Chancellor and all appointments, in particular, were administered centrally although on the recommendation of the Department and through an elected Appointments Committee of the University chaired by the Vice-Chancellor. The devolution of two operations, appointments and finances, to the Deans of Faculties with Heads of Departments reporting to them were the main results of the changes.

My first expenditure was to commission the Tukatuka panels and carvings by Hinemoa and Paki Harrison and link the Faculty to the Waipapa Marae located fifty meters to the south of the Faculty's offices. I was fortunate to have two talented, experienced and respected Professors – Raewyn Dalziel from History and Donal Smith from English accept my offers to be the first Associate Deans.

Initially, we tried to establish with the University Registrar a division between our responsibilities at Faculty level and theirs at the University level. The University failed to respond to this request so I instructed our Faculty Registrar to send anything that was not essential for us to implement back to the appropriate central office. We had many more important responsibilities than acting merely as a conduit. Putting together a strategic plan and budget was one of the first. We put considerable effort into this and it was considered as setting the standard for the other Faculties. In particular, we took the opportunity to establish a stronger budget for equipment than had been the custom. In doing so we improved markedly the information technology of the Faculty. Experience in competing with other science departments proved a huge asset here.

With the University changing rapidly and Deans having more room to move, many challenges came from different parts of the University. Within the first six months of being appointed Dean, I received from the Vice-Chancellor a letter from the Dean of Medicine proposing a new Department of Medical Humanities within the Faculty of Medicine. No discussion with the Faculty of Arts had proceeded this proposal. After a brief discussion with the Associate Deans I wrote a strong dismissal of the idea based on the need for professional training in these disciplines in the same way as it was necessary in medicine. Moreover, research in this area was already vibrant in anthropology, geography, history, sociology and psychology. The Medical School proposal was withdrawn, and our Faculty subsequently established an excellent relationship with Medicine in its research program.

During the five years as Dean I managed to keep my research ticking over. Greg Blunden, who worked with me as a post-doctoral scholar was an excellent colleague. We managed to publish a series of papers challenging some of the research emanating from the United Kingdom on the subsumption of agriculture by capital, locally and internationally. While the New Zealand case is quite different from those of European countries we were able to contribute to this lively debate in the literature as well as at international conferences. Contemporaneously, Nick Lewis was actively reviewing the literature for his PhD thesis on the political economy of New Zealand's educational reforms, and on the role played in these by the Education Review Office of the central government. Nick brought a new set of literature and theory to the discussion. All of this work allowed us to explore the geography of New Zealand's neo-liberal reforms in more depth and from a different perspective.

Before my five-year appointment as Dean ended, I decided that I was not going to seek a second term. Although I was enjoying the job very much I still had research objectives that I wanted to achieve and knew that any new initiatives would be difficult if I still held the Deanship. I gave the Faculty plenty of time to arrange for a replacement by informing the Vice-Chancellor and announcing to the Faculty the year before my term finished that I was not available for a second term. My work in Burgundy had rekindled my interest in the New Zealand wine industry, and I had decided to begin working on it. At the end of my term as Dean I spent most of a sabbatical leave at INRA, Dijon, again working with Philippe Perrier-Cornet who was conducting a large research project on the Burgundy *filière* with emphasis on its regional appellations. This coincided with a series of projects that Serge Wolikov had launched on a reinterpretation of the history of the Burgundian wine industry.

To fund my research I applied for a grant from the recently established Marsden Fund. The title of my project – *Enterprises and environment in the geographical evolution of the New Zealand Wine Industry* captured the essence of my approach. I wanted to take up the themes that Dion (1959) had expressed so effectively, and study the New Zealand industry from an international perspective. The proposal was approved and the grant allowed me to buy myself out of some teaching and to fund Masters and PhD students on aspects of the topic. The main source of data was a series of over 120 interviews as well as archival and fieldwork. My approach in this research relied heavily on the French and international literature on the *filière*, and the way that different enterprises colonize parts of this from grape growing to final demand. Once I had begun the interviewing and the literature review I realized the extent of the task and also the richness of material available. A James Cook Fellowship in Social Science gave me the opportunity to work full time on the project, to involve a larger number of students and to publish my results. A formal relationship established between the Université de Bourgogne and Auckland allowed two students, John Barker and Steve Kelly to complete their PhDs on aspects of the French industry, and three French students in turn worked in New Zealand.

At the time, the University of Auckland and the New Zealand Government were actively supporting the formation of multidisciplinary research institutes and I was encouraged to organize one. The Wine Industry Research Institute was the result and I served as its inaugural Director. It was established in conjunction with an MSc program in wine science. In all of this I was assisted by the support of the Vice-Chancellor and the New Zealand and international wine industries. I was also fortunate to have Nick Lewis as a post-doctoral scholar serving as a continuing source of criticism and good ideas. The publications deriving from this work focused on the elusive concept of *terroir*. Invitations to give keynote addresses at various international conferences enabled me to develop a more sophisticated reading of the interaction between social, economic, political and physical forces in the interpretation of this territorial idea. Without having read the work of Dion and other French scholars my efforts would have been much less convincing.

## Some concluding thoughts

The mix of both the British and North American geographic traditions with a strong indigenous component gave New Zealand academic geography a distinctive flavor. It was reinforced by the continuing flow of New Zealand and Australian academics to these places on sabbatical leave and especially by the successful PhD graduates returning to academic positions in both Australia and New Zealand. This mix was not without its controversies. In the 1970s, when New Zealand born but largely overseas trained geographers began to form a substantial group within departments, initially at Canterbury University, they began to lobby vociferously against the tendency for British geographers being appointed to new positions while New Zealand graduates were ignored. In most disciplines, the colonial origins of the New Zealand universities and the powerful positions held by academics of British origins had a lingering effect on the appointment of academic staff.

A group of Australian and New Zealand geographers have always remained in North America and many of them have had very successful careers. Their presence and continuing support of graduate students and staff from the antipodes have been essential components in maintaining the strength of the North American connection. Certainly in my case, after making my way as a teacher in the Canadian educational system, the regular encounters especially at the AAG annual meetings with the Australian-New Zealand mafia who comprised the *Down-under applied geography society* were memorable occasions. Colleagues of other nationalities were occasionally given temporary honorary status in the society.

And what of Marshall's implicitly environmentally deterministic argument that we New Zealanders should all be geographers 'by instinct'? Without the efforts of Jobberns and Cumberland in the 1930s and 1940s to establish geography in the Colleges of the University of New Zealand, the discipline would not have flourished in the way that it has. They had to convince the Senates and Councils of their institutions that this subject should be included in the offerings of both the Arts and Science Faculties through to graduate level. Their case may have fallen on receptive ears given the regional diversity of the country and the strength of the field disciplines in New Zealand but without their efforts it is highly unlikely that geography would have flourished.

Once geography was established in the universities their staff, often supported by the geographers in the teachers' colleges, put considerable effort into organizing a comprehensive secondary school curriculum and providing the written and graphical material to support it. The emphasis given to New Zealand in the curriculum received warm approval from parents while the case for New Zealand citizens needing to understand the rest of the world was irrefutable, especially after the Second World War. From the late 1940s and early 1950s a high proportion of graduates was absorbed into the teaching profession. Opportunities quickly diversified as the two issues of town and country planning and flood and catchment control were incorporated into legislation. For the next three decades, high enrollments in secondary school geography together with widening job opportunities for university graduates specializing in both physical and human geography saw the discipline flourish in all of New Zealand's universities.

An argument can be made that a convoluted environmental determinism is a partial explanation for the approach taken to their research by some of the first professionally trained British geographers who came to New Zealand. They reacted strongly to the New Zealand environment because they read it differently and emphasized the impact of people on it. For instance, Cumberland's first book, *Soil erosion in New Zealand* (1944), for which he received a D.Sc., was the response of a trained geographer whose intimate experience had been with the manicured British rural landscape. Many New Zealanders of the time saw soil erosion as a 'normal' part of the developing rural economy but Cumberland saw it differently. He had been alerted to the politics of soil conservation through Jobbern's close association with the rural community of Canterbury and his famous 'eye for country'. But it was Cumberland, the trained geographer, who took the lead from some of the early soil conservationists and wrote the book that received international acclaim.

I have no doubt that there is a geography of the discipline geography and of geographers. I believe as Livingstone (1992) argues, that the approach of all disciplines is dependent on the place and time they are practiced. I find it inconceivable that the place we live in and the people we encounter does not influence how we think and behave and how we interpret. The interplay of forces that shape places and people at particular times elicits responses from academia.

## REFERENCES

Anderson, A. G. 1980 (ed) *The land our future: essays on land use and conservation in New Zealand in honour of Kenneth Cumberland* (Auckland: Longman Paul/New Zealand Geographical Society)

Britton, S., Le Heron, R. and Pawson, E. eds. 1992 *Changing Places in New Zealand* (Christchurch:New Zealand Geographical Society)

Bryant, C. R., Russwurm, L. H. and McLellan, A. L. eds. 1982 *The city's countryside: Land and its management in the rural-urban fringe* (London, Ont.: Longman)

Cumberland, K.B. 1944 *Soil erosion in New Zealand: a geographic reconnaissance* (Wellington: Soil Conservation and Rivers Control Council)

Cumberland, K.B. 1946 'The geographer's point of view' *Inaugural lecture* (Auckland: Auckland University College)

Curry, L. 1963 'Regional variation in the seasonal programming of livestock farms in New Zealand' *Economic Geography* 39, 95-118

Dion, R. 1959 *Histoire de la vigne et du vin en France des origines au XIX siècle* (Paris: Les Belles Lettres)

Le Heron, R. and Pawson, E. eds. 1996 *Changing Places: New Zealand in the 1990s* (Auckland: Longman Paul)

Livingstone, D.N. 1992 *The geographical tradition: episodes in the history of a contested enterprise* (Oxford: Blackwell)

Moran, W. 1993a 'The wine appellation as territory in France and California' *Annals of the Association of American Geographers* 83, 694-717

Moran, W. 1993b 'Rural space as intellectual property' *Political Geography* 12, 263-277

Olmstead, C. 1970 'The phenomena, functioning units and systems of agriculture' *Geographia Polonica* 19, 31-41

# 'ON THE EDGE': GEOGRAPHICAL ADVENTURES IN FAR-AWAY-PLACES

## Brian Murton

IN DECEMBER 2003, the 12th International Conference of Historical Geographers met in Auckland, New Zealand. The conference paid special attention to relationships forged 'on the edge', and asked participants to think from the edge rather than the center, reflecting New Zealand's location on the 'leading edge' of the world. I was one of four plenary speakers and I took the opportunity to talk about my recent work on Treaty of Waitangi claims, exploring conflicts over toheroa, the giant surf clam, on a Northland beach from the perspective of cultural politics. This stimulated me to think further about the role of 'edges' rather than 'centers' in my life, not only academically and intellectually, but in terms of where I have mostly lived.

### From the 'Edge' of the World

I was born in 1939 in Gisborne, a town on the eastern edge of New Zealand, with the Pacific Ocean opening up before it and backed by steep hill country. The railway to Gisborne from the south was only completed in 1942, and before and even after that travel over tortuous and steep roads was difficult, making the area one of the most isolated and least accessible in New Zealand . To children growing up there the rest of the world was far away as well, though our family always took a lively interest in what was happening elsewhere. We often spoke about how we seemed to be on the 'other side of the world' from where so much of what seemed to matter to New Zealanders back then was happening. Our family had been in New Zealand for a long time and we had no family connections to Britain, which we never were taught to think of as 'Home'. We would give thanks to where we were, Gisborne and the East Coast, which seemed to be such benign and gentle places. Of course this was wishful thinking because even in the 1950s and 1960s all was not beautiful in and around Gisborne. The rivers flooded and the hill country was eroding away, and there was much poverty and hardship. But for young people, those were golden times, and Gisborne seemed to be immune to the problems that we read about in the newspaper or heard about on the radio.

This sense of being on the edge, of growing up in a place that was isolated but beautiful, a place where the interface between land and sea was so poignant, and where the rest of New Zealand, let alone the world, often seemed far away, contributed strongly I believe to the intense sense of belonging to a place, as well as to a curiosity about other places. It may be going too far to suggest that something intangible, even magical, about the Gisborne area, contributed to my becoming a geographer, but I believe that to be the case.

There was another set of human factors that was important. As I reflect upon the kind of geographer I became, I turn to the influences of family. My mother's family arrived in Gisborne in the 1890s, just after the first freezing-works was opened. Both of her parents' families had been in New Zealand from the 1850s and 1860s, her mother's in Dunedin (they were Scots) and her father's in Hawke's Bay (they were English and Irish). During the late 1940s and early 1950s, I spent much time with my maternal grandfather, time which was very important in generating a connection to place and people. He had grown up on the outskirts of Gisborne and had worked in a range of rural activities, as well as in the freezing-works. Several of his and his wife's siblings married into one of the local iwi (tribes), Te Aitanga-a-Mahaki, and he seemed to know everyone in the country around Gisborne, both Pakeha and Maori. My father's family were relatively late comers to Gisborne, arriving only in 1913, but they were early arrivals in New Zealand, tracing their ancestry back to Kupe. My paternal great-grandmother was of Hokianga Maori ancestry (Te Popoto, Te Honihoni, Te Ihutai dominantly), and my grandmother spoke fluent Maori. Her Irish father, according to his obituary, came off the whale-ship 'John Morrison'. As a young child and through my high school and university years, I spent considerable time at my paternal grandmother's house, and she made sure that I understood where her family was from and who they were.

My grand parents gave me a strong sense of identity without making it an all consuming matter. I knew my place, both geographically and socially, with some degree of certainty. Although aware of our Maori roots and not self-conscious about them, we were brought up as Pakeha, and thought of ourselves that way while acknowledging that we had deeper connections to the land than the mere few generations of our European ancestors in New Zealand.

## Early Years on the 'Edge'

In many ways Gisborne was an ideal place to grow up in during the 1940s and 1950s. My memories of events in World War II are vague, but I remember the end of the war was also a time of celebration. Not only had my father been overseas, but several uncles were also away. After they returned life changed and we youngsters began to follow our father and uncles in their sporting activities. By now I was attending Te Hapara primary school, which I enjoyed, especially the morning and lunch breaks, during which we played the seasonal sport under very light supervision. As we moved through the school we also played rugby and cricket against other schools. During my later primary school years a group of us spent much time roaming through the swamps, lagoons and fields on the southwestern side of Gisborne, and sometimes doing things that would get us arrested if we did them today.

Life and learning continued much as it had done previously through the intermediate school years, but high school brought a number of significant changes. Sport now became much more important and school work even became interesting, especially social studies, history and geography. Some aspects of science, especially biology, were intriguing. Now too, we were old enough to begin to work for money, initially doing tasks like hoeing bean fields and slashing thistles. Eventually, during the Christmas holidays, a number of us began to work at the Wattie cannery, which continued to employ us through our university years, when we were mostly on the field gangs, forking peas around the district.

My experiences growing up on the edge of Gisborne in the late 1940s and 1950s resonate with James Belich's (2001) descriptions of 'wild childhood' and of New Zealand society at that time—conformist, masculist, egalitarian, mono-cultural, and subject to heavy formal and informal regulation. Some of us in places like Gisborne may have been aware that New Zealand was not a mono-cultural society, because many of our school mates, especially on rugby teams, were Maori. Most of the Maori students at high school came by bus from small settlements on the Gisborne plain, many from houses that were fairly rudimentary, and unless a 'townie' was familiar with such places, the poverty of some families, as well as the importance of marae and whanau (family), went unnoticed and unheeded.

## University Years in New Zealand

At high school some of our teachers were excellent, and much of my curiosity about history and geography was fueled by them. Certainly, I was impressed enough to consider high school teaching as a career choice, and was lucky enough to receive a post-primary teachers bursary to attend university.

To go to university from Gisborne involved a journey. Auckland was far distant and most people went to Victoria University College of Wellington, ten hours away by rail-car. But in the immediate years before I began university in 1958, Gisborne students had started going to Canterbury, an overnight trip by inter-island ferry from Wellington. Most notably, as far as I was concerned, was Roger McLean, who reported that the Geography Department at Canterbury was excellent, and that Christchurch was a great place, although cold in the winter. Further, my history teacher during my last year at high school was a recent Canterbury graduate and he spoke very highly of the history department. Given my plan to major in both history and geography, these influences combined to direct me to Christchurch. There, many of us from the North Island resided in Rolleston House, adjacent to the university and very convenient for our attendance at nine o'clock lectures, often with a track-suit pulled over our pyjamas. I did three years of history, learning much about Europe, a little about European colonial expansion including imperialism in Africa, which interested me greatly, but distressingly nothing about New Zealand.

In the 1940s and 1950s geography in New Zealand universities emphasized a historical approach to landscape change. This was very evident at Canterbury where George Jobberns applied Davis' principles of geomorphology to the New Zealand landscape, accompanied by delightful anecdotes, which often located a feature in relationship to the local pub. I had done geology in my first year as well, and felt that studying the dynamic natural landscape of New Zealand was fascinating. But the Stage 2 course on Europe, taught by Leigh Pownall, converted me into a human geographer. In the Stage 3 year, I chose the Asia regional option, taught by Barry Johnson. When the time came toward the end of my third year to select a thesis topic, it seemed natural to chose a historical, geographical one set in Gisborne. It was titled 'Settlement in Poverty Bay, 1868-1889', and focused on the changing pattern of land ownership as a way of understanding the pace and progress of European settlement. At the time, although I did get a couple of publications out of it, I thought that was that. The thesis was available in the University of Canterbury library and a copy was given to the Gisborne (now Tairawhiti) Museum library, but my sense was 'who would want to look at such a document?' It turned out later that I was quite mistaken.

Three of the four seminars I took during my MA year were all on aspects of human geography (urban, economic, historical), and one was on the Pacific. We were fortunate with our teachers in the master's program in 1961. Les King had returned from completing his PhD at the University of Iowa, Reg Golledge had arrived from the University of New England, John Rayner was teaching climatology, and Jane Soons had come in 1960 to teach geomorphology. The MA seminars in 1961 were lively, especially once we learned to read articles critically for ideas, rather than descriptive content. There had always been a procession of visiting lecturers at Canterbury, and while I was there a number of them came from North American universities. This added a dimension to our education and also opened our eyes to the possibilities of doing doctoral work in North America.

In 1961 I applied to a number of departments in the United States specializing either in historical geography and/or Southeast Asia. Minnesota was the first to respond in early 1962 with an offer of admission to the doctoral program and a teaching assistantship. After some discussion, including with Harold McCarty of Iowa, who was a visiting lecturer at Canterbury in 1962, I accepted the offer to begin study in September 1962, intending to work under Jan Broek. My interest in Asia had been strengthened during my Stage 3 year through reading a paper by Broek on unity and diversity in Southeast Asia.

Since leaving Christchurch in 1962 I have returned but five times. The first was a brief visit in 1966 when I went to India via New Zealand (a round-the-world ticket on Pan American was a cheap way to see the world in those days). The next was when I was a visitor at the university in 1976, a very enjoyable year that I look back on fondly. In 1995 I attended the New Zealand Geographical Society conference held at the university, and in 2005 I visited one of my former students, Jay Johnson, who was on the faculty there briefly before returning to United States and taking a position at the University of Nebraska at Lincoln. On the latter visit, Garth Cant asked me to give a talk on my Waitangi Tribunal work, and it was interesting to meet a large number of Maori students and staff, in addition to the geographers.

## Go Golden Gophers: A Sojourn in the 'Center'

As did most students from New Zealand who went overseas in those days, I went by sea, via Tahiti and the Panama Canal to Fort Lauderdale and then to New York, from where I caught a Greyhound bus to Minneapolis. The three week journey was very pleasant and enlightening as many friends from Canterbury were on board, also leaving New Zealand for further study, and there were several from other New Zealand and Australian universities as well. A number of us decided to spend a few days in New York, staying at the YMCA, which proved to be quite an experience.

I was fortunate enough to have found housing in one of the University's halls of residence, and settling in to life in Minneapolis was not too stressful. I was helped greatly by the faculty and graduate students in the department. The three senior faculty (Cotton Mather, the Chair, Jan Broek, and John Borchert) were friendly, but demanding as we soon found out. The junior faculty (John Webb, Phil Porter, Ward Barrett, Ron Helin, Fred Lukermann, and Mei-ling Hsu) were more visible in the hall-ways. A variety of activities (field trips, barbeques) introduced new students to Minnesota, and meetings in the department made us aware of what was expected of us, including attendance at the weekly Friday coffee hour. The latter had become an institution, and over the course of my stay at Minnesota I had the privilege of hearing presentations by many of the notables in geography.

Regardless of students' geographical interests, the Department had a very eclectic approach to graduate education. We were expected to work with a number of faculty, and this led to people with quite disparate interests spending time together in class. It certainly expanded our horizons, especially during the 1960s when geography was undergoing some major transformations. During my time there many students and faculty brought lunches from home, and on most days met in the coffee room to eat and talk, often about the latest developments in geography. For the doctoral comprehensive examinations students were examined on the 'field of geography', usually more narrowly defined through discussions with the faculty selected to be committee members. There was some emphasis in most seminars on the history and philosophy of geography as applicable to the topic at hand.

The historical-cultural approach at Minnesota at the time was different from the more atemporal chorographical approach that had characterized much mid-Western geography in the 1940s and 1950s. Broek had been heavily influenced by Carl Sauer, both when Broek was carrying out his research into landscape change in the Santa Clara valley, and later when he joined the Berkeley faculty. He had returned to the Netherlands after World War II, but had come back to the United States in 1948. Broek disagreed substantially with many of Richard Hartshorne's interpretations of German texts, and was very forthright about this, especially in his seminars where he would expect us to do detailed 'deconstructions' of Hartshorne's writings. To a degree, if you were Broek's student you received a blend of Sauer's approach to the cultural landscape, Ratzell's approach to anthropogeography (notably the more cultural approach found in volume two of Anthropogeographie), Eduard Hahn's cultural approach to the evolution of world economies, Hans Bobek's ways of classifying world economies, and Otto Schluter's approach to landscape, all interpreted through Broek's personal lens.

Exactly how different the education we were receiving under Broek was from that at most other mid-Western departments was highlighted at the first West Lakes division of the Association of America Geographers meeting that I attended in Milwaukee in the Fall of 1962. One of the events on the program was a presentation by the faculty from the University of Iowa on their program and what surprised me were the heated responses to it by some of the more senior geographers present. To young and impressionable graduate students those were heady times, and differences in approaches always good for much discussion over a few beers at West Lakes and national geography meetings.

All doctoral students at Minnesota had to select a minor field for the purposes of developing further expertise and I was advised to look into Asian history. This was the beginning of another adventure. Minor field departments set the rules, including the number of credits required and how and when written exams could be taken. I began with an undergraduate, upper division course on Indian history, and followed it up with two others, plus two full year seminars, and fell under the spell of Burton Stein, the historian then teaching Indian history. Stein was a charismatic, revisionist historian, educated at the University of Chicago where he had pursued cultural history and anthropology under several leading historians and anthropologists. He opened my eyes to the possibilities of doing historical geographical research in India. During the course of seminars with him I encountered the published versions of a set of British records from the late eighteenth century, which I used as the basis for two seminar papers on the agricultural system of a part of southern India in the late eighteenth century.

These records were part of the superb collection of Indian material given to the University by Charles Lesley Ames, and housed in the library bearing his name. The University had also become a depository for Indian books sent to the Library of Congress under the terms of Public Law 480, through which the United States was providing food- aid to a number of countries that paid for it in their own currency. During the early 1960s, Stein and Broek, in conjunction with Ames, were developing a proposal to produce a historical atlas of South Asia. To this end, Ames established a fellowship for a graduate student to do some preliminary work. I was encouraged to apply, and was fortunate enough to be successful. During 1964-1965 and 1965-1966, I worked with a more senior geographer to set some directions for the project. At the same time I began studying Hindi, the only Indian language then offered at the University.

These circumstances resulted in another change in direction. I decided that I would use the work I had been doing in the history seminars as the basis for developing an application for funding to work in India. In the Fall of 1965 I prepared a proposal and submitted it to the American Institute of Indian Studies, and was fortunate enough to receive funding to undertake an investigation of how the agricultural system in one area of southern India changed in the nineteenth century. This research took me to India from September 1966 to early December 1967. I returned to Minnesota early the following year to begin writing my dissertation, teaching a course on 'Australia, New Zealand and the Pacific', and working on the Historical Atlas of South Asia, which by now had received major funding.

During my nearly two years absence the Minnesota department changed substantially. When I had first arrived in Minnesota in 1962, there were nine full time faculty; by the winter of 1968 this staff had increased by one-third and the numbers of graduate students had risen markedly, both in the MA and PhD programs. We had been a small (perhaps 20-25) but reasonably diverse group between 1962 and 1966. When I returned in 1968 a number of these were still around, completing their dissertations and theses, and many more had arrived. Many of those who worked for John Borchert on his various projects became planners in various agencies in Minnesota and elsewhere. Another of my peer group rose to a high position in the Canadian Government, after a brief academic career. Most of the others became university faculty, many in major research universities, and a number chaired departments, became deans, vice-presidents, and chancellors. Several held high office in the Association of American Geographers (including President) and many have been active in the International Geographical Union.

## Indian Experiences, 1966-1984

When my wife and I went to India in September 1966, we had no idea of what we might experience. India and Pakistan had just fought a war, the situation in the Middle East had become very tense, there was a border conflict occurring between India and China, and within India there was rioting, especially in the south, over the implementation of Hindi as the national language, in place of Hindi and English. We flew into New Delhi and after a few days there visiting various sights, we flew to Bombay (now Mumbai). After several days in that city, again seeing the sights and meeting people, we took the train to Poona, where the American Institute of Indian Studies had their headquarters. There were a number of administrative details to take care of, but we also saw much of Poona by bicycle, an often dangerous but useful way to get around in smaller Indian cities. We then traveled back to Bombay by train and flew to Madras (now Chennai) which was to be our base.

Settling in to life in Madras in 1966 took some time. We were fortunate with housing, renting a large and airy second storey of a house from a Tamil family who lived below. Over time we became good friends, and on subsequent visits to India (1975, 1979, 1982) we stayed in the same house. During our times in India we had our share of adventures, and were fortunate to keep healthy most of the time. Away from home we basically ate Tamil vegetarian food and were always extremely careful about the water. Travel in southern India was done by bus and train, and in district towns and cities and even in the countryside, by bicycle. Some of this was done in conjunction with research, but living in southern India also involved visits to temple complexes and hill fortresses, to the great beaches south of Madras and to the tea districts in the hills; we did basket boating (in coracles) on the Kaveri river and I played rugby for the Madras Gymkhana Club (I vividly remember the staff scouring the field to chase away cobras especially during the monsoon season). In 1966 and 1975 the effort required to get a permit to purchase and consume beer and spirits was another aspect of learning to live in a very different place. By 1982 the State of Tamilnadu had abolished prohibition and cold beer was readily available, even in quite remote places.

Over the time I spent in South Asia (in total about two-and-a-half years) I visited most parts of southern India, including some very remote places, saw some remarkable things and had some incredible experiences. I also traveled in northern India, visiting Delhi and the surrounding area a number of times, spent about a week in the area around Meerut, saw quite a bit of the landscape around Varanasi and Calcutta, and visited Bombay and Poona (now Pune) in western India several times. I also spent a couple of weeks in Nepal, visiting former University of Hawaii students in late 1975. During the mid-1980s I also was on a joint East-West Center-University of Hawaii team that visited Pakistan and Bangladesh, spending about ten days in each country. These experiences were part of becoming an 'area' specialist, and there was an expectation from the American Institute of Indian Studies that we would be able to relate our in-depth understanding of India to our students, and convey a positive sense of India to a wide range of people.

In 1966 it took a while to get my research started. Permission had to be obtained to work in the archives. This meandered through the bureaucracy, but eventually it was granted, and I could begin work. At that time the space allocated to scholars reading materials in the Madras Records Office was basic, and for most of the time I was there I was the only person doing research. Procedures had to be followed, but it was quite relaxed and requested material arrived promptly. In contrast, by 1975 the number of scholars, mostly Indian, using the archives (now named the Tamilnadu Archives) had increased exponentially and there was a new reading room, well lighted and with well located ceiling fans (very nice when temperatures rose into the 90s, and even into the low 100s in April-May).

During our first stay in Madras, after settling in and getting my archival work under way, I made a number of lengthy visits to Salem, the area where my research was set. I often stayed with an anthropologist, Geoff Burkhart, who was doing his doctoral research in a village in Salem District, and we traveled around the district by bicycle and bus. To do any research in a district it was necessary to receive official permission from the District Collector, which I did, and obtained permission to work in their library and archives. It helped in these expeditions that we were studying Tamil five to six days a week under the guidance of a tutor, and by the middle of 1967 I knew enough to get along at a basic level. On visits to Salem in 1975 and 1982 I also arranged to meet with the Collector in order to let officialdom know what I was doing.

Over time I developed a wide network of Indian colleagues and friends, and visited a number of their universities, especially throughout southern India. By 1975-1976 Professor A. Ramesh was head of the Geography Department at Madras University and he and his young and energetic staff were managing a number of funded research projects involving PhD students. Logical positivism and the 'quantitative revolution' had come to Indian geography and most student research involved applying some model or method to the voluminous statistics collected by the Census of India and other government agencies. Some of the more creative dissertations, as well as research by faculty, were based on field data, but there was a tendency to slavishly use techniques without any discussion of their applicability to specific sites. As part of my affiliation (required of Senior Fellows of the American Institute of Indian Studies) with the Madras Department, I gave a number of seminars, mostly on research design, and I tried to suggest that more critical approaches were required. I was also asked to give talks (illustrated with slides) at a number of the Arts Colleges (undergraduate institutions) throughout Tamilnadu State. Through these talks I met a number of people, was well hosted in many of the smaller cities of Tamilnadu, and was very fortunate to be given local perspectives on many of the sites and sights. In 1982, when my family was with me, on visits to places like Salem and Madurai, we were welcomed by the local geographers and their families, as well as a number of other people, and through such contacts I was able to visit many places central to my project and meet many people who became informants, including a number of aging British who had 'stayed-on' in India after Independence in 1947.

## Doctoral Research in India, 1966-1970

When I went to London in April 1966 to begin my research, I discovered the map collection of the India Office Library, including a series of incredibly detailed one inch to one mile maps, the result of a survey carried out in the area I had chosen to focus on, a swathe of territory known as 'Salem and the Baramahal' in the late eighteenth century, and then Salem District until it was divided in two during the 1960s. After beginning my archival research in Madras, I uncovered the original survey and settlement (for land taxation purposes) materials for Salem and the Baramahal, carried out during the 1790s. This material included maps locating every settlement, as well as sets of records detailing numerically the acreages of land under different kinds of cultivation, population, caste, who controlled the land, livestock, looms, and so on, for every village in the area, plus some at the scale of individual fields. There was also the correspondence between the British officers who carried out the survey, and between them and the Board of Revenue in Madras city, as well as all the orders that flowed the other way from headquarters.

To say that I was overwhelmed is an understatement. Fortunately, in early 1967 Burton Stein my mentor historian at Minnesota, arrived in Madras for a lengthy stay. After much discussion he advised me to concentrate on the late eighteenth and very early nineteenth century material. Some of the records actually gave insights into the area in the late seventeenth and early eighteenth centuries that were helpful in understanding the later farming system and I decided to collect as much such information as I could. This took me into inscriptional materials, collected and published, some in translation, by the Epigraphical Survey of India, and into other old records in southern Indian languages, originally written on palm leaves. A huge collection of these had been made by the first Surveyor-General Of India, Collin Mackenzie, most of which were in the Governmental Oriental Manuscripts Library in Madras.

This latter material became part of a longer term project and my immediate doctoral research focused primarily on the agrarian system, or as I called it then 'a peasant production system' in the late eighteenth century. Completed in 1970, it was a study of how in a harsh, frontier environment, society had adapted and developed a range of strategies to combat both environmental and human hazards. Conceptually, it drew on the natural hazards research of Gilbert White's group, on the research into agrarian systems being carried out in India, primarily by historians, on the emerging field of cultural ecology, on ideas on risk and uncertainty in agriculture from agricultural economics, and more heavily on the ideas about frequency of cultivation and agricultural intensification of Boserup (1965). Because I used agricultural proverbs to give insight into the knowledge system about agriculture, my study tied in with the interest in indigenous knowledge systems that had begun to emerge in the 1960s, and more broadly with the concerns about people's attitudes and perceptions of the environment. It was, in sum, a rather eclectic dissertation, substantially different from what I had proposed doing.

## Later Indian Research, 1970-1990s

Between 1970 and the early 1990s I continued to devote much of my research to agrarian change in nineteenth century southern India. A 1975-1976 project funded by the American Institute of Indian Studies, involved a testing of some of Boserup's ideas on agricultural intensification in three areas of Tamilnadu. Another project a few years later focused on the development of commercial agriculture, through a case study of a rather idiosyncratic English family, resident in southern India from the 1790s until after Independence in 1947.

I also continued to collect inscriptions and other material dealing with the period before 1800, and finally put much of this together during the late 1980s to address issues about how southern Indian agrarian systems had changed over the thousand years before 1800. In this work I integrated ideas derived from Emmanuel Wallerstein (world systems theory), with ones drawn from the arguments about the nature of capitalism, and examined whether such a system had existed in South Asia before the emergence of the European world system. Many of the papers emerging from this research were presented at the South Asian conference held annually at the University of Wisconsin-Madison each Fall from 1972. These activities, along with meetings of the Association of Asian Studies in the United States and conferences held by IGU commissions and study groups, provided numerous opportunities to meet colleagues from a number of disciplines and from different parts of the world. However, they did take me beyond the boundaries of geography as it was developing in the United States, and at times I seem to have been considered to belong rather to a very small group of historians (perhaps as few as fifteen worldwide) doing research on medieval and early modern southern India.

It was impossible to be working on India and be unaware of the way that famine not only periodically devastated the countryside, but had become ingrained in the psyche of scholars interpreting India's past. In the late 1970s, along with one of our former students, I became part of a famine research project in the Environment and Policy Institute of the East-West Center in Honolulu. This led to my involvement in an International Geographical Union study group, 'Famine Research and Food Production Systems'. The group held a number of well attended meetings including ones which I organized in Honolulu held in conjunction with the Pacific Science Congress in 1990, and at Tufts University in Boston, prior to the International Geographical Union Congress in Washington D.C. in 1992. Much of the work of the group emphasized the idea of a 'space of vulnerability', conceived of as the outcome of the operation of the political economy, of the ways in which entitlements are lost or gained, and of the ways in which levels of empowerment are increased or diminished. These were seen as intertwined sets of relationships, all necessary to the understanding of how deprivation and impoverishment, and increased vulnerability to famine can happen. This approach further identified three analytical concepts, economic capability, property regimes, and the operation of political power as crucial to an analysis of vulnerability. Some of these ideas I found particularly useful when my research changed directions after 1995.

## *At The University of Hawaii, An Edge and a Center, 1969-1992*

During the first part of 1968 I had job interviews at several departments as I had decided to stay in North America. My first position was at York University in Toronto, Canada, where I taught rural geography and worked on my dissertation. The department was an interesting and vibrant one and I was prepared to stay there for an extended period, the more so as my wife and I found Toronto a very pleasant place to live. However, in early 1969, Roland Fuchs, the chair of the department at the University of Hawaii visited, and a little later he offered me a position to teach cultural ecology and tropical geography. I had to think long and hard about making another move, but ultimately decided to do so, influenced in part by the fact that Burton Stein, my history mentor, had taken a position at Hawaii. After teaching South Asian geography at the University of Washington during the summer of 1969, we moved to Honolulu at the end of August, joining three other New Zealanders on a faculty of fifteen, which increased to twenty in the early 1970s through the judicious use of joint appointments.

After statehood in 1959 the University of Hawaii had undergone rapid expansion. Doctoral programs which had been restricted earlier now blossomed including that in geography which was approved in 1967. The Federal Government had established the East-West Center, an institution to facilitate cultural and technical interchange between countries in Asia and the Pacific and the United States and several geography faculty members held joint appointments with the Center, and over time many other notable geographers spent time in it on short and long term appointments. The importance of the Center to the Geography department was reflected in the way we organized our graduate program specialties during the 1970s and 1980s to align with the Center's research institutes (environment, population, and resource management). Especially important was the funding for graduate students, and at times during the late 1970s and early 1980s, as many as twenty-five of them in any given year held East-West Center fellowships. Furthermore, many East West Center appointees held adjunct and affiliate appointments in the department, serving on graduate committees, and teaching seminars. It is little wonder that the department's graduate research and teaching focused on issues and topics set in the Asia-Pacific region, and while disciplinary theories and methodologies were not neglected, graduate student programs were quite eclectic and idiosyncratic. In addition to connections with the East-West Center, many of our faculty were affiliated with area studies programs in the Center for Asian Studies, as was I for a number of years, often helping to teach the South Asia graduate seminar.

At the undergraduate level in the department I taught a range of courses, including introductory level courses, a course in cultural geography which I initiated and which evolved over time until I retired in 2005, a course on the geography of the tropics (later tropical agrarian systems), and for many years I contributed to a team taught course on the geography of agriculture and food systems. Every couple of years during the 1970s and 1980s I also taught a regional course on South Asia. When I began teaching cultural geography, I focused on cultural ecology, with a strong emphasis on historical changes in both land cover and land use. Over time I became more oriented toward landscape studies, especially from a humanistic perspective, notably emphasizing a 'biography of landscape' approach and later one that emphasized the landscape as 'text', and as the outcome of 'performance'.

At the graduate level my primary responsibilities were teaching a seminar in some aspect of cultural geography, and occasionally one in resource management. Between 1969 and 1971 the cultural geography seminar was a joint one with anthropology, as it was a key component in the interdisciplinary program in human ecology involving geography, anthropology, and the School of Public Health. This program was funded by a National Science Foundation Grant, a part of NSF's Special Projects in Graduate Education and it involved a summer field program for graduate students set on one of the neighboring islands. Over the years, the themes and issues discussed in my seminars in cultural geography changed considerably, especially with the emergence of 'new cultural geography' during the 1980s. Eventually cultural ecology became political ecology, and development studies issues were integrated into the seminar.

But by the mid 1990s the seminar had come to focus on aspects of the intersection of cultural geography and imperialism and colonialism, an outcome of my own historical work in South Asia, and the new research I was beginning to undertake in New Zealand to support claims to the Waitangi Tribunal. The seminars were populated by a numerous and diverse group of people including many non-geographers. Feedback from students in the seminars, especially those of indigenous ancestry, directed attention to indigenous perspectives, and to how geography, and especially cultural geography, might (or might not) resonate or reverberate with indigenous understandings of the world. Many of the students were grappling with the 'colonial' natures of their disciplines, and with how they might overcome some of the biases that they saw in western research. Many were wanting to use theory deriving from their own traditions, but realized that to satisfy disciplinary demands at the doctoral level they had to engage with western theory. Questions were raised, such as how can geography as a 'colonial' discipline move toward geographies that acknowledge, perhaps even embrace, alternate assemblages of power? How can the seeming 'historical amnesia' of the discipline be tackled? Is it possible to de-center a discipline, or do attempts to do this simply refine a discipline's pre-existing way of knowing? Does geography have a place for a 'native voice' in its theoretical formulations? A number of issues also emerged about authority in relation to research subjects, as well as who should define research questions when working in indigenous communities. This led into examinations of research approaches variously called collaborative research, participatory action research, and action research, as well as into the literature on de-colonizing methodologies.

Ultimately these seminars focused on the question of knowledge in cultural geography, almost as slippery an endeavor as trying to define an 'indigenous person', as the concept of knowledge moves back and forth between ontology and epistemology. As cultural geographers we were particularly interested in ontological binaries such as nature and culture, individual and society, and the space and place, features absent within indigenous knowledge systems which are holistic in nature. This led us into the recent literature dealing with space and place and nature and culture, and with indigenous knowledge. Many students became critical of the recent attempts among anglophone geographers to heal some of these divides, notably nature-culture, through approaches such as hybrid geographies or actor network theory, and of social constructionist approaches generally, especially those concerning place.

As the advisor of many graduate students, I have tried always to get them to be critical of accepted approaches and methods, to be thoroughly versed in the subfield of the discipline in which they are specializing as well as in the appropriate cognate fields, and to draw them along, showing them different possible paths to the joy of discovering knowledge. I seem to have had some success in this as all of my former graduate students (thirty at the doctoral level and nearly fifty at the master's level) have found professional employment, many are actively involved in a wide range of disciplinary and professional activities, and several have published extensively. I am especially proud of the fact that of the nearly thirty students who have completed, or will shortly complete, dissertations and theses under my supervision, since 1998 , about half have dealt with indigenous issues of one type or another, and four of the students involved are on the board of the Association of American Geographers' 'Indigenous Peoples' Specialty Group. A former student, Jay Johnson, is the chair of the newly formed International Geographical Union Commission on 'Indigenous Knowledge and Issues', another sits on that body as the Indonesian member, and another, a Hawaiian, is serving as the secretary of the commission. Interestingly, given my academic orientation, about half of my former doctoral students have found employment outside of universities, notably with the Food and Agricultural Organization of the United Nations, the World Bank, the United States Agency for International Development, Oxfam, Rural Development Associates, as well as research positions in government agencies in Australia and New Zealand. When I reflect upon my career at the University of Hawaii, graduate advising and mentoring has been where I have made a major contribution.

The late 1980s, when I was chair of the department were particularly busy times. Roland Fuchs, who everyone thought of as 'chair for life', moved to the United Nations University in Tokyo. He had done much to bring the department into the national and international spotlight, and the faculty who he had appointed in the 1960s and early 1970s were extremely active in research and publication. Roland's departure, plus the retirement of most of the faculty hired before 1969, resulted in much of my time as chair being spent in hiring new faculty, and between 1986 and 1992 seven such persons joined the department. In most cases these people had done their own research either in Asia, or in other tropical areas, but to the regret of some the strong area studies tradition in the department began to wither.

While the department at Hawaii during the 1970s and 1980s considered itself very much a part of the discipline in the United States, because of its location and the composition of its faculty it frequently looked beyond what local residents call the 'mainland' or the 'continent'. Through the mid 1980s American born and foreign born faculty were equally represented but some of the latter showed little interest in the professional geography organizations in the United States. Additionally, over the years up to 1990 at least half of the visitors to the department were from departments in the Asia-Pacific realm. The department usually had at least one visitor a year from a major department on the 'mainland', a conscious effort to maintain linkages, and during the 1980s we were able to develop theme seminars for which we brought in a number of experts, each for a week at a time. Through this period too, Hawaii was an airline hub in the Pacific and this brought many geographers from Pacific rim countries through Honolulu, where they frequently broke their travel and often gave talks. The Asia-Pacific focus of most of the faculty tended to set us apart, with few other departments claiming this as a major focus. Another factor of difference, was that the Hawaii department never developed a strong program in spatial analysis, though a number of its members did use highly sophisticated models and techniques. More of our faculty professed to interests in human-environment relationships but again, as most of these were focused on non-Western settings, we seemed to be outside of the mainstream of North American or even European human-environmental concerns.

## *A Return to an Earlier 'Edge'*

In the spring of 1995 I took a six month sabbatical leave, intending to complete several papers on southern India (which I did do), and take a trip to New Zealand to explore two research ideas that had been in my mind for some time. One involved constructing a biography of the changing landscapes of New Zealand, using the experience of our family. To do this I needed to learn more about the family, especially my father's, when various members of it had arrived in New Zealand, where they had lived, and what they had done. The second, and not unrelated idea, was to revisit and extend the historical geographical research that I had carried out for my MA thesis.

I began in northern New Zealand, following up on some leads left by my grandmother relating to her family. I was successful in this and was welcomed as family (whanau), taken to the Oturei marae and cemetery near Dargaville where many ancestors are buried, and began to learn about them. In July 1995 I spent a longer period in the north and visited Puketawa marae at Utakura on the Hokianga Harbour, where our family is tangata whenua.. After this last northern excursion I went to Gisborne where I had been asked to meet with a team carrying out Waitangi claims research for Te Aitanga-a-Mahaki. They had begun their research early in 1995, and had found my MA thesis very useful. After I met with them I volunteered to help in any way they wished. Later that year, I was again in Gisborne and I met there with the Te Aiatanga-a-Mahaki Claims Committee. When they 'placed' me and realized my connections to Gisborne and to some of their own families, they decided that they could find a project for me to work on, eventually settling on a socio-economic impact report. I had no idea what this might entail, as there had not been many of these done at the time and the one that I examined was very sketchy. Nonetheless, I said I would do a report as a volunteer researcher and would spend the northern hemisphere summer of 1996 in Gisborne working on it. Little did I know that Waitangi claims research would almost consume all my time and energy until 2005, and that the experience would lead to involvement in a project funded by the Marsden Fund of the Royal Society of New Zealand.

Since 1996, with the exception of completing some work in progress on southern India and writing several more general pieces on famine and food systems, my research has dealt with issues of deprivation and resource access and control to support claims of six Maori groups to the Waitangi Tribunal. From 1996 to 2005 I spent three to four months each year in New Zealand and when in Honolulu, devoted all my time outside of my university work to preparing lengthy reports. Initially, I worked in Gisborne on two socio-economic reports for Te Aitanga-a-Mahaki and Ngai Tamanuhiri (another of the Gisborne, or Turanganui-a-Kiwa, tribes) to support their claims. Te Aitanga-a-Mahaki had established a research unit in Gisborne and work space was available in it. I came to know many members of this iwi very well, especially the group of elders (kaumatua) who were working on its traditional history. To say that they taught me a tremendous amount is an understatement, and I received much help in the work I was doing on economic and social deprivation. I was also recounted a vast amount of Te Aitanga-a-Mahaki history, which helped me understand much of what I was seeing in the archival sources.

In 1998 I also began work for the funding agency, the Crown Forestry Rental Trust, on a report that addressed how Crown legislation, policy, and actions had impacted Maori resources and landscapes around the Kaipara Harbour. The study was based upon archival sources obtained for me by a research assistant working for the Trust, upon my own research in Auckland, and on information from the three major claimant groups involved. As the Dargaville branch of our family at Oturei marae is intermarried with two of these groups, this research brought me into constant contact with many family members. Again this proved to be an immensely valuable experience, far beyond the fact that I was now being paid to do the research. My last report, a lengthy socio-economic one for Te Urewera, was based primarily upon materials from the National Archives in Wellington and Auckland and from various other libraries and archives obtained for me by several archival research specialists. The materials were couriered to Honolulu, where I wrote the bulk of the report, only venturing to places in Te Urewera for meetings with claimant groups.

Central to the work I did was the identification of any actions and omissions of the Crown (Crown culpability) which impacted Maori. It was a type of advocacy research, but the research product had to have the rigor to withstand the scrutiny of Crown historians and lawyers, and meet all the standards of academic scholarship while being empathetic and culturally sensitive and related to key Maori values. My reports generally have been received and reviewed favorably by members of the Waitangi Tribunal, by the Chief Judge of the Maori Land Court, by counsel for claimant groups, and the claimants themselves. The Crown has taken a more circumscribed view. Richard Boast, Associate Professor of Law at Victoria University appraised my Kaipara report as 'a very impressive, important, and methodologically sophisticated statement', noting that he had also read my earlier one for Te Aitanga-a-Mahaki and 'was equally impressed by that'.

Although such reports can be prepared without resort to theory, as I was already familiar with some of the literature dealing with the processes of impoverishment, I decided to use these as a framework, and found that three operational concepts— economic capability, property regimes and power relations—to be especially valuable in the New Zealand context. Economic capability (the extent to which an individual or a group has the freedom to achieve economically) has been identified by Sen (1981, 1999) as crucial to understanding the processes involved in impoverishment and deprivation because it shifts the analytical focus from measures of economic achievement towards the question of whether people are able to access the means to function economically. To address this question involves deciphering the 'entangled web' of Crown policy, legislation and practice that had the potential to impact prejudicially Maori economic capability, and detailing how this played out in specific situations. Property rights issues had important bearing upon Maori economic capability, as did politics and power relations.

As a claim progresses from the research to the judicial stage, the role of the academic changes from that of researcher to that of expert witness. Much of my time was involved with the preparation of materials to assist claimant counsel at Tribunal hearings, and in preparing written answers to questions from the Crown and counsel for other claimant groups. The actual presentation of evidence before the Tribunal (under judicial rules) also involves written submissions, and cross-examination by Crown Counsel, as well as other claimant group counsel. In December 2001, for example, my testimony and cross-examination at the Te Aitanga-a-Mahaki hearings took the best part of a day, although in January 2005 at Ruatoki, it only took about four hours. These experiences were rich and rewarding, and intersected very nicely with the literature and concepts being pursued by many of my students.

I also continued to visit family in the north. When visiting the Hokianga I stayed in Kohukohu with a cousin who is a genealogist and cultural expert, and who serves as the research administrator for Ngati Hine, whose territory is in the southern part of the Bay of Islands. In 2002 a number of Ngati Hine elders and leaders decided to become involved with a project that dealt with landscape change and human interaction in the Bay of Islands, 1769-1840, that had been initiated by Geoff Park, an ecologist and environmental historian in 2001. After several iterations, during which it became both bicultural and multidisciplinary, it was funded by the Marsden Fund for three years, 2004-2006. The project is premised upon the idea that while European voices have spoken frequently and loudly about events leading up to the signing of the Treaty of Waitangi, a Maori perspective on the landscape in which the Treaty was signed has been virtually ignored. My role is an ambiguous one, as I am both an academic and part of the Ngati Hine team. One of the difficulties we have encountered is the very different understandings of a number of concepts, which has involved digging deeply into epistemological and ontological matters, especially from a Maori perspective. The research is completed and various parts of it are being written up, not without difficulty. It is a venture onto another 'edge', and it will probably occupy the rest of my working life.

**REFERENCES**

Belich, J. 2001. Paradise Re-forged. A History of the New Zealanders From the 1880s to the Year 2000. ( Auckland: Allen Lane, The Penguin Press)

Boserup, E. 1965. The Conditions of Agricultural Growth: The Economics of Agrarian Change Under Population Pressure. ( Chicago: Aldine)

Sen, A.K. 1981. Poverty and Famines: An Essay on Entitlements and Deprivation. (Oxford: Claredon Press )

Sen, A. K. 1999. Development as Freedom. ( Oxford: Oxford University Press)

# REFLECTIONS ON A PERIPATETIC CAREER

## Robert H. T. Smith

I SPENT MY childhood in rural Australia, my earliest memories being of the small town of Inverell on the McIntyre River in northern New South Wales (NSW) where I completed my primary (elementary) education. 'Geography' in the sense of regional differences was taken for granted: I recall frequent family visits within a 100-mile radius to relatives and friends who lived on mixed (sheep and wheat) farms. My parents both came from rural backgrounds; after marriage in 1930 they moved to Coffs Harbour on the coast of NSW where they rented a dairy farm. The timing was not great as their move coincided with the beginning of the Depression: displacement followed quickly and my father entered the ranks of the casual rural labour force. Eventually he found some employment continuity in sheep shearing, an occupation that invariably took him away from home, sometimes for long periods. His work-related travels became another source of regional knowledge (albeit second hand) for me. Like my peers, I saw life in country NSW as preferable to life in the city, although few of us had any basis in experience for this view. A major event in the lives of children of my age at that time (1940's) was an occasional summer holiday at the beach, so I was very much aware of the differences in the landscapes of the northwest slopes and plains of NSW and the north coast (as well as the mountain ranges in between).

By the time I reached secondary school age, my parents had acquired a sheep and wheat farm. Because the nearby school did not go beyond what was then called "intermediate" (roughly junior high school), the decision was made for me to attend a state boarding school. This agricultural high school was some 120 miles from home near Tamworth, quite a large country town with a productive hinterland. The boarding fees in 1948 were 50 Australian pounds a year; I have a recollection that my parents thought this was a good deal as they doubted whether they could keep me at home for that amount! This school, the Farrer Memorial Agricultural High School, had been established in the late 1930s and was named after a pioneer agricultural scientist who had bred rust-resistant varieties of wheat. While geography was one of eight subjects I studied for the first three years, and one of six for the final two years of secondary school, I have no enduring memory of outstanding teachers or experiences from that time. Most boys who completed the Leaving Certificate at Farrer either returned to the family farm or entered agricultural-related employment; a very small number went on to study agricultural science at the University of Sydney. I did well in the final year public examination (known then as the Leaving Certificate), but my plan, largely due to the influence of the fifth year English teacher, was to take an Arts degree and to major in English Literature – a study choice hitherto unknown at Farrer.

I was duly accepted into the Faculty of Arts at the New England University College of the University of Sydney in Armidale, about 60 miles north of Tamworth. The college was later, in 1954, to become the University of New England (UNE). The four subjects I chose in my first year, with the assistance of the NSW Education Department to which I was bonded as a teacher-trainee, were English, geography, history, and psychology. The standard pattern of a three-year 'pass' Arts degree was to study three subjects in second year and to major in two in the third and final year. My earlier planned commitment to English literature soon waned and 1955 saw me concentrating on geography and psychology, with more of my energy and attention going to the latter than the former. I realised several years later my good fortune in having been introduced to descriptive and inferential statistics in my third year of psychology.

Much to my surprise, and I suspect to the surprise of the staff in each of the geography and psychology departments, I qualified to do a fourth honors year in both subjects. In the event I decided to concentrate on geography first and to spend a second honors year on psychology, although I had no plan for the financing of such a second year. As it happened, I became committed to geography and did not pursue further studies in psychology. In a sense then, my entry into geography was a fortuitous choice but having made it I embraced the subject with alacrity.

## Early influences

A major influence in shaping my career in geography was the friendship and guidance of the late Ellis Thorpe who was Head of the Department of Geography at Armidale from 1953 to 1956. Ellis' own academic achievements were modest but he had an immense influence on the lives and careers of a large number of people and I am proud to say that I was one of them.

Geography was an 'evening' subject then with classes scheduled after 4 pm and on Saturday mornings. This meant that the classes included several mature-age students, comprising schoolteachers and others. One of these was Jack Caldwell, who went on to work with the Population Council in New York, and subsequently was Professor of Demography at the Australian National University in Canberra. It was during this time that I met Mal Logan who had enrolled in some economics subjects in the evening. Reg Golledge commenced at UNE the year after I did although we saw more of each other after we left there. There were only three students in the geography honors year, and from the beginning there was a great sense of collegiality in the very small department where we were accepted as equals by the staff .The major component of the honors year was the completion of a research thesis. There was some course work, involving the history and philosophy of geography, for which Richard Hartshorne's *The Nature of Geography* was the text, as well as some instruction in scientific German. Little did I realise then, that within six years I would be a departmental colleague of the 'great man' Hartshorne.

The subject of my research project, suggested by Ellis Thorpe as I recall, was the movement of beef cattle from Queensland into NSW. Data to establish the location and volume of these movements were available in the office of the District Veterinary Officer in Armidale and I spent an enjoyable year recording and processing flow data, transforming the data into maps, and writing descriptions and explanations. I supplemented the statistical data with some visits to border centres where I met with stock and station agents and others who had some knowledge of cattle movements. In retrospect, the field enquiry part of the project was rather amateurish. Further, the study was not convincingly placed in any broader context, although I became aware of the emerging field of transportation geography.

## Graduate study in the USA 1957-58

Another major early influence on my career was the year spent at Northwestern University in the United States in its Masters degree program. During the latter part of my honors year in 1956, and in 1957 when I served as a 'demonstrator' in the department, I resolved to pursue postgraduate study, either in Australia or overseas. Ellis Thorpe and others all suggested that I explore opportunities in the USA and the UK. After competing unsuccessfully for several UK awards, I took the advice of a Canadian faculty member at UNE and submitted applications to a large number of departments in the United States. I was surprised and encouraged to receive positive responses from several of them. I accepted an early offer of a teaching assistantship from the University of Kansas, where expatriate Australian David Simonett was a faculty member, but subsequently withdrew in favour of Northwestern University. I was attracted there by its courses in transportation geography and by the presence of the Transportation Centre. Further, the prospect of living in the Chicago metropolis was exciting to say the least to someone whose entire urban experience had been in centres of less than 10, 000 people. With the confirmation of a Fulbright Travel Grant, I left Armidale in July 1957 for Evanston.

There were brief stopovers in Auckland, where Bryan Farrell who years later was to establish the Australian Studies program at the University of California Santa Cruz, gave me a tour of the city, and Honolulu where the spectacular Diamond Head made the first of many impressions on me. I arrived in San Francisco early one morning and made my way via a cab to the Greyhound Bus depot. The highlight of the cab ride occurred when an inebriated woman leapt into the front seat when the cab was stopped at a red light; she told us quite a bit about the all-night party she had attended before the cabbie persuaded her to alight! The coach trip from San Francisco to Chicago via Lawrence, Kansas, was then and remains something of a blur due to jet lag and the lack of sleep. I do however recall the gracious hospitality extended to me, when I paid a brief visit to the Kansas Geography Department, by its chairman Walter Kollmorgen.

Soon after arriving in Evanston, I had to attend the department's five-week field course in Platteville,Wisconsin. Satisfactory completion of this course, which included field observation, land use mapping, and urban land use and social structure surveys was a requirement of the Master's program. It also provided a valuable induction experience for overseas graduate students such as myself. Later that fall the department hosted the meeting of the West Lakes Association of American Geographers and there I first met Les King with whom I became a firm friend.

The teaching assistantship that I had been awarded carried a tuition scholarship, a substantial benefit at a private American university, and a small stipend that was sufficient to cover room and board. It also required that I lead four physical geography discussion or laboratory groups weekly throughout the academic year. I found balancing these teaching responsibilities with my own study quite a challenge and, in retrospect, I doubt that I gave my students value for money.

I had left UNE with a first class honours BA and, while I think I was typically Australian in that I did not trumpet my own achievements, I suspect I thought I was at the top of the academic heap. A few months at Northwestern corrected that impression. I came up against serious intellectual competition for the first time, and rubbing shoulders with students ten years my senior, some with Korean War and Malaysian combat experience such as Frank Thomas and Peter Gould, proved quite challenging. I found that I could compete but I had to work hard.

The Northwestern program required candidates to prepare for oral examination in a regional specialty, a systematic speciality, and 'world patterns'. I chose Latin America, mainly because that part of the world was largely *terra incognito* for me, and transportation geography. These choices meant that the two faculty members with whom I had the most interaction were Clarence F (Pappy) Jones and Edward J. (Ned) Taaffe. I worked closely with Ned Taaffe from whom I learned a great deal, not only about transport studies but also quantitative methods and their applications to geographical research. It was he who made me aware of the fact that empirical research without a sound theoretical context was rather shallow. He was a great inspiration: approachable, modest, helpful and a really fine man.

My knowledge of descriptive and inferential statistics, acquired from my studies in psychology at UNE, proved to be quite useful. At a more general level, my initial impatience with the structure of the Masters program and its formal course requirements gave way to a genuine appreciation of the opportunity it afforded to fill in gaps in my undergraduate background, for example by way of a course in transport economics taught by Charles Tiebout. When the year at Northwestern was coming to an end, I was fortunate to have several options from which to choose— a Transportation Centre doctoral fellowship, a lectureship back at UNE, or a research scholarship for the PhD at ANU. I chose the latter and left Chicago for New York in July 1958, again by Greyhound bus.

The Northwestern experience had given me a real sense of purpose in my geography career. I felt better prepared for research and had a much wider sense of the diversity of the discipline than previously.

## *The ANU experience 1958-61*

I enjoyed a leisurely return to Australia in the northern hemisphere summer of 1958, travelling first by ship from New York to Southampton, then around England and continental Europe, and then again by ship from Naples to Sydney. It was on the last voyage that I first met my wife Liz. I commenced in Oskar Spate's Department of Geography in September 1958.

The Department was housed administratively in the Research School of Pacific Studies, which meant that there was a strong research focus on field studies in such adjacent Pacific countries as Papua New Guinea, Fiji and Noumea. My proposal to pursue a transport topic in Australia was very different from most of the research of the other human geography students. The department also had a strong focus on geomorphology led by Joe Jennings but despite these two quite distinct foci, the students and staff were a cohesive group. Research presentations occurred from time to time but I recall very little discussion of trends in the discipline. Oskar Spate was quite a dominant (if eccentric) presence, especially after his well-publicized attack on quantitative work in his 'Lord Kelvin rides again' guest Editorial in *Economic Geography*. In retrospect, I suspect that his description of me as a 'gentle quantifier' was less a compliment than an epithet.

My initial assignment to Harold Brookfield for supervision worked well: we knew each other from UNE days and, while his focus was very much on Papua New Guinea, he was supportive of my plans for research in the transport field within Australia even though economic geography broadly defined was not emphasized in the department. The subject of my research was transport competition in the Riverina area of southern NSW, an area that had long been subject to intense competition between Sydney, the state capital, and Melbourne which was geographically closer and capital of neighboring Victoria. By the end of 1958 I was well launched on data collection from the NSW Railways and had familiarised myself with the area of study. From my studies at Northwestern I had a clear context in which to place the research and took as a focus the pattern of commodity flows that might have been expected according to population, land use, and distance from the rival capital cities.

At about that time, Godfrey Linge was appointed as a Research Fellow and he replaced Brookfield as my supervisor. An LSE- trained economic geographer who had recently completed a PhD at the University of Auckland on New

Zealand industrial development, Linge was more attuned to what I was doing. I made rapid progress and was able to submit my dissertation for examination early in 1961.

### A foot in the door - The University of Melbourne 1961-62

I had stayed in touch with colleagues from Northwestern and had resolved to return to the U.S. when my PhD was in hand. A delay in the overseas external examination of my thesis and the prospect of our first child arriving late in 1961 prompted a re-thinking of my plans. My scholarship at ANU was coming to an end and the Lectureship offered to me at The University of Melbourne seemed a prudent option. The recently-established Geography Department there was led by John Andrews, formerly a long-time staff member in McDonald Holmes' Department at Sydney. Andrews suggested I take responsibility for economic geography at the second and third year levels. This was still the era of 'God Professors' in Australian universities, and John Andrews was not a department chairman in the North American sense. However, he was satisfied for the staff to handle courses pretty much as they saw fit within broad curriculum guidelines. I enjoyed introducing students to location theory: while we made good progress with von Thunen, Weber and Christaller, neither the students' mathematical background nor mine was up to August Losch. My departmental colleagues were congenial but there was little of the rough and tumble of life as a graduate student that I had come to know at Northwestern. Les King, then at the University of Canterbury, established contact and our exchange of course outlines helped to keep me in touch. I used the time at Melbourne to develop courses and to 'harvest' my dissertation but I was impatient to be on the move again across the Pacific. The period at Melbourne also introduced me to some of the ambiguity that often surrounded geography as a university discipline: in addition to the recently-established Department (in the Faculty of Arts), there were staff members in the Faculty of Commerce who offered economic geography as a subject in the Commerce degree while geomorphology was offered as a subject in the Geology Department in the Faculty of Science. I was far too busy however, with course preparation and research to worry very deeply about the significance of this unusual situation.

There was an aura of uncertainty about this time as the months rolled by without any response from the overseas external examiner (Edward L Ullman at the University of Washington in Seattle). Eventually Spate decided to appoint a second, local external examiner for my dissertation, and I met for the 'defense' with Peter Scott and Max Neutze (Urban Studies, ANU) at the University of Tasmania in January of 1962. Things moved quickly thereafter, and I focussed in earnest on returning to North America. I found my initial correspondence with Andrew Clark at the University of Wisconsin a little forbidding— 'if you were to become a faculty member in this department you would be expected to teach successfully at all levels (introductory undergraduate, upper division, and graduate) and to publish regularly in both length and depth'. Nevertheless, we reached agreement on the terms of an appointment without difficulty and I arrived in Madison in the summer of 1962. Generally, I was to assume responsibility for many of the courses previously offered by John Alexander (who had been elected Chairman of the Department) and to introduce courses on quantitative methods.

## *The promised land: Madison, Wisconsin 1962-70*

I have a jumble of memories about my eight years at Wisconsin. The twin first impressions in 1962 were first, of an age-skewed department (I was 27 and the next youngest person was 40—Karl Butzer, also in his twenties was on leave and I did not meet him until my second year), with a majority of the faculty having been there quite a long time; and second, of a comfortable, almost complacent conviction of the excellence of the department, based on a recent assessment by the American College of Education that had ranked it as number one in the nation. I was welcomed warmly to the department and the only indication of my being low man (and they were all men) on the totem pole was my assignment to 7:45 am classes – but this suited my lifelong habit of being an early riser. Ostensibly the department ran on democratic principles so that by and large the chairman was careful not to exceed his authority but there was a small number of the senior faculty who were very influential. Perhaps because of my albeit brief Australian experience with 'God professors', I was much taken initially by what I saw as a passion for democracy in departmental (and university) governance. My first encounter with departmental politics occurred when John Alexander resigned from the chairmanship during 1962 to assume a national position with the Inter-varsity Christian Fellowship: there was no consensus that the obvious successor should be appointed and after an intense period of lobbying an alternative candidate was elected.

My Wisconsin experience falls neatly into three distinct phases: 1962-64, 1964-66, and 1966-70. Soon after arriving in Madison in 1962 I discovered that my visa was incompatible with my tenure-track appointment, and that to remain in the USA I would need to leave the country in 1964 for a two-year period before returning as an immigrant. While this unexpected bureaucratic impediment cast something of a shadow over those first two years, it did not unduly distract me from the development of graduate and undergraduate courses in quantitative methods and economic geography. I found working with graduate students (who included Julian Wolpert and Robert Aangeenbrug amongst others) very stimulating and challenging in contrast to the situation I had experienced at Melbourne. I also found colleagues such as Fred Simoons very refreshing although his background and research interests were very different from mine. Through this association, complemented by later interactions with David Sopher and Phillip Wagner, I formed a deep respect for cultural geography as developed and practised by the Berkeley school. However, my research was cast firmly in a problem-oriented scientific method framework and I saw this as the main game. It was during this time that I worked with Les King and Ned Taaffe on a book of readings in economic geography which had a particular focus on location theory. The book's eventual publication in 1968 was a source of great satisfaction, but I doubt that it was a commercial success for the publisher.

My horizons broadened when I was presented with an opportunity to spend at least a year of the 1964-66 period at the University of Ibadan in Nigeria. Simoons had involved me in the African Studies Program at Wisconsin and Akin Mabogunje from Nigeria, who I had met in 1963 at an NSF Summer Workshop on Quantitative Methods at Northwestern University, encouraged me to come to Ibadan. In the event, the African Studies Program made it possible and I was appointed as Honorary Visiting Lecturer at Ibadan. I spent July and August of 1964 in London where an affiliation with the department at University College afforded a convenient base and occasional interaction with colleagues. Then, with Liz and our two small children I flew to Ibadan in late September 1964. As it happened, Michael Chisholm of Cambridge University (and his family) was also in Ibadan in 1964-65, and I recall many stimulating conversations with him during that year. Several outstanding Ibadan students from that year subsequently came to the US for graduate work: Nurudeen Alao to Northwestern, and Sam Onakomaiya and Jonothan Ekpenyong to Wisconsin.

As a result of my sojourn in Nigeria my research interests moved away from contemporary economic geography. I became involved in a study of interregional trade and money flows in Nigeria under the auspices of the Nigerian Institute for Social and Economic Research. This was eventually published as a book jointly-authored with Alan Hay who was then a research student at Cambridge University ( Smith and Hay 1970). There were two results of my involvement: first, I became more aware of the policy implications of what I was doing and second, I developed an interest in the infrastructure, both physical and organisational, of internal trade and marketing in Nigeria and in developing countries generally.

A Guggenheim Fellowship gave me the flexibility to spend the following year in the Geography Department at The University of Sydney where I was able to write up the Nigerian research. Also, after Mal Logan left on leave I offered a course there in transport geography to third year students. My association with George Dury who was then Professor of Geography at Sydney was to become even closer several years later.

During this two-year period, none of the several flirtations with the idea of returning to Australia was pursued and it was with a sense of excitement and relief that Liz and I and our two children travelled back to Madison in the summer of 1966, with 'green cards' in hand. During my absence, David Ward had returned to the department and with several retirements looming there was an air of anticipation about what shape the department would take.

The four years 1966 to 1970 were a period of great activity. I was very much involved in building what became a pluralist department, including Bill Clark, Tom Eighmy, John Hudson, Jim Knox, Mal Logan and Joel Morrison. The attraction of George Dury to a joint appointment with the Department of Geology was seen as a major coup, signalling as it did an acceptance of process geomorphology as an integral part of the department. While I became increasingly interested in African Studies, my research on internal trade and markets received a major boost by the award of a National Science Foundation grant that supported field studies for several years. At the University level, I became a member of the Research Committee of the Graduate School, an assignment that continued for three years and involved assessing research proposals from faculty members for summer or semester salary support. A stint as chair of the African Studies Program, a decidedly interdisciplinary group, complemented my work on the Research Committee. I suspect these experiences contributed to the emergence of my interest in university governance several years later.

At the wider discipline level, I was appointed to the AAG's Commission on College Geography, assumed the chair of its panel on Resource and Technical Papers, and sat as a member of the AAG Council. My related work with John Lounsbury, Warren Nystrom, Les King, Paul English, Ed Soja and others was a real pleasure. At the time, I was convinced that the effort was well worthwhile in terms of providing content and approach materials that could be used in college and university courses. The parallel High School Geography Project was also an initiative with great potential to effect much needed change: the 'mush' known as 'social studies' had made vast inroads into the schools' curriculum territory formerly occupied by geography and history and determined responses were required.

The second half of the sixties was a turbulent time on US campuses, indeed in US society generally. I found this troubling, especially seeing the campus in a haze of tear gas, occupied by the National Guard and with police engaged in pitched battles with students. At this time, I also found my interests widening to include departmental leadership and management. I had reassessed my initial embrace of the purely democratic approach that I found when I joined the department and concluded that effective departmental governance required a chair or head with appropriate authority and discretion. I became increasingly dissatisfied with the proposition that 'the executive duties of a university department can be amply performed by a chairman, or other competent drudge' offered in in an early AAUP Bulletin that I came across. Thus, I began to examine seriously opportunities available elsewhere.

## *A taste of administration - Queens University, Ontario 1970-72*

I assumed the Headship of the Geography Department at Queens in the summer of 1970. Liz and I often joked about the fact that for two people who had found the Wisconsin winters a trial, southern Ontario was a peculiar choice. The Department comprised a core of long-serving senior faculty members and several more recently-appointed younger faculty members who brought energy and a variety of approaches and experiences. I think it is fair to say, albeit in retrospect, that the department had not realised its potential in a university with significant strengths in several cognate disciplines.

I had many opportunities to develop leadership and management skills while at Queens. An immediate challenge was to build university consensus around a proposal that the department be authorised to offer the PhD degree; while there were healthy enrolments in the masters program (both MA and MSc), there was a strongly held view in the department that the lack of a PhD program constrained both staff and student recruitment. The task of obtaining support and approval involved an immense amount of advocacy within the University and with the Ontario Council on Graduate Studies which was essentially a Provincial regulatory body whose task was to bring some order into the establishment and offering of graduate programs, and to control thereby the expanding demand for Provincial funding.

During my second year at Queens when the PhD proposal was well on track, I was approached by Mal Logan about the possibility of joining him at Monash. This required an excruciatingly difficult decision: we had come to enjoy living in Kingston (a rather quaint town of 60,000 with a great deal of history) which was close to Toronto and Montreal, and the department and University were most congenial organizations within which to work. However, the fact that the approval of the doctoral program at Queens was imminent made the decision to return to Australia a little easier, and we spent several weeks of the northern hemisphere summer on an ocean liner travelling leisurely from Vancouver to Melbourne.

The Kingston experience remains in my memory as a highlight of my career. Queens was then, and I assume is still one of Canada's stronger national universities, and the quality of students and faculty was quite high. Further, its size, then about 10,000 students, gave it a 'manageable' character. I enjoyed thoroughly leading the department and had many opportunities for involvement at the university wide level. As I recall, all of Ontario's universities had a geography department so there was a large community of colleagues with whom interaction was possible, including Les King's group at McMaster. I was able to continue working with the Commission on College Geography, as well as on my research program on internal trade in West Africa. I also commenced a ten-year association with a colleague in West Germany with whom I established a Working Group on 'Market-Place Exchange Systems' under the auspices of the International Geographical Union.

## Returning home - Monash University, 1972-75

I had become somewhat involved at Monash even before I left Queens in the summer of 1972. Mal Logan had been very successful in securing additional positions for the department and we worked together to fill them, preferring younger staff members with North American experience. A particular objective was to add strength to the postgraduate programs in the department. The last few months of 1972 were quite exciting as I settled in to the department along with Gale Dixon (from Oregon), Chris Maher (from Toronto), and John McKay (from Ohio State). The presence of Larry Bourne, also from Toronto, for a few months was an added source of stimulation. Nationally, it became a time of near-euphoria with the election of a Labour Government, the first since 1947.

Departmental governance presented no problems as Mal and I had agreed to alternate as chair. It was about this time that challenges to the scientific method research paradigm began to emerge generally in the social sciences. A continuing and sometimes spirited dialogue arising from this challenge permeated the department during my three years there. By and large this was conducted in an atmosphere of reasonable tolerance, if not mutual self-respect, by most members. Although the department was administratively housed in the Faculty of Arts and did not offer a degree in the Faculty of Science, there was a substantial physical geography presence which had particular resource and staffing implications. The department attracted large numbers of students, many of whom went on to honors and graduate degrees. Two students from the Faculty of Economics and Politics who were unable to complete a geography major in their commerce degree subsequently completed an MA preliminary year in our department and went on to stellar careers: one, Gary Johns, in Federal politics, and the other, Gordon Clark, after obtaining a PhD at McMaster to appointments at prestigious US universities and then to a distinguished Chair at Oxford.

University-wide governance was built around Faculties led by an appointed Dean with budget and personnel responsibility. This was the exception in Australia, the normal pattern being deans elected by the Faculty and having student administration responsibilities. Faculty Boards were responsible to the Professorial Board which was chaired by the Vice-Chancellor (President). This arrangemement of a senior academic governance body composed on a principle of status was new to me and in the event I found myself more comfortable at the Faculty level.

The logistics of continuing my research in West Africa were prohibitive and I initiated a project on internal trade and marketing in Papua New Guinea. That this did not develop the momentum that had characterised my West African work was due partly to the immense differences between these two parts of the world; and partly to the fact that my interest in this field of research was beginning to wane. North America beckoned again and I was approached early in 1974 about my interest in the Headship at The University of British Columbia. This appointment was finalised in mid-1974 with a start date of July 1975 (an excruciatingly long interregnum as it happened). I spent my third and final year at Monash as chair of the department, as well as Associate Dean in the Faculty of Arts. Amongst other things, this enabled Mal Logan to continue a part-time policy involvement role with the Commonwealth Department of Urban and Regional Development.

## Opportunity beckons - The University of British Columbia 1975-79

My assessment of the UBC department was that it faced three major challenges: first, to secure a place of respect in the large Faculty of Arts which was its administrative and therefore budget home; second, to overcome internal dissensions between physical and human geographers; and third, to build a culture that would re-engage several long-serving members with the objectives of the department as a whole. I pursued these three isues vigorously with moderate success. I found myself again enjoying the challenge of helping colleagues identify and clarify their objectives and assisting in their achievement. It was a very pluralist department, with 'humanistic' and cultural/historical geographers working alongside regional scientists, climatologists, geomorphologists, and traditional regional geographers. I was aware that we were regarded as somewhat eccentric by other departments in Canada, and possibly the US, but that was not a source of concern for me.

A recently-concluded 'special plan' for collective bargaining between the University and the Faculty Association (on compensation and conditions of appointment) provided an explicit context for personnel decisions in the department. This area consumed a large amount of my time and energy and I became very familiar with the criteria and procedures for appointment, reappointment, promotion and tenure – but no more familiar than any self-respecting department head should have been. I took the personnel and performance management part of my role very seriously: I instituted a process that required each faculty member to prepare an annual report in a consistent format for distribution to all faculty members, and gave each faculty member an opportunity to comment on the performance of colleagues. Decisions about salary adjustments remained with the Head but I undertook to consider carefully any comments made by colleagues. This process effectively removed the air of secrecy, even envy, that in the past had surrounded the delicate matter of salary adjustments.

My research interest in internal trade and marketing continued although there were few if any opportunities for field studies. I had continued working with Erdmann Gormsen of Mainz University on the IGU Working Group, but largely in a coordinating rather than a research role. I was very much aware of the fact that I was not as productive in research and publication as I had been in the past. and in an attempt to retain some standing as a scholar I decided to seek sabbatical leave. In the winter of 1978-79 I prepared a proposal that would take me back to Australia and to Papua New Guinea for the 1979-80 session, by which time I would have served four years in the role of Head of the department.

## The watershed - drifting away from geography

In the spring of 1979 the Vice-President (Academic) invited me to join him as an Associate from July 1. The initial understanding was that the appointment was for one year and that a decision on whether it would continue would be made by 31 January 1980. The role included assistance to the Vice-President across his portfolio, as well as a major involvement in collective bargaining (initially with the Faculty Association, and subsequently with the teaching assistants after they organized as a local of the Canadian Union of Public Employees).

After due consideration our plans for a sabbatical leave were shelved, and I focussed on the new role I was about to assume. I found the work enjoyable and developed a good relationship with the Vice-President so that my decision on January 31 1980 was to resign from the Headship effective 30 June 1980. In the ensuing four years I effectively withdrew from the Department: I ceased teaching after the first term of the 1980-81 session and had only sporadic involvement in doctoral and other committees of the department and the Faculty. However, I retained memberships in several associations and subscriptions to several geographical journals so my withdrawal from the discipline was not total.

During this period I increasingly developed the capacity to 'think university', a relatively rare exercise at the departmental level where colleagues usually expect a Head (or chair) to be an effective advocate for their department, in competition with others. With a fixed pool of resources, the situation that had increasingly emerged in the 1980s, any successful advocacy by one department for additional resources usually meant a reduction for others. The new challenge I faced was to identify the set of university-wide priorities that would provide a consistent context for such decisions. This was no small challenge in a university with twelve faculties and upwards of 30,000 students.

A new President appointed in 1983 delegated the entire academic budget to the Vice-President (Academic), a marked change from past practice in which Faculty Deans reported directly to the President. Even prior to my appointment to this role, growth in the annual Provincial operating grant to the University had begun to level off. There was desultory talk of program reductions and discontinuations but I think most faculty members saw this as a highly unlikely outcome. The Faculty Association took the view that under the Special Plan, the University was severely constrained in what it could do in a situation of financial exigency. When it became obvious that the grant for 1984-85 would constitute an absolute reduction on the previous year, program reductions and discontinuations —- and the associated and inevitable terminations of appointment for some— became a realistic prospect. Late in 1984 I commenced a review process with an exacting timetable to be applied in all Faculties and budget units, which was designed to meet the shortfall. An explicit assumption was that 'redundancies' could not be avoided.

This was a difficult enough time if only because of the University's deteriorating financial situation and the demands of managing the process that I had established. However, it was made the more so by two other unrelated developments. First, in 1984 I was approached by two Australian universities about my possible interest in the position of Vice-Chancellor. Second, I was aware that the UBC President was under considerable political pressure and was exploring possibilities elsewhere. In February 1985 I met with the selection committee for the Vice-Chancellorship of The University of Western Australia in Perth. My return to Vancouver in early March coincided with the UBC President's resignation after two years of his five-year term. The University's Board of Governors resolved to accept the resignation with immediate effect, and I was asked to assume the role as President *pro tem*. The urgent priority was to implement the outcome of the process that had been established earlier. Under the Universities Act of British Columbia, the Academic Senate (chaired by the President) was required to approve discontinuation of some ten programs that had been identified. Ultimately, the Senate spared one. The Board of Governors then asserted its authority to terminate the twelve faculty appointments associated with these programs, although this was hotly disputed by both the UBC Faculty Association and the Canadian Association of University Teachers (as well as by sibling bodies elsewhere in the English speaking world).

In April I was offered and accepted the Western Australia position, to assume office in November 1985. However, the ensuing nine-month term as UBC's President *pro tem* was anything but a picnic in the park. Further, accounts of events at UBC, some more accurate than others, were rapidly and widely disseminated to Australia and it seemed that my reception at UWA in November would be less than warm. In the event, these apprehensions proved to be groundless and I found myself in a University community that was justifiably proud of its accomplishments. At the same time, it was somewhat uncertain about its future in what was an increasingly different and differentiated higher education landscape.

## *The drift is complete*

During my three years at UWA until early 1989 I kept my distance from the Geography Department for no particular reason other than the fact that it would have been untenable for the Vice-Chancellor to be seen to be too close to what had been his discipline. I do recall opening the annual meeting of the Institute of Australian Geographers hosted by the UWA department, but this was no more than I did for numerous other disciplines over the three-year period. The leadership and management challenge at UWA was to introduce and have accepted a new structure that devolved budget and resource responsibility to appointed Faculty Deans. Externally, I was involved in a major review of medical education and the medical workforce, the report of which was placed in the 'too hard' basket by the responsible Minister. Also, I was one of several

Vice-Chancellors and others whom the new Commonwealth Minister, John Dawkins, consulted about future directions for higher education. This group, known pejoratively as 'The Purple Circle' by the Commonwealth bureaucrats whom Dawkins had sidelined, was quite influential in the Green Paper-White paper process that occurred in 1987 and 1988.

My one foray into government service in Canberra occurred in 1989 when I was Chair of the National Board of Employment, Education and Training (a statutory, not a ministerial appointment) in which role I reported to John Dawkins, the portfolio Minister. While the Board supposedly had a major role in advising on higher education policy, as well as in several other areas, I do not think I was particularly effective in the role. I was unaccustomed to policy work and I found working within and with the Commonwealth bureaucracy a real challenge. I missed the collegiality of universities and the presence of colleagues (even though as a Vice-Chancellor one often was quite alone), and I was by no means convinced that the advisory structure of the Board was particularly effective. Therefore, an approach from The University of New England in the latter half of 1989 to consider becoming Vice-Chancellor fell on receptive ground.

In 1990 I commenced appointment as the second Vice-Chancellor of the amalgamated University of New England, which encompassed the former UNE, the former Armidale College of Advanced Education, the Northern Rivers College of Advanced Education in Lismore, the Orange Agricultural College, and the small UNE presence in Coffs Harbour on the NSW coast. As at UWA, I maintained a nodding acquaintance with the Geography Department on the Armidale campus, but avoided any closer contact for the same reasons that guided me in the past.

The amalgamated UNE had been created under the policy initiatives that flowed in part from the work of 'The Purple Circle', so I was seen (especially on the Armidale campus) as being in a position of 'put up or shut up'. The task was to persuade the faculty and staff members of four predecessor institutions that their future was brighter in the larger, federated institution that had been created by legislation in mid 1989. This proved to be impossible for several reasons and I spent the last two of my four-year appointment managing the dissolution process – quite a challenge as legislators are not especially receptive to arguments that legislation passed a few years previously was flawed. Liz and I decided that a change was desirable after four years of managing conflict so I declared no interest in the Vice-Chancellor positions of the two successor universities, the reconstituted UNE, and Southern Cross University.

My UNE appointment concluded at the end of 1993, and we repaired to our recently-acquired home in Ballina on the north coast of NSW to spend some months unwinding. Early the following year I was approached about the possibility of becoming Executive Director and President of the Australian Education Office in Washington DC. While the Office was located in the Australian Embassy, it was not a government function but was an entity owned by twenty-five of the Australian universities. It enjoyed some support from the Commonwealth but effectively it was a small business, promoting Australian education and training in the US and Canada. This role was immensely satisfying and when I left the AEO three years later, it was on a sound financial footing with a small but very good staff, a clear understanding of its role and responsibilities, and a valued presence in the Embassy. Being in Washington DC enabled me to renew some geographical links although largely on a social basis. Thus, I met with Ron Abler, the Executive Director of the AAG and some of his colleagues on several occasions, and while on a visit to Penn State met with with Peter and Jo Gould, friends from my Northwestern days.

When my contract and work permit expired in mid-1997, I decided to leave the full-time paid work force and return to Ballina. The subsequent years have been taken up with a variety of consulting and project assignments especially on issues of university governance and related matters. I was privileged to serve as Deputy Chancellor of Southern Cross University from 1998 to 2002 and then beginning in January 2005 as Chancellor of the University of Ballarat in Victoria – a far cry from my first academic position also in Victoria, as lecturer in geography at The University of Melbourne.

## Retrospect

When I reflect on my earlier career as a geographer I think that my work in Nigeria in the mid-1960s was a major turning point. Much of what I had done previously arose from themes in my doctoral research, the functional classification of urban centres, the measurement of complementarity in commodity flows, and so on. The Nigerian interregional trade project alerted me to the variety of infrastructures that supported and facilitated this trade and made clear to me the essential role played by the network of periodic markets that existed in Nigeria and, as I subsequently discovered, in many other countries. The work by Ed Ullman and James Stine on space-time relationships, and the emerging work on the informal sector in developing countries, provided me with a context within which to examine these periodic markets. This became the focus of my research activity and I spent considerable time on empirical research on the location and characteristics of periodic market systems in various parts of the world, especially tropical Africa. A theoretical synthesis of this work was presented in Smith and Hay (1969). Perhaps, had the opportunities for continued research on this subject been more attractive, or perhaps had the options of involvement in university administration been less attractive, I would have chosen differently at later points in my career.

Over the years I have maintained my life memberships in the Association of American Geographers and of the Institute of Australian Geographers. I peruse publications as they arrive and often note the names of former colleagues amongst authors and editorial boards. I admire greatly those who continue to contribute to the discipline despite their assumption of major university leadership and management roles. This I was unable to do.

I have also become aware, sometimes with regret, of how much the discipline has changed since I was an active participant. I retain however, a genuine appreciation of my time as a geographer and I am grateful for the academic foundation that the discipline provided. I cannot be sure whether this contributed to the way my career unfolded but I have always felt that amongst academics, I could usually rely on geographers to bring more than a modicum of common sense to the argument and debate that ebbs and flows across campuses everywhere.

**REFERENCES**

Smith, R. H. T. and Hay, A. M. 1969 'A theory of the spatial structure of internal trade in underdeveloped countries' *Geographical Analysis* 1(2), 212-236
Smith, R. H. T. and Hay, A. M. 1970 *Interregional trade and money flows in Nigeria, 1964* ( Ibadan: Oxford University Press for the Nigerian Institute for Social and Economic Research)

ISBN 1425127517-7

9 781425 127510